Between Witness and Testimony

Between Witness
and Testimony

The Holocaust and the
Limits of Representation

Michael Bernard-Donals
Richard Glejzer

State University of New York Press

Cover photo: Eric Block

Published by
State University of New York Press, Albany

Printed in the United States of America

For information, address State University of New York Press,
90 State Street, Suite 700, Albany, NY 12207

Production by Judith Block
Marketing by Michael Campochiaro

Library of Congress Cataloging-in-Publication Data

Bernard-Donals, Michael F.
    Between witness and testimony : the Holocaust and the limits of
representation / Michael Bernard-Donals, Richard Glejzer.
        p. cm.
    Includes index.
    ISBN 0-7914-5149-6 (alk. paper)—ISBN 0-7914-5150-X (pbk. :
alk. paper)
        1. Holocaust, Jewish (1939–1945)—Personal narratives--History
and criticism. 2. Holocaust, Jewish (1939–1945)—Influence.
3. Holocaust, Jewish (1939–1945)—Psychological aspects.
4. Holocaust, Jewish (1939–1945), in literature. 5. Holocaust,
Jewish (1939–1945), in motion pictures. I. Glejzer, Richard R.
II. Title.

D804.3 .B4445 2001
940.53'18'092—dc21   2001032205

10 9 8 7 6 5 4 3 2 1

Contents

Preface

Forgetfulness would not be emptiness, but neither negative nor positive: the passive demand that neither welcomes nor withdraws the past, but . . . refers us to nonhistorical forms of time.

Blanchot

Fragmentation, the mark of a coherence all the firmer in that it has to come undone in order to be reached . . . [is] the pulling to pieces (the tearing) of that which never has preexisted (really or ideally) as a whole, nor can it ever be reassembled in any future presence whatever.

Blanchot

To what extent can a disaster, or an individual's attempt to respond to it, be considered redemptive? This is a particularly dangerous question to ask in connection with the events of the Shoah. How is it possible to redeem one of the most horrifying events of the century, to bear witness to the nearly six million Jewish lives destroyed, the millions of Roma, gay men, Poles, and other individuals who resisted either the political or ideological will of the Nationalist Socialist government in Germany? It seems preposterous to suggest that we can represent—by literary or any other means—the individual horrors, or the collective destruction, of the Final Solution in a way that brings the viewer, or hearer, or reader anywhere near the events themselves. And yet we have discovered over the fifty years since the disaster, but particularly in the last fifteen, that Adorno's insistence upon the barbarity of Holocaust representation has been mooted by a flood of words and images and testimonies of the events that occurred between 1933 and 1945 in Europe and in the years immediately following in countless other locations. In memoir after memoir, in narrative after narrative, survivors and bystanders obey the compulsion to speak, bringing the memories that haunt them to language. Organizations like the Fortunoff Video Archive at Yale University, Steven Spielberg's Survivors of the Shoah Foundation, and the Yad Vashem Heroes' and Martyrs' Memorial Authority in Israel have all made strong efforts to search out those who have endured the miseries of the camps and the ghettos and exile. These efforts have given witnesses the opportunity to speak, so the images that passed before their eyes, and the traces that are imprinted upon their bodies, can be translated into the language of narrative so that others may be made aware of what history can come to. And for those who were not there, those whose place or date of birth, or family religion, or simply sheer luck kept them away from the events of the disaster, there has been nonetheless a need to confront the language of the witness, and the traces of the dead, on their own terms. In short, the resounding response to Adorno's claim is that although representations of the Shoah may be barbaric, they are unavoidable.

But the simple reality of these representations does not respond to the question of their redemptive nature, the extent to which the testimonies allow us to see, to witness, the events themselves. In point of fact, there has been some fierce debate over their adequacy. The sometimes ugly quarrels over the movie *Schindler's List* are only one case in point. In a forum printed in the *Village Voice* some months after the movie's release, Ken Jacobs complains both about the hyperrealism of the movie and its fakery. It's so real as to allow viewers to mistake the film for the fact of the Holocaust; but it's so fake as to play to viewers' stereotypes of Jews, Nazis, and Christians. It's too much Holocaust, and not enough. His double-edged complaint was echoed in the following months by film critics and viewers alike, and it suggests two of the difficulties inherent in terms like witness, testimony, and redemption in connection with the Shoah. The shock or pain the viewer feels upon seeing a movie or reading a memoir or novel is related to the horror and pain felt by those whose experiences are written or depicted, and the viewer is tempted to say that his pain redeems the victim's. Or representations are understood *as* representations, mediating the viewer's reaction to both the medium and its object, distancing the viewer from horror, and giving him access to the event by transforming it into knowledge. Representations redeem the event either by allowing the viewer to identify with the witness or victim, or by allowing the viewer to come to "know" something about the event (or individual) being depicted.

But both of these models equate the object of representation with either the viewer's own experience or with his ability to construct a knowledge that makes the experience commensurable with other objects or events. If what we have heard for the last fifty years is true, and the Shoah is a limit event whose status as experience exceeds our ability to know it, then either model is inadequate: how is it possible to say that any experience can be likened to the experience of the panicked citizen of a Polish shtetl loaded onto a windowless gas van with his family, whose destination was a forest outside of Chelmno? How is it possible to say that we understand the event—the death of a single person, or that person's family, in the midst of a process of slaughter that would annihilate two-thirds of the Jews of Europe—in common-sense, or even analytical, terms? Both models of witness and testimony, in other words, suggest that by bringing the experiences of individuals to life on the printed page, or the film screen, either through feeling or through knowledge, we can bring back the experiences themselves, thereby redeeming the dead. But neither of these models allows for the possibility that there is something in the experiences and events of the Shoah that exceeds our ability to identify with or to come to know them. Neither of these models allows us to understand the grief or revulsion that the reader experiences reading Christopher Browning's accounts of the Einsatzgruppen and their police escorts as they made their way through the Baltic states. Neither does justice to the inexplicable grief associated with seeing photographs of individuals or couples in a small town in Poland, towns that were emptied of Jews and bulldozed into the ground. And neither of these models allows us to understand what exceeds the limit of knowledge.

We have endeavored, in this book, to reexamine a relation between witness and testimony that can account for what exceeds the limit of knowledge. Witnessing in this sense is founded upon a moment of seeing, of glimpsing what escapes understanding. What we glimpse in such moments is not history but the event as it precedes our ability to bring it into language at all. It is our sense that some representations of the Shoah manage to write or to inscribe a kernel of what Maurice Blanchot calls the in-experience of the disaster (50–51), an "experience that is not a lived event" because it exceeds the regularities of knowledge and the language that could contain it. In a curious passage in *The Writing of the Disaster*, Blanchot makes reference to "the God of Isaac Luria," calling the disaster that which is withdrawn from experience rather than expanded to form it (13). Though it is a withdrawal from writing, from memory, and from knowledge, the disaster nonetheless leaves a mark on each one. Blanchot, in his own way, is attempting to understand the ways in which any attempt to write the disaster, to testify, fails to redeem the events as we can *know* them. But testimony also succeeds in presenting, through a failure of representation, an opportunity to *see* the events (if only for a fleeting but powerful instant) as they indelibly mark both the writing and the reader of the writing.

The reference to Luria, however, is not as out of place as it seems. Isaac Luria was a mystical teacher of a Judaism at odds with more orthodox understandings of Torah and the tradition of commentary that surrounds it. One of his most radical revisions was of the creation myth, in which the divine source does not materialize the world through utterance of the word (as most readings of the Genesis texts have it) but instead withdraws into itself to make room for something else—something material—to inhabit the void. For Luria, divinity was not the purely positive entity whose absence embodies evil; divinity was both presence and (through its withdrawal) absence, and it was only through divine absence that the material world could be brought into existence. In Luria's cosmology, the materiality of the world could not be bound in the divine vessels intended to contain it and—as it shattered them—that materiality became commingled with the shards of those vessels. The fall, in this creation myth, is the dispersal of divine shards among the materiality of the world; the task of redemption is to recover the divine spark—shards of the vessels as they are matched piece to piece—through ethical activity, through prayer, and through the rhythms of daily life as they follow the laws of God. "The God of Isaac Luria," then, is a divinity marked by both presence and absence; good and evil; ecstasy and agony. And redemption is possible not through the eventual recuperation of the vessels entire, but in every moment as humans engage in activity that recovers shards of divinity and glimpse the shape of the whole.

To speak of divinity in a book about the Holocaust is, like speaking of witnessing or redemption, a dangerous act. Elie Wiesel's famous question about the whereabouts of the divine as a young boy is hanged in Auschwitz before the eyes of the Jewish inmates is answered with the terse revelation that God has been killed along with the boy on the gallows and the millions who preceded him and would follow (*Night* 62). But our thesis here is that the divine, like the God whose image is banned by the Second Commandment, is defined by excess, something quite outside the limits of the knowable that can only be indicated and only leaves a trace.

The God of Isaac Luria is intimately related to the God of Immanuel Kant, the divine presence that lay completely outside of human experience and human knowledge, but which could be indicated—fleetingly glimpsed—only through a feeling of sublimity. As we'll explain in the book's opening chapters, the feeling of sublimity—the palpable anxiety and fear that is experienced when we confront an object or event that is too much for the faculties that regulate knowledge—indicates both the limit of human knowledge, and shows us that, were it not for this sense of limit, we wouldn't finally be aware of those faculties whose limits we have reached. The commingling of pleasure and pain, of fear and ecstasy, in sublimity results from our dual response to limit. But the sublime also indicates something beyond human knowledge—something in the natural world whose behavior creates in the observer this feeling of fear—of which we can be aware (which, in Kant's terms, we can "think") but which ultimately we cannot know; it is something the witness sees but cannot say, and acts as the limit of testimony. So in the sublime—as in a recuperation of the divine—we are confronted with both the limit of knowledge and an uncanny sense of what lies beyond it. And this impossible pairing—of fear and ecstasy, the natural and the divine—compels explanation, demands testimony. Like Blanchot's disaster, the horrifying experience—the murder of a child, the day-to-day fear of death by starvation, the uncanny sense that you will be the only human survivor as all those around you are sent to the gas chamber—indicates where knowledge and testimony break down, as well as where the *compulsion* to explain and to speak (for Blanchot, to write) begins. We will argue that the disaster of the Shoah—in which the victim and the survivor find it impossible to know, or put words to, the experience in which they find themselves—is located at the junction of the compulsion to speak and failure of speech, where the witness manages to redeem the moment (to finally see what lies beyond or behind what can be told by history), to "fall victim" to it, and leave a trace of it in language. The witness, confronted with the sublime object, is rendered both speechless and is compelled nonetheless to speak.

In countless videotaped and written testimonies of the Holocaust, witnesses succumb to precisely this twin impulse of speech and its failure. Lawrence Langer has called it a tension of selves, in which the "self" that remains in the camp or ghetto is at odds with the self who has survived to tell the tale, and that the silences or stutters in these testimonies are a result of this battle. But what we'd argue instead is that the witness participates in a moment of sublimity, or of redemption—a redemption of the moment of horror, a moment that flashes briefly before the eyes of the witness but which can't be fixed by either memory or by knowledge, and which nonetheless compels testimony, a narrative, of an event construed as history. Cathy Caruth and Shoshana Felman both call this moment an instance of the traumatic, in which the victim who has apparently survived the horrifying event "unscathed" undergoes a moment of seeing—of witnessing—but is marked nonetheless by the event itself. But the victim in this case doesn't have access to the event (she does not remember it) because she was not fully conscious at the time of its occurrence. That is to say, the event's sublimity—its unavailability to knowledge—has rendered it absent, and the witness's testimony is marked by this absence. This means that there is a stark difference between witness and testimony, two terms that have sometimes been conflated in the context of Holocaust representation. Witness is the moment of seeing, in which the witness's confrontation with the (sublime) event renders him speechless and terrified; testimony is the witness's obedience to the compulsion to speak, though what the witness says is neither a reflection of the event (which is irretrievably lost to memory) nor unaffected by it. But this also means that the relation between the event that forms the core of traumatic memory and the testimony that provides the only access that we have to the event itself is a vexed one, all the more so because of the nature of sublimity and the possibility of redemption implied by it.

The foregoing has significance for pedagogy as well. It has been suggested that, in the wake of the events that comprise the Holocaust, the work of redemption—*tikkun olam*—is all the more imperative. Not only is there an urgency to repair the world that could produce such suffering and lack of reason and compassion, but there is an additional urgency to reconcile civil and moral law with a new knowledge of what occurred, an urgency to teach the events of the Holocaust so that such a thing could never happen again. This was, in effect, the pedagogical/ethical imperative put forward by Elie Wiesel: never forget. Never forget so that the world will remember and learn.

However, if the Holocaust as an event complicates the work of redemption, it also complicates the work of learning. The events of the Holocaust have been made material through witness testimonies, documents, photographs, and by means of fiction and other media of representation, but that material is, essentially, testimonial. It is the result of the compulsion to speak, which itself is the result of the effects of trauma or sublimity experienced by the (first- or secondhand) witness. If we take pedagogy to mean the inculcation or the transmission of a body of knowledge or the creation of new knowledge, then we have to recognize the possibility that whatever knowledge is transmitted or created bears only an oblique relation to the events that form its source. If we take pedagogy to be synonymous with redemption, and conflate witness and testimony—thereby redeeming the events for history—then it's altogether possible to "rebuild" the Holocaust (see Spiegelman, *Maus* v.2 98). But what is rebuilt through testimony and what has been seen (but lost to memory) by the witness are not the same, so a pedagogy of transmission that doesn't recognize the inherent failures of testimony will also fail in its aim to provide knowledge of the Holocaust. What may be needed, instead, is a pedagogy of trauma, in which the teacher recognizes that the students themselves are also witnesses to a witnessing; they are witnesses to testimonies that are shot through with a kernel of the event. The sublime moment, presented by means of a failure of representation, has an effect on the secondhand witness, but it is not an effect of knowledge. It is, instead, a mark of the traumatic, and whatever knowledge the student tries to produce will likewise be affected by the sublime object. The consequence for pedagogy, though, is that we may not be able to transmit a knowledge of the Holocaust, and may never be able to recognize another Shoah before it befalls us. Still, it may allow us to understand the structure of trauma inherent in witnessing, and the nature of a redemption that doesn't simply mean a recuperation of history but that involves access to what lies beyond it.

We intend to work out the implications of the connections among sublimity and redemption, witness and testimony, and their relation to pedagogy in seven chapters that roughly follow the argument presented above. The first chapter lays out two terms fundamental to notions of representation and its limits, redemption and sublimity: sublimity is located at the moment of seeing; redemption speaks to the difficulties inherent in representing that moment. As we suggested, the term redemption is founded in the mystical tradition of Judaism, one given substantial contemporary relevance in theology by Gershom Scholem and Moshe Idel, and in debates surrounding representation and philosophy by Walter Benjamin and (in a book on Benjamin, Scholem, and Levinas) Susan Handelman. What interests us here is the relation between the historical real—the materiality of the world in all its positive and negative aspects—and what lies beyond it. It was just this relation that troubled Walter Benjamin who, at the brink of the disaster, wondered whether it was possible to write in such a way as to "release the divine spark," and provide access to—but not knowledge of—the events that found the historical real. Benjamin contends that certain translations, in their relation to the "original," manage to do this, but he also contends that what is important in such translations is not the distance (or lack thereof) between original and translation but the distance between the two texts and "God's language." Translations redeem language by indicating its point of origin, much like sublimity redeems the phenomenal world and humans' place in it by indicating the limit of experience. For our purposes, Benjamin's contentions about the task of the translator suggest an aesthetics of redemption useful to scholars of Holocaust representation. It is an aesthetics that depends less upon mimesis than upon sublimity, an attempt to present, through the failures inherent in representation, that which can only be hinted. We heed, in this section of the book, Dominick LaCapra's warning that sublimity may involve something like a "troping away" from the material consequences of disaster by paying close attention to the ways in which sublimity has effects both upon the reader and upon the witness, and in a sense everything else we do in this book traces just those effects.

Though history may be an inherently fallible testimonial trace of events irretrievably lost, still the historian needs a way to understand the relation between a language of testimony and the shape of events. Hayden White may be right to assert that all historical accounts are emplotted as narratives, but that does not mean that all historical narratives are created equal. White puts a great deal of faith in what he calls "intransitive writing," which indicates the writer's place in the writing itself, and makes clear the distance between what the writer sees and the experience of what he sees. But what are we to make of a diary written in the three years of the Warsaw ghetto, in which the distance between the time of the writing and the events at its source is collapsed to nothing? Here the language of the witness appears to be quite transparent—events are recorded in a kind of shorthand—but also quite painful in its record of individuals killed, familiar streets turned into blind alleys, and day-to-day events turned into a litany of atrocity. We argue in our second chapter that the diary is an instance of metonymic displacement, a displacement that creates an uncanny sense that the events witnessed defy any discursive attempt to render them. But it is also a testimony of a writer obeying the impulse to write, to render events for history, that is marked by the effect of the sublime object of history, the event so horrible that it can't be written even as it is written. And what the diary suggests is that even the most transparent historical document is far from transparent—it does not give us a name for the events it depicts—but does provide a record of the traumatic or sublime event, even if only obliquely.

It is specifically the relationship between witness and testimony to which we turn in the third chapter. The traumatic moment can be understood as a point of passage from witness (seeing an event) to testimony (telling the event) and it is a movement that situates what we have called the real or the divine. The act of seeing (bearing witness) and the act of testifying are radically incommensurable moves, and the point that divides them is the movement into discourse. More precisely, the passage from seeing to testifying is a passage that tears the fabric of the language of testimony and that manifests itself in stutters, silences, and nearly uncontrollable fits of violent speech that sometimes (as in some cases of videotaped testimonies collected by the Fortunoff Archive) scare the interviewer. What concerns us here is the way in which that kernel of the disaster—what is seen but lost to language and, ultimately, memory for the witness—moves from witness to witness through testimony. Does the language of testimony pass on a trace of the event to the secondhand witness (does it "pursue" her, in Shoshana Felman's terms), and if so, what are the consequences of this transmission? For Felman, the answer is that the secondhand witness has an obligation to "work through" the trauma of the encounter by identifying the language of other testimonies and connecting her response to that language. But we wonder whether such a working through will have the intended effect. In an examination of several witness testimonies, and of a secondhand witness account written by Art Spiegelman (*Maus*), we contend that witness cannot be a collective act—that only individuals can witness the events of history, and that testimonies produced by them have radically unique effects that cannot be shared across groups or communities. For inasmuch as Art Spiegelman or the witnesses interviewed in person or on tape are attempting to leave a historical record that may be read collectively as a bulwark against the disaster, the effect of such testimonies—as excessive—cannot be forecast by rational means.

It is not an historical record that novelists have in mind to leave, but an imaginative one. James Young pointed out some time ago that one way novelists have an effect upon readers is to adopt the trope of the eyewitness account to lend a certain authority to language that is otherwise obviously fictive. But Young's work on the historical language adopted for fiction, though it complicates how we come to *know* history, doesn't get at the question of the very real *effects* novels and stories have, and the means by which they produce them. For narrative works by means of figures of speech, figures that—as we suggest apropos White and the language of history—both do and do not have the ability to make present the events represented. What interests us in a chapter on literary representation of the

Shoah is whether a language of "presence"—an attempt to fill in the details of the event primarily through the trope of metaphor—or the language of "absence"—a metonymic displacement of signs that empties the events of detail altogether—works most effectively to bring a trace of the event before the reader. We examine the fiction of three canonical writers (Tadeusz Borowski, Aharon Appelfeld, and Cynthia Ozick) and find, perhaps ironically, that it is Ozick, the nonwitness, who most clearly approximates an aesthetics of redemption, an aesthetics that works by means of an oscillation between a plenitude of detail and the void of nonmeaning. All three authors, in making the language of the work incommensurable with itself and with the event, produce moments of recognition, as an excess of knowledge, in their fiction. Plato's injunction against direct representation and the Second Commandment's prohibition against graven images are instructive here: narratives of the Holocaust provide a clear sense of that which refuses to be connected to the (historical) event. Idolatry is at least as dangerous as it is hubristic, for if we could redeem moments beyond history in all their fullness, what is it, precisely, that we would see?

That question arises again in our examination of how films create instances of seeing. In an analysis of *Schindler's List*, *Shoah*, *Night and Fog*, and *Life is Beautiful*, we argue that film, in its ability to place the viewer in the position of witness, forces upon her a recognition that works against a knowledge of the events depicted. The debate over the realism of *Schindler's List* is a case in point: the film was damned because it "showed too much" by following women into the showers or by forcing viewers to bear witness to executions; and it was damned because it didn't show enough. By treading lightly in scenes depicting the liquidation of the Kracow ghetto or the brutality of Amon Goeth, critics complained, Spielberg suggested that the Holocaust wasn't as bad as we were led to believe. But what the debate missed was the degree to which Spielberg placed the viewer in the position of witness—in which the viewer mediates the position of the one who sees (in some cases Goeth, in some cases Schindler, and in some cases minor characters) and the event that is seen—and how that position stands in the way of knowledge rather than provides it. Miriam Hansen reminded us several years ago that *Schindler's List* is not *Shoah*, and examined the ways in which the eye of the camera in the former film problematized "seeing" altogether; we take Hansen's essay as a point of departure and contextualize what the camera sees in terms of witnessing, testimony, and the rupture of knowledge.

In our sixth chapter, we contend that memorials and monuments to the Holocaust (including the United States Holocaust Memorial Museum and the complex of memorials and museums at Yad Vashem in Jerusalem), provide a narrative point of departure for the visitor, and confront them with just such ruptures of knowledge, fragments of events that cannot be narrated, and that instead rupture narrative. The museum provides not a way to learn about the Holocaust but a way to confront its ethical effects. At the permanent exhibit at the United States Holocaust Museum, for example, visitors walk past photographs of the liquidations of European ghettos, Torah scrolls desecrated in Czech synagogues, artifacts of unimaginable misery. One of the sections of the exhibit that evokes the most intense wonder and emotion, however, is a two-story wall of photographs taken over sixty years in a Lithuanian shtetl, including candid shots of picnics, posed sittings of families in their homes, and other scenes of ordinary lives. These representations seem, in some ways, out of place in a building whose purpose is to document the destruction of a culture and of a people. They don't seem to offer evidence, or to provide knowledge, of the events taking place in Europe in the years between 1933 and 1945; and they don't seem to give us knowledge of the Holocaust and of the series of events that the Museum wishes to commemorate. The photographs—as well as other artifacts, other stories, other representations—don't provide knowledge; instead they provide something like trauma, a sense that even in the connection between the lives seen in the representation and the viewer's own lived life, there is something that powerfully exceeds both. They provide, in Walter Benjamin's terms, "moments of danger" that brush historical narrative—the language we use to give our lives and the lives of those we do not know a certain coherence—against the grain.

We conclude by offering some of the pedagogical implications of a redemptive theory of witnessing for Holocaust representation. Following Augustine, Benjamin, and Blanchot—who argue that teaching as the dissemination of knowledge is a retelling of things that the hearer already knows—we argue that if we take representation to be a retelling or a teaching of the Holocaust, we impoverish not just the event but also the human capacity to think the event, and foreclose the incommensurable in favor of a secure position from which to speak. Humans have a tendency to elide incommensurabilities by inserting them into systems that have already been devised, into positions of identifying or naming (and therefore misrecognizing) trauma. This is the danger in Holocaust education: learning the Holocaust as a knowable event may not prevent future Holocausts, since we'll think we can see it coming. The ethics we propose here is not the universal ethics (capital "E") of system, but a particular ethics, one that insists that the impact of the Holocaust as a human event is so great because it resists such a universal ethics. This does not mean, of course, that we turn our backs on the ethical imperative to teach the Holocaust; rather, we want to rethink that imperative so that, in teaching the event, its capacity to traumatize and to allow for the intervention of the divine through a different sort of redemptive power is not lost.

We began this project as a way to work across a number of disciplinary lines—philosophy, theology and religion, history, literary and cultural studies, among others. Part of the problem we've seen in even the most cross-disciplinary work on the Holocaust and representation, beginning with Langer's pathbreaking work but including recent work like Young's and La Capra's, is that it tends to work at the level of historical documents or survivor testimony or the narrative of a memorial. Our intention is to go farther, to investigate what such narratives *do*, and to begin to characterize their effect. This is not simply a study of representations of the Holocaust, but of how such representations help us to understand the nature of the human subject. In particular it attempts to investigate those aspects of the subject—the divine, the material, the real—that don't bring the reader or viewer or participant to meaning but bring her to note meaning's complexity and frailty in the face of something like the Shoah.

Acknowledgments

We are grateful for the support of many institutions and individuals who have made this book possible. Albertson College of Idaho provided a generous grant to support initial research at Yad Vashem during the summer of 1997 that served as groundwork for our thinking on trauma, history, and identity. During the fall of 1998, the graduate school at the University of Wisconsin at Madison provided a semester's leave, during which a good deal of the project was drafted. The George L. Mosse/Laurence A. Weinstein Center for Jewish Studies granted funding for course development, part of which allowed travel to Yad Vashem in 1999 and research for some of the work on pedagogy developed in the book's conclusion. The work done at Yad Vashem was also partly funded by the offices of Academic Affairs and International Programs at North Central College. Finally, the Faculty Development Committee at North Central College funded research during the summers of 1999 and 2000; both grants provided time for drafting and completing different parts of the book.

This book began in the aftermath of a panel at the 1995 Conference on College Composition and Communication in Washington, DC; it was at that conference that we first realized the pedagogical imperative we set forth here. The International Symposium on German/Russian Cultural Interaction held at the University of Missouri at Columbia in 1996 provided the opportunity to do some of the research that eventually became part of the chapter on the United States Holocaust Memorial Museum and Yad Vashem; we thank Gennady Barabtarlo, the symposium organizer, and the symposium participants for their indulgence of a paper that was at best tangentially related to the interests of others gathered there. Thanks are also due the program committees at the Modern Language Association, the Rhetoric Society of America, the Legacies of the Holocaust conference at the University of Nebraska at Omaha, the Midwest Modern Language Association, and the Yad Vashem International School for Holocaust Studies, which allowed us to present and develop much of the work that we include here.

This book could not have been written if it weren't for the patience and generosity of our colleagues and students. We are especially grateful to Dominick La Capra, Geoffrey Hartman, Sara Horowitz, James Young, Mark Pollock, and Jane Bellamy, with whom we shared the podium at conferences and who helped us by arguing with much of what we had written. Thanks are also due to our colleagues Howard Hinkel, Tim Materer, Sandy Camargo, Kerry Walter Ashby, Diane Raptosh, and Denny Clark for their encouragement at early stages of the project—and those who sustained us as we slowly completed it—Lisa Long, Sara Eaton, Tom Schaub, Susan Bernstein, and Elaine Lawless. Our involvement with our students was perhaps the most rewarding aspect of our work, for it is through them that we understood just how high the stakes of witness and testimony are. We want to thank, in particular, Greg Sturgeon, Lucy Stanovick, and Reinhold Hill; Mary Juzwik, John Drake, Melissa Walter, Tisha Turk, and Kim Rostan, as well as several classes of writing and theory students at North Central College, Albertson College of Idaho, and the University of Missouri. We acknowledge Rebecca Mitchell, Amanda Buchanan, Andy Young, Danielle Rubin and Bill Morgan for their unflagging interest and their intense engagement with the difficult material we presented in the classroom. We owe a special debt to Janet Alsup, whose acuity and intelligence as both a teacher and co-investigator of this material was invaluable. Most of all, we are immeasurably grateful to Syd Bernard, whose commitment to the difficult task of bearing witness and to the work of Jewish memory in the wake of the Shoah, was and continues to be a inspiration to us.

This project could not have been possible without the love and support of Hannah Bernard-Donals and Lynn Jankiewicz.

We are indebted to those at SUNY Press who showed us great patience and encouragement throughout the writing of this book. The generous comments from our readers and the production guidance of Judith Block all have made for a much better book. Most of all, we wish to thank James Peltz whose initial and continued enthusiasm for the project helped us remain focused on what the book could become.

Some of the material in this book has appeared in significantly different form elsewhere. Portions of chapter 1 were published in *Mosaic* in the spring of 2001; portions of the chapter on history appeared in *Clio* during the same year. A section of our chapter on testimony appeared in *College Literature* in the spring 2000 issue, and a portion of the chapter on museums was published in *Cold Fusion: Aspects of the German Cultural Presence in Russia*, edited by Gennady Barabtarlo.

We dedicate this book to our children and our students.

1

Sublimity, Redemption, Witness

If thought is not measured by the extremity that eludes the concept, it is from the outset in the nature of the musical accompaniment with which the SS liked to drown out the screams of its victims.

Adorno, *Negative Dialectics*

With enigmatic eyes, the machine angel [Klee's Angelus novus*] forces the viewer to ask whether it proclaims complete disaster or the rescue hidden within it. It is, however, to use the words of Walter Benjamin, who owned the picture, an angel that does not give but takes instead.*

Adorno, "Commitment"

A historian . . . establishes a conception of the present as the "time of the now" which is shot through with chips of Messianic time. . . . For every second of time [is] the strait gate through which the Messiah might enter.

Benjamin, "Theses on the Philosophy of History"

There are obvious risks involved in using the word "redemption" when talking about the Shoah: it seems counterintuitive that we could redeem the suffering of the millions who were systematically rounded up and killed during those years, or that there might be a way to somehow retrieve the lives, or even the traces of the lives, that were ended. Even the two most central injunctions to have become linked with the aftermath of the Holocaust—"never forget" and "never again"—cannot be said in any way to imply redemption: it may well be that by remembering the events of the Holocaust, in their individual cases or in their staggering totality, they will be burned into our collective consciousness; and it also may be true that the trace of the events that remains there may hold individuals to an ethical standard that will keep a series of events like it from happening again. But neither act—of remembrance or ethical action—can either roll back history or provide a sense of what it was like to be there, to allow us to see what it was like. A different kind of risk is involved when using the term "sublimity" in relation to the event, one that Dominick LaCapra has warned us about: sublimity seems to call for silence rather than utterance or representation, thereby working against the imperative to write the Holocaust; and sublimity, at least in Lyotard's formulations of it, evacuates history and historical specificity in favor of the negative (and perhaps negative pleasure) of ultimate trauma (LaCapra, *Representing* 95–106). If we confront the Shoah and the Final Solution as events that evoke sublimity, though we may "well recognize the special demands placed on language" and representation, we nonetheless risk "celebrat[ing] transgression, abstractly affirm[ing] limits, or confid[ing] in one aesthetic or another" (110). Essentially, the appeal to the sublime for LaCapra is a move away from the particularities of the horror of the Shoah and toward the more comfortable realm of theory.

But we want to call into question the more or less orthodox understandings of both sublimity and redemption in order to suggest that it is in their *relation* that we can begin to understand the traumatic effect of certain representations of the Shoah. One warrant for this relation is found in Kant's *Critique of Judgment*: "Perhaps the most sublime passage in the Jewish Law is the commandment, Thou shalt not make unto thee any graven image . . ." (134). The commandment against idols, the image that would stand for itself and take the place of the (absent) object of representation, is a commandment guarding against the quid pro quo of a simple representative redemption—this act redeems this object. It reminds that representation does not give us the sublime object in the case of God. Instead it presents what George Steiner calls "an in-gathering of all existence into a 'oneness' of strictly inconceivable compaction, and a zero-point" ("The Great Tautology" 355). Such representations—particularly certain representations of the Holocaust—complicate the imperatives of remembrance and of historical vigilance because rather than see their task as calling to mind or imagining the events they purport to represent, they instead confront the reader or the viewer with the extremity that eludes the concept, what Kant called the "abyss of the imagination." It is an abyss, however, that calls forth not silence, and not the historical or novelistic narratives that so trouble Berel Lang or Saul Friedlander, but representations that present what exceeds the name, that present the oneness of the inconceivable and the zero point.

The meaning of redemption, as it is generally accepted, carries with it a notion of exchange, of a quid pro quo, whereby that which is lost may not be recovered but for which we may gain something of equal value in return. As traditionally understood in theological terms, redemption refers to the performance of an ethical act or an utterance that can bring into being a state of affairs different from, and qualitatively better than, the one currently in existence. In Jewish theology, redemption carries with it the idea of healing—*tikkun olam*, to repair the world—the crux of which is that by working to fulfill the law and by bringing yourself, through prayer and activity, into community with other Jews and with God, you are bringing the world closer to its perfection. Kabbalistic (or messianic) notions of redemption go farther, suggesting that by repairing the world we not only redeem ourselves and this world but also hasten into existence the potential unification of the human and the divine.

There exists, in this assumed relationship of equivalence, an odd symmetry—one term may stand in for another as a figural sign may stand in for another, different sign, so that, in Anthony Hecht's poem, in which "A Luger settled back deeply in its glove" ("More Light! More Light!"), we are able to let the glove be redeemed for a hand, and the meaning of the synecdoche here becomes clear: the gloved hand of an SS officer is a more sinister image than an ungloved one, and we understand, now, the image that is called up, either for us or in spite of us. Poiesis, here, functions redemptively: through a series of figural equivalences, in which terms are substituted for one another, either in logical terms or—sometimes—in illogical ones, the result is the aesthetic completion of the image, achieved by bringing signs into accord with one another on a recognizable paradigm. As if by invocation or prayer, we bring terms into alignment so that they make sense, so that we build a knowledge from them, so that we are able, in poetic terms, to read the poem.

It works in similar ways if we suggest that in creating representations of the Holocaust, we may be participating in an act of redemption. Adorno's fear, in the years immediately following the war, was that by daring to write poetry—by engaging in any act of representation that allows us to build a knowledge that brings us pleasure by means of poiesis—we would engage in such an act of alignment. By equating the object represented with the image—by transforming "the physical pain of those who were beaten down with rifle butts" into something that appears to have meaning ("Commitment" 88)—we forget that there is something of that pain, and some aspect of the lives that surround those moments of pain, aspects that include joy and drudgery, that escape the equation. Adorno,

quoting Sartre, favored works of art that do "not have an end . . . [but
which *are*] an end" (89), works that did not run the risk of commensurat-
ing the suffering of the victim of the Shoah, or its potential victims, with
some moral lesson or pleasure. The risk of committed art, art that attaches
itself to a political rather than to an aesthetic ideology, is that the substitution or alignment or redemption simply takes a different form. Instead of
turning the image into an object of consumption for what Adorno called
the culture industry, it is instead redeemed by its connection to political or
moral agendas, agendas that may work against the pleasure principle of au-
tonomous art (art that redeems by providing pleasure in the place of language or medium) but which are agendas nonetheless. Better, suggests
Adorno apropos of Brecht, to dismantle the illusion of exchange by "ex-
plod[ing] the art from the inside" than to subjugate it from the outside either in the name of aesthetics or of politics (90). Representations of the
Shoah are instances of this conundrum par excellence. The redemption of
1100 Jews by Oskar Schindler, and its representation in the hands of
Steven Spielberg in *Schindler's List*, has itself been seen as something like
an act of redemption: here, finally, we are able to begin to understand both
the nature of the events of the Holocaust and the potential goodness that
it may well have spawned in individuals. And yet if we take seriously Spielberg's offer of the film to any school that wants to use it as a way to teach
(about) the Holocaust, the redemptive value of the film becomes suspect:
for some, *Schindler's List* has become the Holocaust, and Schindler's redemptive act is substituted for the unseen and unrepresented cruelty and
violence in Jewish communities in France, and Hungary, and other parts
of Poland and Russia. As powerful and unswervingly valorous a film as it
is, *Schindler's List* is redemptive in the sense that it provides a way to know
the Holocaust, and for us to believe that we can prevent something like it
from happening again. "Never forget." "Never again."

But what we want to argue here, and in the chapters that follow, is
that representations of the Holocaust—and, one could make the case that
this is true of representation in general, but this is a case that we will let the
reader make on his or her own—do not allow us to see or redeem the
events of history because the equation of sign to sign (of "hand" to
"glove," of over a thousand Schindlerjuden to six million Jews from Europe and the East, of the effect of a work to its conceptual organization as
knowledge) works to produce a harmony, either in the form of knowledge
or in the form of aesthetic pleasure. But to witness redemptively is much
closer to the sublime than it is to the aesthetic, much closer to a rupture
than to harmony. Contained in the idea of redemption—in traditional

terms as well as in those related to Orthodox and mystical Judaism—is a sense that there is, in the transaction between the human and the community, the human and the world, something *beyond* the human and the worldly that is generated to lift up or to advance the individuals and the communities that work toward the world's perfection. The kabbala suggests that there is released a divine spark, a fragment of the state prior to the fall and potential in the messianic age. In more conventional terms, what is produced—in prayer, in the encounter between human and divine in the work of the world—*exceeds* the work itself, and also exceeds our human capacity to describe it. It is the equivalent of Steiner's zero point.

We will argue here that what is redemptive in representations of the Shoah—what one sees—is precisely the production of this sublime excess, which troubles testimony and narrative and forces the reader to confront the horror of the limit, rather than (in conventional terms) the presence of the object or event itself. If we take the sublime to be something like Adorno's "extremity that eludes the concept," that elusiveness can only be made manifest in representation itself, and it is made manifest in what Geoffrey Hartman calls, apropos of Lyotard, "a *differend* (between what is conceivable and what is presentable) that challenges" representational harmony. It is this extremity, the differend between the conceivable and the presentable, that is redemptive, in work that presents both disaster and rescue, the sacred and the profane, the face of God and the abscess of evil.

It will be the task of this chapter to make clear the connection between a sense of redemption consistent with a strand of mystical Jewish theology that cares deeply for how one can present the excess of the knowable, and the feeling of the sublime in which the events of history disturb the witness and stand full force in the way of writing.

I. Redemption

The Shoah is so difficult to understand in terms of historical precedent that it has been likened to a break or a discontinuity in historical time. David Roskies begins his book on Jewish responses to catastrophe by wondering whether the Holocaust is destined to become "the crucible of [Jewish] culture" because of its status as "Event," an abyss of history, in which we can no longer use traditional narratives or rituals of remembrance to understand or contextualize it. His response is to suggest that "to approach the abyss as closely as possible and to reach back over it" is "a much more promising endeavor than to profess blind faith or apocalyptic despair"

(Roskies 9). The motif of the break or rupture has made its way into the memorials created in Europe to commemorate the Shoah, as James Young notes in his studies of Holocaust memorials: in Kazomierz, Poland, a wall has been built of shards of tombstones that had been used by Germans as paving stones, a wall whose predominant feature is a jagged breach which commemorates "the devastation that remains" even after fifty years (Young, *The Texture of Memory* 203). Roskies and Young both recognize that the breach of historical time embodied in the Shoah and the repair that is compelled by it are irreconcilable: redemption is both necessary and impossible by tangible means. It is, however, by means of the intangible, the unrepresentable—by what might even be called the sublime representation—that redemption is made possible.

Redemption, as found in the rabbinical literature, is seen essentially as the end of history and a return to the world outside or beyond history. In the days of the messiah, there will be a reconciliation of the natural and the divine law, and justice will be meted out accordingly: those who broke the law but who went unpunished will be punished, and those who profaned the divine will likewise be punished regardless of their adherence to the (fallible) human law. The diaspora will be ended, despotic rulers will be crushed, and Israel will live on the holy land on intimate terms with God. Harmony between God and humans will be restored, and creation will be returned to a "future time" that abolishes history in favor of the pre-Fall state of being (for details see the third chapter of Kaufmann's *The Religion of Israel*).

There is no irreconcilability in these accounts of redemption between the divine and the human because they were never reconciled to begin with. As Gershom Scholem noted in what turned out to be a life's work on mysticism, "Judaism aimed at a radical separation of the three realms [of cosmos, God, and human]; and above all, the gulf between the Creator and His creature was regarded as fundamentally unbridgeable" (*On the Kabbalah* 88). Needless to say, such a view of redemption is especially troubling in view of the events of the Shoah. Roskies devotes a chapter of his book to the image of the crucified Jew, the Holocaust survivor or victim as the ultimate witness and the archetypal sufferer upon whose pained shoulders the burdens of the world are laid (see *Against the Apocalypse*, 258–310). In terms of redemption, this is a chilling thought—the Jewish Holocaust victim, offering himself up willingly like Christ to pay for the suffering of the world, cleansing the world of evil by taking upon himself the catastrophe and being immolated (an etymologically honest holocaust). Such a view assumes a theodicy in which the good suffer pain alongside those who ignore the human and the divine law, but in which only the truly observant will be restored. There is a direct correlation between the obedience to the law and the redemption to come, a correlation in which the effects of the divine—the effects of an order that is beyond comprehension upon the material and rhythmical lifeworld of, say, a fourth-century rabbinic community or of an early twentieth-century shtetl in northern Romania—are ignored in favor of a stoical, forward-looking knowledge. Such a stoicism, a view of suffering whose foundation is a recognition that it will be repaid in future generations, is cold comfort for the father in the ghetto who watches as his children die of starvation one by one.

Thus Scholem's interest in mysticism: he was concerned that the rabbinic tradition in Judaism was more concerned for a rational divinity—one that speaks the world into existence by naming it and thereby establishing, in the name, the thing itself—than that which escapes the neat categories of the logic of a Maimonides or, more recently, a Hermann Cohen (see Idel, introduction and chapter 1, for another interpretation). "Once the fear of sullying God's sublimity with earthly images becomes a paramount concern," Scholem writes, "less and less can be said" about the divine and its effects upon the earth whose image is all we have to go on (88). These effects are apparent in the material realm through an excess of feeling, the sublime's "beyond" of representation that commingles pleasure with pain.

This commingling is evident, in the mystical tradition, in the emanation of the divine itself. Particularly in the texts originated by Isaac Luria in the sixteenth century, the *shekhinah*—the in-dwelling of the divine, the presence or "face" of God—is characterized by a radical otherness. In this view, God is at once entire and yet exiled from itself, both beyond the human and firmly represented by the human being. In orthodox convention, the coming of the messiah heralds the restoration of Eden and the ultimate good in the form of the divinity, and every injustice delays the restoration and forestalls the arrival of the ultimate good. But the *shekhinah* is an aspect of the divinity itself, and the fall represents not a further division between human and divine but simply an articulation of the otherness of the divine (and thereby the human) attributes themselves. As a result, both righteous acts and the perpetrations of disaster are different aspects of the divine. If the Fall is the moment in which the Tree of Life is distinguished from the Tree of Knowledge (in which divine language is distinguished from human languages), every historical moment carries with it both the potential for disaster and the potential for reunion of the human and the divine, the complete disaster or the rescue hidden within. Every historical moment, in the words of Walter Benjamin—wayward fellow-traveller of Scholem and the mystical tradition—is "the strait gate through which the Messiah might enter." (We'd argue that the radical otherness of Edmond Jabes's fiction—his "writing from the break" of Auschwitz—in which what is written is the disarticulation of word from world, is an instance of this kind of redemption, a redemption not of history but of the divine in all its aspects in the events of the Shoah as it precedes history. See Jabes 57–68; Patterson 15–16; for a different view of Jabes, see Lang, *Act and Idea* 103–16.)

In a version of the Creation and Fall from the mystical tradition that rang true to Benjamin, who was eventually caught in the maelstrom, the divine essence is withdrawn into itself to create a space that makes possible the existence of the world's matter, but also chaos and evil. This volatile mixture of order and chaos is harmonized and contained by ten divine spheres or vessels. In Luria's cosmology, however, the mixture was too volatile and the vessels were shattered, and it is the shattering of the vessels that serves as the paradigm for the state of the contemporary world: its shards combine the divinity and the materiality of creation. The aim of redemption (*tikkun*, restoration) is to release the divine spark through human activity and especially the act of speaking and of prayer. Through utterance and righteous action, we may experience the completed aspect of the divine—pleasure/pain, order/chaos—if only momentarily, and in that act or utterance glimpse what exceeds the merely human.

Redemption, the process of releasing the divine spark in human ethical and creative activity, was an extremely urgent task for Benjamin (and, to a lesser extent, Emmanuel Levinas; see Handelman, 262–305, especially 271–8). Levinas was held in a detention camp during the war, and lost most of his family in Russia. Benjamin saw his world, that of Weimar Germany and its intellectual efflorescence and of the utter failure of the state and his own intellectual enterprise, as an example of "crisis time," a state of emergency. The emergency was an historical one—in which the threat of national dissolution and the advent of fascism seemed to be one more historical moment, strung like pearls on a necklace, in the long march of oppression that the Jewish people in particular seemed destined to follow—but it was also a suprahistorical one. For Benjamin, the crisis he saw in Germany was not the latest crisis but simultaneous to other crises, like the destruction of the Temple, the diasporas, the Flood. As Susan Handelman puts it, this was not peculiar only to Benjamin: "In

Jewish historiography . . . the ancient rabbis used the interpretive technique of compression and anachronistic simultaneity to construct their own species of dialectical images" (150).

For Benjamin in particular, redemption is a process that takes place in terms of discursive representation, one that followed closely Scholem's understanding of the various kabbalistic literatures: at the moment of Adam's fall the world, which had been governed by the Tree of Life in which the divine and the mutable were in communion, and its elements become differentiated. Humans resort to the Tree of Knowledge, which enables them to distinguish between good and evil, holy and unholy, the truth and the lie. The primary means by which humans do this is through the senses and through language. There's an implicit link between sense experience and experience of the divine, and between human language and divine language, but it has been rendered invisible by language's (and sense experience's) tendency to naturalize existence and the name. Though God created the world through an act of divine language, "the Fall marks the birth of the *human word*, in which the name no longer lives intact, and which has stepped out of the language of names . . . the word must communicate *something* (other than itself)" (Benjamin, *Reflections* 327). And yet it was still possible to glimpse the original link between the heterogenous human language and the Divine *Ursprache*, and it is the task of revealing the shape of this link, if not the link itself, that was the task of redemptive criticism.

But this work must take place in the realm of the profane: historical time. Our narratives of ourselves and our places in the world have so naturalized human language as to stand full force in the way of redemption, of the recovery of the divine, of the original, structurally determinate moment in which material content and truth content engage in relation. In order to engage in the work of redemption, our job is "that of rescuing the few unique visions of transcendence that grace the continuum of history, the now-times (*Jetztzeiten*), from the fate of oblivion which incessantly threatens to consume them" (Wolin 48). Redemptive critique is "a work of *re-membrance*: it is a process of preserving the truth content or idea of a work [or an object] from the ever-threatening forces of social amnesia to which humanity has over the ages become inured" (Wolin 45). Such work involves the piecing together of languages: rather than try, in Benjamin's oft-cited example, to match a translation to the original (trying, in effect, to match historical narrative to the event it purports to narrate); and rather than try to write a translation that sounds as if it had been written originally in the language of the translation (trying, in effect, to match historical narrative, by means of contextualizing it in the language of the narrative itself, to an interpretive "truth"); the translator—and by extension, the historian—must "constellate" the original and the translation so that their superimposition releases "that pure language which is under the spell of another" (Benjamin, *Illuminations* 80). The writer has before him "fragments of a vessel which are to be glued together" so as to match one another, and must "incorporate the original's mode of signification, thus making both the original and the translation recognizable as fragments of a greater language, just as fragments are part of a vessel" (78).

But redemption here doesn't mean trying to recuperate the events that, in Pierre Vidal-Naquet's terms "precede discourse" if by that we mean getting the historical moment, the minutiae of the Holocaust's horror, right. Events of history are heterogenous because their interpretive significance and their effect upon the participant's and the observer's lived lives are by definition incommensurable. As with the mystical notion of the divine, in which the material and the immaterial, the sacred and the terrible, are commingled, any point of history is a disorderly intersection of moments—of pleasure, pain, logic and chaos—that resist narrative closure. Representations of such historical moments will show the pressure of this historical incommensurability, despite their attempts to do otherwise, in their effects upon readers or their figural displacements, but they don't provide access to—stand in for—the events. What can be written is the impasse between what we can imagine and the conventions available to us to express them. It is this impasse, "the strait gate" in kabbalistic terms, "through which the Messiah might enter" (*Illuminations* 264), through which we have a sense of something simultaneously human and beyond the human, of something both distressingly recognizable (providing us comfort or pleasure) and impossibly painful as well. In Handelman's terms, "for Benjamin the stripping or the mortification of the works" either of history, or of literature "was only one part of the dialectic of allegory; in making things 'other,' there is a countermovement toward redeeming them as well. On another level, Benjamin could be said to be endeavoring to relate the sacred and profane" (128).

On this view, redemption is a discursive operation. To return to the problem with which we began this chapter, can we say that redemption of the six million is possible, given the difficulty if not the impossibility of recovering what has been lost? To suggest to the child of a survivor, or to a survivor herself, that life before the Shoah can be recovered, or that her experiences at Majdanek or in hiding in Czechoslovakia that are constantly recalled to memory are moments "through which the Messiah might enter" might sound to the survivor or her child crass at best. But on the reckoning of a Benjamin, and that of Luria and the other mystics, there is no way to equate the experiences of Majdanek and their memories or their representations because they comprise material that can never be completely recovered—the sacred and the profane, the experienced and the remembered, the instant and the representation of it. They may not be made commensurable because the days of the messiah present themselves every day in the flashes of pain and pleasure—and in representation, flashes of "extremity eluding a concept"—and not in the crashing down of some historical curtain. These horrifying moments—the irreconcilability of, for example, the warm spring breezes that met allied troops in early 1945 as they entered the gates of Dachau to "liberate" it, and seeing sights that "beggar the imagination," Eisenhower put it then—are redemptive in Benjamin's terms, not in conventional ones, precisely because the commingling of irreconcilables presents what defies presentation. What is redeemed here is what exceeds representation, perhaps in Steiner's negative terms, certainly not as positive or transcendent; in the facets of the creative or the destructive forces of both history and of representation, but not the lives lost or the experiences that traumatize a life.

II. Sublimity

In *Critique of Judgment*, Kant was attempting to work through the relation between what we are able to perceive and to think, and our *capacity* to perceive and to think. From the beautiful we learn how the demand for an end, the demand for a name or for learning, can be suspended in favor of a self-consciousness about learning itself. Aesthetics began, once and for all, to lay the foundation for the universality of the human ability to think and to know: it is through the ability to bring into "agreement" the imagination and the understanding common to all humans that we also have the ability to say something about the capacities that exist, a priori, enabling us to do so.

Such a harmony bears a resemblance to the notion of redemption that is commonplace in rabbinic theology. Though the epistemologies of theology and phenomenology have distinct aims, Kant is quite clear that he is concerned with humans' relation to the divine, and this connection is one that has been advanced by Geoffrey Hartman, among others (see "The Book of Destruction;" Blanchot also obliquely links Kant's sublime to God in *The Writing of the Disaster*). In the aesthetic moment, though we are not able to understand the relation of the divine and the human, we are nonetheless able to bring into accord (if not make commensurable) rational capacity, that which makes us human, and the sensible world. That accord allows us to understand the perfection that is achievable through human capacities to know and to do, but is a perfection that has little to do with the God of the supersensible because that supersensible realm is simply not something we can know. It may be there, and we must trust that it is there, but we ought not try to reason the divine, just as we ought not try to reason the theodicies about which midrashim were written and told after the destruction of the Temple in the first century, and after the diasporas of the fourteenth century, or after the destruction of European Jewry in the twentieth. God and the messiah are not our concern, though a reconciliation of the human and the natural law are.

But the sublime is different. Whereas the apprehension of the beautiful has to do with the form of the object and our ability to make sense of it, the sublime is the "exhibition of an indeterminate concept" that is "unbounded" (II.§23, 244). Kant goes on: "what is sublime . . . cannot be contained in any sensible form . . . which, though [it] cannot be exhibited adequately, [is] aroused and called to mind by this very inadequacy" (II.§23, 245), and "carries with it, as its character, a mental agitation" (II.§24, 247), an agitation that isn't harmonious but is instead irritating, troubling, traumatic. If the imagination's tendency is to organize sense data, and understanding's is to bring those data (as *quantum*, in Kant's terms; as an object of knowledge) under a concept, or without naming them, then the mind is presented with something it simply cannot do in the sublime. It is forced to deal with something completely boundless. In the feeling of the sublime, "our imagination strives to progress toward infinity": as Russian and American troops entered the camps in Poland and central Germany in late 1944 and early 1945, they were confronted with the most unimaginable sense data—walking corpses, bodies piled upon bodies, the smells of decay and defecation and the sounds of suffering, and of death, and of birds, and breezes, and the vaguest feeling of warmth that comes after the edge of winter has been tempered. In comparison to what these soldiers may have seen in their travels toward the camps—in wartime, with the atrocities associated with the belligerence of nations—these "data" were infinitely more difficult to organize, because they were unassociated with the war: whose enemies were these, and by what combination are the chills of typhus and the warmth of earliest spring to be brought under a concept or unified such that they can be combined with understanding?

The sublime moment is, like redemption in the mystical texts, a highly ambivalent one. The excess represented by the sublime moment is also a radical simultaneity.

> If a [thing] is excessive for the imagination (and the imagination is driven to [such excess] as it apprehends [the thing] in intuition), then [the thing] is, as it were, an abyss in which the imagination is afraid to lose itself. Yet at the same time, for reason's idea of the supersensible [this same thing] is not excessive but conforms to reason's law to give rise to such striving by the imagination. Hence [the thing] is now attractive to the same degree to which [formerly] it was repulsive to mere sensibility. (II.§27, 258; brackets appear in the translation)

The sublime is exhibited in a simultaneity of pain and pleasure, revulsion and attraction—pain at the realization that the mind simply cannot comprehend the magnitude of what is presented to it, pleasure at the recognition that it must have the capacity to feel such pain; revulsion at the horror of the image; attraction to the supersensible, to God, that provides the position from which to be revulsed. It is also a simultaneity that, like the moment of redemption, annihilates time. "Comprehending a multiplicity in a unity (of intuition rather than of thought), and hence comprehending in one instant what is apprehended successively, is a regression that in turn cancels the condition of time in the imagination's progression and makes simultaneity intuitable" (II.§27, 258–9).

It is the moment of pleasure and pain that characterizes the feeling of sublimity that seems to be the source of Adorno's admonishment to poets (and writers in general) to avoid the pleasure afforded by works of art that represent the immeasurable suffering of the victims and survivors of the Shoah. In Kant's *Critique of Judgment*, the sublime is a key moment in a theory of knowledge because it is the moment at which a person, in the presence of an object that is so overwhelming as to defy reason, is presented with the limit of her capabilities to judge, to reason, to understand. It is a moment "beyond representation." Sublimity is the means by which the *presentation* (*Darstellung*) of the trace of the event of the Shoah itself is accomplished by a failure inherent in *representation* (*Vorstellung*).

The sublime, Kant claims, involves *negative* presentation, an experience of the breakdown of the accord between the imagination and the understanding. In the words of Irving Howe apropos the Shoah, "it leaves us intellectually disarmed, staring helplessly at the reality or, if you prefer, the mystery of mass extermination. There is little likelihood of finding a rational structure of explanation for the Holocaust" (Lang, *Writing* 175). In the face of such a vastness, such a mystery, reason, the faculty that exhibits entireties to the mind, demands absolute totality. But in the face of such a vastness, our inability to produce the image of this totality "is the awakening of a feeling of a supersensible faculty within us; and it is the use to which judgment naturally puts particular objects on behalf of this latter feeling, and not the object of sense, that is absolutely great" (Kant, §25, 97). The supersensible—that which beggars the imagination, to use General Eisenhower's words, that which is beyond what is capable of being presented to the mind—and not the sensible object is the source of our feeling of the sublime.

The sublime is the experience of a lack, as the no-place, of the idea, a necessary absence that summons the presence-through-absence of the power of reason. The infinitely possible is called up in the space of impossibility.

> We need not worry that the feeling of the sublime will lose something if it is exhibited in such an abstract way as this, which is wholly negative as regards the sensible. For though the imagination finds nothing beyond the sensible to support it, this very removal of barriers also makes it feel unbounded, so that its separation from the sensible is an exhibition of the infinite; though an exhibition of the infinite can as such never be more than merely negative, it still expands the soul. Perhaps the most sublime passage in the Jewish Law is the commandment: Thou shalt not make unto thee any graven image, or any likeness of any thing that is in heaven or on earth, or under the earth, etc. (General Comment 135)

The sublimity of the Second Commandment is that it understands the risks inherent in mistaking the image—that which has the appearance of the natural, of that which bears a resemblance to the everyday objects and occurrences to which we have become accustomed—for that which exists beyond it. That risk is a risk of equation, in which we call the divine the beautiful or—worse—something that can be brought under a concept in knowledge. The Second Commandment recognizes the sublimity of the divine, the sense in which the sublime resists representation altogether, and that for it to be made present, the sublime object—God, the object or event itself, the moment that precedes history or the trace of a life that precedes our capacity to imagine it—must be *presented* not by the graven image but by some other means.

"Poetry," for Kant, does not succumb to the threat hanging over mimesis (or the graven image), the threat that we mistake the object represented for some permutation of the "Idea," the event as it precedes discourse. The means by which the trauma of the (sublime) event is best presented is through indirection, not through the language of the name, the language of instrument, in which we believe we recognize the object represented in its image. Poetry does not, according to Kant, allow us to generalize from the particular image presented to the Idea itself, but rather presents a sense in which there *may* be a relation between the particularity of the image and the Idea, if only through the suspension of knowledge brought about by the failure of language to provide a comprehensive name for the event itself. Appelfeld's dictum—to refrain from directly representing the event of the Shoah—here may be borne out by Kant's sense of the presentation of the image through poetry: the events of the Shoah are best represented not through the language of metaphor, of presence, through the recognizable figures by which we give shape to our lives—"oven," "gas," "transport," those phrases that we have learned to identify as measures of pain and of inconceivability that have now nonetheless become (or so we think) conceivable—but through the language of absence, in which "such a multiplicity of partial presentations [are created] that no [single] expression that stands for a determinate concept can be found for it" (Kant §49, 185). Direct representation—the graven image (like Kosinsky's *The Painted Bird* or even Borowski's *This Way for the Gas*)—ought to be thrown over in favor of the more oblique but nonetheless more suggestive *The Book of Questions* or Appelfeld's own *Badenheim 1939*. But to suggest as much is to forget that the object of representation in this case is itself sublime, is itself incapable of being rendered by the faculties of the human mind in such a way that an "expression" could be found to present it. The feeling of the sublime that is aroused in the face of the event that defies our capacity to present it to the faculties of the mind nonetheless forces a recognition of an entity—a nothing, a no-place—that exists, as a void or an abyss beyond that capacity; and the presentation through narrative, through the "aesthetic idea," of that which suspends knowledge in favor of a vertiginous sense of what lies beyond it, are intimately connected.

In the aesthetic idea, the intuition is too rich with what Kant calls aesthetic attributes for the concept it is associated with, and it is this richness that stimulates the rational movement that produces the feeling Kant associates with the aesthetic idea. While the sublime pushes the imagination to its negative limit, the symbol pushes the understanding to its negative limit, passing over to the faculty able to think beyond the limit of the understanding: reason. Where the sublime produces an accord between the imagination and reason by forcing the imagination to break down and then respect reason, the symbol induces such an accord through the expressive power of the imagination in its production of thought that exceeds reason.

Symbolism, writing, is not really about the putative object of writing, but about "language only and not the object itself" (*Prolegomena* 105). Language can never give a pure presentation of supersensible objects. Its symbolic presentations always carry with them an excessive element, an unintelligibility at the heart of the presentation of the supersensible that prevents language from ever announcing its object. Representation contains its own limitations as it projects the narrative of purposiveness beyond discursive knowledge, installing it against a "ground" of concepts in terms of time and of space and of duration—in terms of what we can know. Yet these grounds themselves contain their own excess and in the incommensurability between them announce the impossibility of the immediate, intellectual intuition that would fuse intuition and concept in a single, nontemporal instant. It is in that instant that we are confronted by the abyss, silence, and the end of representation.

Two of the risks of connecting sublimity to the disaster of the Shoah are the risk of silence, and the risk of dissolving the particular horror into the ether of a broadly defined "discursivity," in which—with reference to Lyotard—"the Shoah is transcoded into postmodernism" (LaCapra, *Representing* 98). We want to briefly address these risks, because the fears directly expressed by LaCapra, as well as indirectly by Berel Lang (*Act and Idea in the Nazi Genocide* 165–206) and to some extent Saul Friedlander (in *Reflections of Nazism*) are essentially a fear that by naming the Shoah—either as sublime object, or as redeemable—we domesticate it and sidestep the unnameable horror that it was. (Lang goes further, linking Kant's metaphysics to the logic of the Final Solution, though—interestingly—he says little about sublimity as such.) But these fears do not account for the implications of the sublime and redemption that we are attempting to outline in this chapter. In an analysis of Lyotard's *The Differend* and *Heidegger and "the Jews"*, LaCapra notes that Lyotard's view "of the 'excess' of the Holocaust whereby one is recurrently confronted by the need to put into language what cannot as yet be acceptably 'phrased'" is convincing (97). He goes on, however, to suggest that this same confrontation leads ultimately to a sublime silence, whereby one "'trope[s]' away from specificity and evacuate[s] history by construing the caesura of the Holocaust as a total trauma that is un(re)presentable and reduces everyone (victims, witnesses, perpetrators, revisionists, those born later) to an ultimately homogenizing yet sublime silence" (97). In later work, LaCapra wonders whether the Kantian sublime, and its theorizations by Lyotard and others, offers different modalities, in which silence, terror, and elation are but three distinct manifestations of sublimity (*History and Memory* 27–42). Here the urgent question is whether, in speaking of the sublime in relation to the Shoah, we aren't finding a way to name it, finding a way to make of the Shoah a divinity, not Steiner's negative divinity, but a divinity in whose presence we dare not speak, as Moses dared not, whose negative presence calls forth silence, or flight, or pleasure. As LaCapra put it to us at an MLA session in 1996, what does the sublime obligate one to do?

A careful reading of Lyotard, however, suggests that his understanding of the sublime—one closer to Blanchot's disaster than to the "uncanny" of the *Rausch* (in Friedlander's terms) or a secular displacement of the sacred— involves an obligation to utterance rather than an insistence upon silence (Friedlander, *Memory, History, and the Extermination of the Jews of Europe*; his discussion relating *Rausch*—the elation of killing—and excess, is in pages 80–114). The section of *The Differend* entitled "Obligation" makes this clear: when faced with the differend—the sublime object, that which exceeds understanding—the subject is obligated to respond, though not in the form of narrative, but of rupture. Lyotard provides the example of Abraham: the impossible command to kill his son is responded to ethically and discursively, but that response, the willingness to destroy his son whom he loves, is utterly excessive—it cannot be understood, and yet he responds affirmatively and in full grief—and that excess points both to the radical otherness of the character of Abraham and the impossibility of hermeneutic closure in the narrative (107–15). The act of witnessing to the voice of God, or of confronting the event of the Shoah, obligates individuals to, in Kant's terms, obey the moral law while recognizing that there is something that exceeds it, will abrogate it, and potentially lead to its undoing (see 125–6). Sublimity does not call forth "'appropriate' response[s]" (LaCapra, *Representing the Holocaust* 106) because it is experienced uniquely, with each individual responding to the event or object differently from every other individual. The "silences" so important to Lyotard in the section entitled "Result" are the silences of Blanchot's disaster, but they are silences that precede experience, that precede the understanding that allows us to name the event or to respond sensibly to it. Those silences that "interrupt the chain [of discourse] that goes from them" (Lyotard 106), are written in the language of representation and provide the glimpse, the divine spark, the potential for destruction and completion, inherent in redemption. Though LaCapra is right to worry about the ethical consequences of understanding the Shoah and representations of it as sublime, it is likewise true that we simply cannot guarantee instances of sublimity or trauma will call up "appropriate" reactions. This is what Benjamin meant when he suggested that we can never know whether an instance of historical time that any one of us may experience is the one in which the messiah will arrive or whether it will be the moment of catastrophe.

It could be argued that redemption is par excellence a discursive dynamic rather than a cognitive one precisely because it is the elusiveness—and the horror that results from it—of the attempt to match the infinite sense data of our life worlds to the capacity of reason that would hope to bring some kind of pattern or unity to it. It is the elusiveness of what Blanchot has called the "disaster," the "force of writing [that is] excluded from it, is beyond the pale of writing or extratextual" because it is what writing—that most reasonable of the capacities that organizes knowledge—follows and what writing nonetheless hopes to bring to the present (Blanchot 7). Particularly when that force of writing originates with the events we have come to call the Shoah (but whose name we realize is inadequate), it is imperative that we recognize the potential for writing to generate the excessive, perhaps traumatic effect: the unease of the sublime, the potential and simultaneous risk of redemption.

III. Witness

To suggest that the sublime can be attached to any kind of truth seems to fly completely in the face not only of Kant's own understanding of it but also the reasoning behind the Second Commandment prohibition. First, how can we call a work of human production (like a testimony, or a novel, or a play) sublime, or even say that the feeling one has when reading or encountering a work *as a work* is sublime, since to consider it as such would be to bring the work under a concept—we know that it is "x", a movie, a book, a *representation*—and rule it out as either aesthetic or sublime. In an example we'll return to, one of the reasons the discussion of *Schindler's List* as a representation of the Holocaust shed so much heat but so little light is that participants in the debate failed to distinguish between considering the work as a representation—a testimony—and considering moments of sublimity—of witnessing—that may have been experienced by (some, a few, all) viewers of that film. The complaints leveled against Spielberg's film—that it was not accurate enough, that it was too accurate, that it focused too much attention on non-Jews, that it relied too heavily on conventions of filmic representation—say very little about the dynamics of the sublime that are encountered by viewers at certain points throughout the film (in some cases, in complete contradiction to those very same viewers' disdain for the film as film). In judging the film, or any work, we are using judgments of taste, and we are creating knowledge based upon what we already understand (for example) about Shakespeare, about the unities, about stage convention, but such knowledge cannot be equated with the object or event that lies beyond representation itself.

But what Kant tells us over and over again is that the feeling of the sublime is the feeling one gets at the edge of a precipice, "an abyss in which the imagination is afraid to lose itself," and in which it *does* lose itself in spite of reason's ability to provide the imagination with the awareness that it is doing so. To suggest of the feeling of the sublime—whether it is encountered in the deeds or creations of humans or in the natural world—that it embodies the truth, that it instantiates in a fleeting moment a sense of all there is beyond our limited abilities to know it, is to miss the underside of that moment. To suggest this of the sublime is also to suggest of witnessing that in the act of piecing together the shards of the vessel, the bits of what we know, that we remake the vessel. It is to say that we can match testimony to testimony, or image to deed; can force together, as in Hecht's poem, the Luger and the glove in the presence of the non-Jewish Pole who has dug the grave of two Jews and, unwittingly, his own; can force together, in Spielberg's film, the bittersweet shattering of a glass under the wedding huppah, the *rassenschande* of Schindler's kissing a Jewish woman and her daughter who have, miraculously, baked a cake for his birthday, and the violence of camp commander Goeth's sexual battery of his servant Helen in a damp wine cellar. It is to say that we bring into being the horror of the seen by forging together testimonies and narratives until, taken together, they stand in for the events themselves.

But to do so would be to lie. Representation—like redemption—is par excellence a discursive dynamic rather than a cognitive one precisely because of the event's elusiveness in the presence of the word, and the horror in the face of that elusiveness. It attempts to match the infinite sense data of our life worlds to the limits of the capacity of reason that would hope to bring some kind of narrative pattern or unity to the event. But in the case of what Blanchot has called the "disaster," the "force of writing [which is] excluded from [testimony] is beyond the pale of writing or extratextual" because it is what writing comes after, while at the same time it is the thing which writing hopes to bring to the present (Blanchot 7). The force of writing—the moments of the lives of the six million Jews of Europe and the innumerable millions of others, the words of prayer uttered before the gas silenced prayer altogether, the moment of realization that comes with the closing of a van door in Kulmhof that you are the last one alive—is itself so inconceivable that any attempt to testify to it is altogether doomed to failure. But knowing, saying, and acting are themselves acts of representation, attempts to equate what one sees to cognitive categories that may or may not provide such an equation but which in the end provide access, if not to the events themselves, to the structure of witness.

The sublime moment is that in which the witness knows that she is seeing, but can't say what it is, and yet must say what it is; it both compels speaking and limits speaking by withdrawing the event. Adorno is right: it is barbaric to create poetry after Auschwitz. There is a certain barbarism, a certain horror, involved in representations of the Holocaust, or involved in any representations at all in a world that made the Holocaust possible. But this is not a barbarism that can be avoided by ruling such representations out of court, either by banning graven images or by insisting on a "modernist" rendering of the events of the Shoah. Because the utter burn of the events of the Shoah are in some sense paradigmatic of the immensity of the objects or events that Kant would say arouse the anxiety or trauma of the sublime, they will just as certainly give pain to the creator and the viewer of the works as they will give pleasure to them. They will provide the momentary pleasure that comes with the sense that but for this desperate rupture of reason and knowledge I could not have believed that these were the lineaments of human reason and knowledge. And they will provide the crushing blow that comes with the realization that along with knowledge and reason—the genius with which such a work, as a work, could be generated—comes the impossible act, the act in the world that is impossible. These two moments, of pleasure and pain, of exhilaration and doom, are the twin moments of redemption. In prayer, or in the work of representation, or in the observation of that which defies the limits of reason, we make material the unification of the present moment and the moment before time (the unification of the *urprache* and the language of the written work). In doing so, in making flesh the world and that which exceeds it, we likewise withdraw the divine from the moment in order to make room for that material presence—the representation, the embodiment of the disaster—and at the very moment at which the coming of the messiah is made possible (at the moment at which we catch the most fleeting glimpse of the supersensible in the suspension of reason and imagination, in the subreption in the exhibition of the sublime) the moment is withdrawn.

There is no need for the Second Commandment prohibition in the face of the sublime, just as there is no need to take Adorno's statements about art after Auschwitz as an injunction against representations of the Shoah. The Second Commandment was crucial for Kant because it prohibited the creation of those representations that would stand in for the objects of representation themselves, and that would therefore place discernable limits upon what sensibility would "know" of those objects. This is especially true in the case of the divine itself: rather than use the name of God, the traditional reference to the divinity in Jewish ritual is *ha-shem*, the name. On the logic of the Second Commandment, to substitute the name of God for the divinity itself, individuals using the name would also be compelled to substitute other names for God, in a sense putting limits upon the divinity itself—God would be brought under a concept. But what we have learned after Auschwitz, among the many traumatic lessons, is that the act of naming, or limiting, even those things "on earth or under the earth" let alone those things "in heaven," such as God, is itself a sublime act whose vertiginous possibilities are so many as to paralyze reason itself. If Blanchot (and Lyotard with him) is right, and naming is an act of impatience (39) because naming tries desperately to limit those possibilities, then the sublime is the recognition that with every act, including acts of representation and of utterance, there is something untrue. By untruth we do not mean falsity, but a sense that there is something that can't be brought under the concept, something that withdraws from knowledge ("in the manner of the God of Isaac Luria, who creates solely by excluding himself" [Blanchot 13]), or lies at its foundation.

There is no sense in which we can recover the loss of the lives of the six million, and there is no sense in which we can have knowledge of their suffering, or the suffering of the survivors (or their children). There is no sense in which any testimony can adequately describe either the lives that preceded the disaster or the disaster itself. To assume that we could is to assume that it is possible to work our way back along the chain of signification, along the path of history and testimony, and see what they saw, bear witness to the moment that is, for all intents and purposes, lost to history. And yet we are affected by the words, and the images, and testimonies that, in spite of our foreknowledge that it really isn't so, provide for us the merest glimpse of those lives, and those deaths, whose powerful traces affect us still. Whether we see, impossibly, the face of a loved one in a photograph from a shtetl, or we stand before a defaced ark of the covenant recovered from a synagogue somewhere in Poland and remember the words of the *shema* that would have sounded simultaneously in Hebrew sixty years earlier in that synagogue and in your father's, we witness—in the extremity that eludes the concept, in the impossible connection that is a connection nonetheless—the effect of the sublime. Like the possibility of redemption it is fleeting and full, and like the possibility of redemption it carries with it the risk that we name it—make it into testimony once again—and close the gate through which revelation (whether it be in the form of the messiah or the idea of the supersensible that underlies the moral law) may pass. Because the Shoah is, perhaps like nothing else written in and through history, the extremity that eludes the concept, and because both redemption and sublimity are defined as the act that tries nonetheless to bring into relation extremity and concept, witness and testimony, it seems to us that we cannot avoid understanding them together, both for their barbarity and also for their promise.

2

History and the Disaster: The (Im)possibility of Writing the Shoah

The disaster, unexperienced. It is what escapes the very possibility of experience— it is the limit of writing. This must be repeated: the disaster de-scribes. Which does not mean that the disaster, as the force of writing, is excluded from it, is beyond the pale of writing or extratextual.

Blanchot, *The Writing of the Disaster*

The disaster is related to forgetfulness—forgetfulness without memory, the motionless retreat of what has not been treated—the immemorial perhaps.

Blanchot, *The Writing of the Disaster*

If you were not there, you cannot imagine what it was like. . . . I was not there.

Raul Hilberg, "I Was Not There"

On the afternoon of August 3, 1942, the liquidation of the ghetto in Warsaw had been under way for nearly two weeks. On July 19, Himmler had sent a directive to the head of the police forces in the Polish General Government that set the deportations in motion, but the policy of deportation and liquidation had been set six months earlier during the conference on the "Final Solution" held in Berlin in January 1942. For anyone in attendance either at that meeting or at a meeting one month earlier, all doubt as to just what the policy meant was dispelled by Hans Frank, the governor of the area.

I want to say to you quite openly that we shall have to finish with the Jews one way or another. . . . Certainly, a major migration is about to start. But what is to happen to the Jews? Do you think they will actually be resettled in the *Ostland* villages? We were told in Berlin: Why all this trouble? We can't use them in the *Ostland* either; liquidate them yourselves. (quoted in Hilberg, *Destruction* 308)

With the killing centers already set up, the logistics of the deportations themselves were developed and by July 16, a local solution to the problem of transport had been found: a train would run daily between Warsaw and the center at Treblinka carrying no fewer than 5000 Jews from the ghetto. On July 20, the *judenrat* in the ghetto was presented with the order to prepare the population for resettlement, which would begin on the 22nd. All were to report voluntarily to the Umschlagplatz (the "gathering place"), with the exception of those registered for certain kinds of "valuable" work in industry, the ghetto bureaucracy, and those who were not fit for removal. Those in the ghetto were told that the deportations would total no more than about 60,000 people; no one could imagine that nearly ninety percent of the population of the ghetto—over 300,000 of the 380,000 Jews crammed into a corner of Warsaw—would be in Treblinka by the beginning of 1943.

That afternoon, on the third of August, Abraham Lewin, who was born in Warsaw fifty years earlier, wrote in a diary that he had kept probably since the establishment of the ghetto in 1940. That diary along with several others written by members of the Oneg Shabbas organization (which was formed with the expressed purpose of recording "the martyrology of the Jews of Poland") was eventually buried in a milk can in a basement in the ghetto. Those accounts, along with the remembrances of those who survived the deportations and the camps, form the core of the historical record of the liquidation of the Warsaw ghetto, which is itself the basis of the most comprehensive histories of the Holocaust (those written by Martin Gilbert, Lucy Dawidowicz, Raul Hilberg, and—most recently—Saul Friedlander). Those historical accounts, superimoposed upon one another, provide a broad account of the events that occurred during the days and weeks of the deportations from Warsaw: Hilberg's account relies primarily on documents retrieved from archives in Israel, Europe, the United States, documents that record the meticulous care with which the German government planned and executed the Final Solution. Gilbert and Dawidowicz tend to focus, in their accounts, upon the communities of individuals who lived in Warsaw during the concentration and the deportations, and upon the individual reactions by those Jewish eyewitnesses to the logistics of the roundups and their human consequences. Accounts written or told of the events occurring on the afternoon and evening of August 2 and the morning and afternoon of Au-

gust 3, 1942, are harrowing—of ruses used by government forces to separate children from their parents, of acts of brutality both by the German mil-
itary police and by the Jewish police, of the political and theological
convolutions of the *judenrat* and by the other Jewish organizations as they
tried to justify a consistent response to the orders to be "resettled"—and in
many cases those accounts are powerful enough to bleed through the fabric
of the historical narrative itself and (to use a phrase of Blanchot's) to burn
themselves upon a memory that is simply not our own:

> Several vans went by, loaded with Jews, sitting and standing, hugging
> sacks that contained whatever pitiful belongings they had managed
> to gather at the last moment. Some stared straight ahead vacantly,
> others mourned and wailed, wringing their hands and entreating the
> Jewish police who rode with them. Women tore their hair or clung
> to their children, who sat bewildered among the scattered bundles,
> gazing at the adults in silent fear. Running behind the last van, a lone
> woman, arms outstretched, screamed:
>> "My child! Give me back my child!"
>> In reply, a small voice called from the van.
>> "Mama! Mama!" (qtd. in Gilbert 393)

Between the language of the historian that sets these memories into
a coherent order, so that we understand the course of the events, and the
language of the eyewitness, whose task is to match the contour of her
memory with the language that will inevitably fail it, something occurs that
allows us to see the precarious position in which the historian finds himself.
On the one hand, the historian's task is to understand, from the evidence
that is available, the coherence of the course of events, events whose coherence may be immanent in their occurrence but which cannot be
matched by a language that follows its own order. On the other hand, the
historian's task is to render those events in such a way that they may be
conveyed to those who were not there. In Siegfried Kracauer's words, he
must "establish the relevant evidence as impartially as possible" and he
must "try to render intelligible the material thus secured" (47). Kracauer
goes on to suggest that these two tasks are not only impossible to separate
but that history is so heterogenous as to suggest that the successful combination of the two in a coherent historical account is impossible.

One assumption generally prevails among historians about writing
and memory—about the problem of writing on a subject that one has not
himself experienced—regardless of whether one takes the position of a

Hayden White, who assumes that there is no categorical difference between the document-as-situated-text and the historical account that situates it and other documents in turn, or maintains a distinction between the
document's material or temporal closeness to an event and the historical
narrative in which it is contextualized. That assumption is that the event
somehow makes itself present in the writing, or has an effect upon writing.
This is true whether one assumes that language and memory somehow de-
flect the event or one assumes that the array of evidence and the comprehension of it may be combined to approach it. In the words of Louis
Mink, after all historiographical options have been considered, "the con-
viction returns that the past is after all *there*, with a determinateness beyond and over against our partial reconstructions" (93). Mink suggests
that the paradox—that history is made and that history happens—cannot,
as is the case with any paradox, be solved but that we "oscillate" between
its two irreconcilable poles. For Mink, this is the best description not only
of history but of the dilemma of living a life embedded in history itself.

In this chapter we want to examine that assumption about the pres-
entness of history and about just how an event like the Holocaust may
exert its presence over us regardless of our acknowledgment that we are always writing or rewriting the effect of its presence in historical terms. Our
point of reference will be eyewitness accounts, like Abraham Lewin's diary
of the deportations from Warsaw in 1942, accounts seen as the material
of history. In Dawidowicz, and Hilberg, and Gilbert, we are given to understand events like the deportation so that we know them—through their
skillful (or perhaps, at least in Gilbert's case, artful) abilities the writers are
able, in Lore Segal's terms, to "translate" another's memories into a language that is serviceable to the memories of readers who were not there.
And, in Gilbert's case, those histories provide accounts of eyewitnesses
whose language is a sometimes breathless narrative of survival and of terror that has been filtered through the years of amazement that accompany
the experience of survival of what was assumed to be inescapable death.
But what to make of an account like Lewin's, which is written at the time,
and whose language is the language of abbreviation? "A night of horrors.
Shooting went on all night. I couldn't sleep. . . . Yesterday the following
were taken away: Kahanowicz, Rusak, and Jehoszua Zegal's whole family."
And how to account for the language that lists the events of a life in terms
only meaningful for the writer, and for whom the presence of those events,
even in the shorthand of one who breathlessly writes while gazing out the
window at the object of representation, is lost even to him at the moment
of writing? The answer that we will provide is that even for those who were

there, there is a presence—a presence of the disaster, of the occurrence of the event itself—that precedes the experience of the event, and it is this presence that may be available through, but not in, intransitive writing. This presence, like the presence of the divine spark that is known only in its effect upon the material, or like the pain accompanying the sublime, does not so much restore the events of history as it tears its fabric so that we glimpse, in Benjamin's terms, "the time of the now."

I. The Problems of History

Questions of the event's effect upon narrative accounts of that event must be answered in the context of two significant debates among historians of the Holocaust. The first of these debates is that between the intentionalists—a group of historians who focus upon the agents of history when answering questions of how certain events are connected— and functionalists—a group who focus upon the complicated networks of social and ideological material and the ways in which their intersections determine the course of historical events. The second of the debates is between those historians like Hayden White who insist upon a radical subjectivism, the result of which is that we have no access to the events of history that have essentially taken place behind our backs, and historians like Mink or like Vidal-Naquet who acknowledge the subjectivist position but who nonetheless insist that "beyond [discourse], or before this, there is something irreducible which, for better or worse, I would still call reality" (quoted in Ginzburg 86).

Though the quarrel between the intentionalists and the functionalists has mainly to do with the role of the Fuhrer in the execution of the Final Solution, it is worth considering here because the quarrel is essentially over the issue of how to categorize the events of history into a workable narrative. In order to sort through the events of history, historians need a way to distinguish the documents that form the detritus of those events and the events themselves. It is one thing, for instance, to examine the extant documents from the SS and the ministries of transport and from the regional governments in order to determine the intent of those government officials, something which lies "beyond, or before" the documents themselves. It is quite another to substitute those documents, in what amounts to historical metonymy, for intention itself. The intentionalist/functionalist debate, in other words, is a debate over whether it is ultimately possible to avoid the metonymic substitution of document for the act or event beyond

the document, and the resolution of the debate turns on the ability to identify the presence of an event as it disrupts the logic or rhetoric of the documents. The same is true for the debate between the subjectivists like White
and the pragmatists like Vidal-Naquet: both groups of historians eventually
require a language for historical writing that leaves room for the presence of
an event to bleed through the writing or method of the historian. The extent to which it is possible to write in such a fashion depends at least in part
upon our ability to glean an event from historical accounts of it. We want to
spend some time working through these debates in part because it is in the
proposed middle ground between the claims made by both sides that we
see the possibility for the end of historical writing and the inception of what
Benjamin might call redemptive history.

Intentionalist writers, like Lucy Dawidowicz, tend to see causal connections between historical events, suggesting for example that as early as in
his writings in *Mein Kampf* Hitler understood that any war would have to
be a twofold one, for territorial gain and for the annihilation of Judaism
(see, for example, 111; 158). Dawidowicz's argument hangs on the reconstruction of documentary evidence, recovered from archival records left by
the SS, particularly individual reports from Heydrich, Himmler, and those
in their employ; and upon speeches made by high officials of the Reich, including Hitler's speeches in the Reichstag invoking the massacre of Ar-
menians during the First World War and other virulently anti-Semitic
statements made at public rallies. In part founded upon the logic through
which a national bureaucracy would run, and in part founded upon the idea
that one's statements provide a sense of one's intentions, the historian is
forced, in Christopher Browning's words, to extrapolate intention through
documents and testimony "originating outside the inner circle" of those involved in policy-making. "Like the man in Plato's cave, he sees only the reflection and shadows, but not reality" (99). Intentionalist history confuses
the shadows for the historical reality, in part because the question with
which the historian begins—"Whence did the Final Solution originate?"—
predetermines the answers and the evidence that may be adduced.

The functionalists try to circumvent the problem by avoiding the
question of intention altogether. Browning points to Martin Broszat as an
"ultrafunctionalist" on the question of the Final Solution: local pogroms
and spontaneous actions against the Jews, particularly in eastern Europe,
were not the result of an orderly plan that originated with officers of the
German government. They were instead a collective response to an ideological milieu that comprised an anti-Semitism fomented by but not originating with Hitler, and a panic and anger over the losses on the eastern

front in the early 1940s and a lingering question about the link between Bolshevism and Zionism. Like Dawidowicz, Broszat and other less radical functionalist historians must resort to an incomplete documentary record and are forced to understand a relation that lies behind or beyond the language of the records themselves. But rather than attribute a single motive— a single shadow, as it were, on the wall of Plato's cave—to the disparate utterances that can be found in speeches and memos, the functionalist attributes a number of motives to those utterances and, further, examines the cultural and material context in which those utterances were made. But the same error occurs in functionalism as with intentionalism—at a certain point in the reconstruction of the context in which the policy of the Final Solution was formed, a substitution takes place in which the discursive material (in the form of reports and memos by Heydrich, Himmler, and others) is replaced by an actuality, a reality that in this case is not a reality of intention but of material circumstance. And, like the intentionalist substitution, the functionalist one severely limits the kinds of evidence that may be adduced in the analysis, because the "network" of discursive material (like the logical sequence of the same material in intentionalism) all responds to the same general question—"What is to be done with the Jews?"—a question (troublingly) posed by both German functionaries and local authorities.

For someone like Abraham Lewin, the question "What is to be done with the Jews?" takes on an entirely different significance than it would for those involved in implementing the Final Solution. How does the language of a diary, as it functions as evidence of the Final Solution and its implementation in one very local circumstance, mark the limit of both intentionalism and functionalism? For the intentionalist historian, the question of Lewin's relation to the events surrounding the liquidation of the Warsaw ghetto in 1942 might well have to do with his participation in the Oneg Shabbas organization. In effect, the guiding question of the documentary evidence of the diary itself becomes "How could this come to be written?" as much as it is also a question of "What is to become of the Jews?" In an entry dated July 24, at "six in the morning," Lewin writes, "The death of Czerniakow yesterday at half past eight in the Jewish community building" (162), and on the 25th, he wonders, "How did Czerniakow die? 10,000!" (163) The note appended to the entry says of Lewin's odd response that "Many members of the intelligentsia also killed themselves" (187). Like all of the other entries in his diary, it reads nearly the same as the entry of August 3, with its litany of the dead and its occasional record of the feelings of the writer in the face of the oncoming disaster

(July 24: "Terrifying rumors about the night. Will there be a pogrom?"). It would be tempting for the historian who understands the outcome of the events of the liquidation (a brief cessation of the deportations in September 1942 before they began again in January 1943; Lewin's presumed capture and death in Treblinka, probably days—and no more than months—later) to measure the events recorded in the diary—the death of Czerniakow, the annihilation, street by street, of families and of lives—by the agency of the writer. In Lewin we have an individual who, either for posterity through the Oneg Shabbas organization or simply out of sheer will, is the characteristic survivor. Unlike Czerniakow, he refuses to fall into despair even in the face of the deportation of his wife. For Dawidowicz, who did not have Lewin's diary at her disposal but who had others from which to compile her history of the Holocaust, this is evidence of the intentions of a single Jew, one of many who refused to passively go to the slaughter without at least registering its atrocities. The record becomes the event, the words become an act of resistance in the fact of their survival, and the historical event is redeemed by its record.

The functionalist historian will not reduce the record to the event it records through the intention of the writer or speaker. But even Christopher Browning—who calls himself a "moderate functionalist" because he refuses to see a single agency working through documents but nonetheless reads a multitude of intentions leading to a complicated and sometimes unorganized constellation of events (pointing, in the case of his work on the Final Solution, to a set of circumstances that led to the attempt to annihilate Europe's Jews through government policy)—seems to be looking for the object casting the shadow rather than examining the shadow itself. In "One Day in Jozefow: Initiation to Mass Murder," an account of the men of Reserve Police Battalion 101 and their participation in the actions to clear the East of its Jewish population, Browning is very clear with the reader: a note tells us that the study is based entirely on the records of an investigation of the battalion that was undertaken in Hamburg after the war (365), and the question at the conclusion of the study is whether or not the action at Jozefow was "typical." Though the account pieced together by Browning is chilling, its perspective is univocal and its language is authoritative. There is, even in Browning's functionalist account of the action in Jozefow, the assumption that the event may be named, that a question asked about the event may be answered, that—in short—the disaster experienced by the men in the 101st Police Battalion might be described by the historian so that it would be understood or co-experienced by the reader. But what Abraham Lewin understands, even in contextualizing the disaster in biblical terms ("a slaughter the like of which human history has not seen. Even in the legend of Pharaoh and his decree . . ." [178]), is not the continuity of event with experience, or even the continuity of event with its record. What he sees is something like the *discontinuity* between the event and its context, in which the "calamity of the 'dead souls'" is followed immediately with a record of "120,000 fictitious food-coupons" (168). There is no intention, nor even a constellation of events, possible for someone like Abraham Lewin, and it is in the language of the account—the written record—that we have a sense of this failure of experience in the face of the disaster.

II. The Problems of Narrative

Though the debate between intentionalists and functionalists may not tell us how to adjudicate claims made through documentary evidence, a group of historians following the work of poststructuralist philosophy and the radical historiography of Hayden White have argued that we're missing the point if we think we can have access to the events of history at all. More important, this group suggests, is that we look not for the contours of the object casting the shadow upon the cave wall but the contours of the shadow. Though such an examination may not tell us much about the events, it may be able to suggest how to construct a narrative account of history that suggests some of the resonance of its events without conveying the thing in itself. On such an accounting of history, the task would be to understand the narrative as evidence of the problems of the historian's method, drawing "attention to a historicity inhabiting the very presupposition that history is the fundamental mode of being" (Bennington and Young 8). Pushed to its logical extreme, such a position "takes seriously 'language as the origin of history'" (9). White wipes away with one stroke the unwarranted substitution of the event for the narrative account of it by bracketing the former and concentrating on the emplotment of the languages of history. There are other historians—Berel Lang and Pierre Vidal-Naquet to name only two—who are suspicious of this view. Though neither Vidal-Naquet nor Lang are interested in attributing motive to the Final Solution, they nonetheless reach the same conclusion that George Kren does: that there is something in the historical documents and the diaries of those like Abraham Lewin that registers somehow as "sincerity," "honesty" (7), and that this aspect of the historical—the uncanny feeling that this is something quite unlike anything we have the language for—is what lies behind or in historical writing. It may not be the event; but for Lang and for Vidal-Naquet, there is something in history that resists universalization, abstraction, and the language of narrative (see Lang, *Act and Idea* xv–xix), something that finds its way through the surface of narrative to irritate it. White's insistence on the unwritable nature of the historical occurrence forces him to insist upon writing in a "modernist" mode, a mode that focuses the reader's attention upon the difficulties of writing about something you haven't experienced. For Lang, Friedlander, Vidal-Naquet, and others, the events of history obtrude upon the writing of history, regardless of the intention of either the historian or the originator of the evidence.

Hayden White's revolutionary view of history is well enough known that it does not require rehearsal here. He made clear his position on the relation between narrative and histories of the Shoah at a conference at UCLA in 1990, entitled "Nazism and the Final Solution," and in written form in Saul Friedlander's *Probing the Limits of Representation.* On that occasion White was responding to the question of whether "there are any limits on the kind of story that can be responsibly told" about the Holocaust and Nazism, and his essay amounts to a resounding "no." It is true, he suggests, that there are certain ways of emplotting history—as tragedy, comedy, epic, fable, pastoral—that seem more implausible than others, and he cites Andreas Hilgruber's 1986 book, *Two Kinds of Ruin: The Shattering of the German Reich and the End of European Jewry,* as an example of history of the Holocaust emplotted as tragedy, the tragedy of the Wehrmacht's destruction at the hands of the Russian army during the winter of 1944–5. Written as tragedy, the defeat of the Wehrmacht overwhelms and contextualizes the (secondary) tragedy of the acceleration of the Final Solution in the year before the German army was crushed on the eastern front, a defeat that had been foreseen by the German army command during that year. Clearly, this is an emplotment of the events of the Holocaust—events we have access to only through documentary evidence and artifacts—that flies in the face of our understanding of the events themselves, but for White this does not rule the account out of court. Rather, its author "approaches the position of a number of scholars and writers who view the Holocaust as virtually unrepresentable in language" (43). For, if we rule Hilgruber's tragedy as unacceptable historical narrative, what do we do with Art Spiegelman's *Maus,* about which White speaks approvingly, an account that is (at least on the word of Terrence DesPres, quite literally) comic? Hilgruber's account of the Holocaust as subordinate tragedy, like Spiegelman's account of the survival of his father (and his own subsequent "survival") plotted as comedy, is simply one narrative that competes with other narratives of destruction and survival, and each narrative should be judged not on its accordance with the "facts" of history, which are in any event simply inaccessible, but as to whether or not they "violate any of the conventions governing the writing of professionally respectable" narratives of history (42). Analyzing the *success* of the narrative means that we have to determine how its structure—in the case of tragedy, we require a hero, and for Hilgruber the hero is the German army—determines what we can say about the documentary evidence arrayed for the historian. For Hilgruber, European Jewish culture becomes the foil for the hero in the tragic tale of the Wehrmacht, but the reader will find that the first tragedy (the destruction of Jewish culture in Europe) undermines the substance of the second tragedy (the destruction of the German army). It is this contradiction, suggests White, that impugns Hilgruber's narrative, not the fact that it is somehow distasteful to canonical historians or violates contemporary mores, and certainly not the fact that it is somehow out of accord with the events (in White's terms, the "chronicle") of history itself.

But as Carlo Ginzburg has pointed out, this formulation presents a problem: in his response to Vidal-Naquet's writings against Faurisson and the denial of the events of the Holocaust, White complains that there is no warrant with which to assert that the "ideologues" of history—either those who, like Faurisson, contextualize the evidence of the Final Solution in such a way as to minimize it as an event or those, like Zionists "who would exploit the massacres" in order to rationalize political terror—are lying or are mistaken (White, *The Content of the Form* 77). To know if a person is lying, you have to know whether they are asserting the occurrence of an event when they know it has not occurred. But by eliminating the motives for—and, with it, the occurrences of—history from consideration in evaluating histories of the Holocaust or anything else, White is left to assess the effectiveness of competing accounts. As Ginzburg points out—perhaps unfairly—"we can conclude that if Faurisson's narrative [of denial] were ever to prove *effective*, it would be regarded by White"—like Hilgruber's—"as true as well" (93).

To get around this problem, White asserts that the most effective historical writing is "intransitive writing," a term he adopts from Lang (who in turn attributes it to Roland Barthes; see *Act and Idea* xii, 107–9). The common view of narrative is that the language of the story is intended "to be read *through*; it is designed to enable readers to see what they would otherwise see differently or perhaps not at all" (xii). It allows the reader to understand something about the nature of the irreducible object or event that lies beyond discourse, or before it. Intransitive writing "denies the distances among the writer, text, what is written about, and, finally, the reader; they all converge upon a single point," the point of writing—James Joyce's flyspeck period at the end of the penultimate chapter of *Ulysses*, or Primo Levi's act of writing, in *The Periodic Table*, the act that "guides this hand of mine to impress on this paper this dot, here, this one" (quoted in White 53). The act of writing becomes the object of history, in a narrative that tells "the story of the genocide as though [the teller herself] had passed through it" (xii). For Lang, this kind of writing is exemplified in its most extreme form by Edmond Jabes' novels, beginning with *The Book of Questions*, writing that is "nonreferential, nonrepresentational," in which "the subject of discourse is problematic even in its existence" (107). Intransitive writing succeeds, for White, because it brings to the surface of the historical narrative the aporias that exist between subject and object, agent and patient, literal and figurative language, and makes the case for the reader that it is not one or the other of these poles that ought to be the object of historical inquiry but rather the writing itself and the way that it resists reading, or naming, or knowledge. The most effective history of the Holocaust is not necessarily the one that is the most effective or persuasive, the narrative that most forcefully and completely contextualizes the documentary evidence of the event. It is not the account that allows the reader to put himself, through the act of figurative substitution, in the place of the historical actor. The most effective account draws the reader's attention to the *impossibility* of making the substitution, the difficulty of putting himself in the place of the historical actor, of saying "I am here," or "I understand." On such a criterion, the old standard histories of the Holocaust written by Lucy Dawidowicz (who has been accused of overplaying Jewish resistance) and Raul Hilberg (who has been accused of paying scant attention to the culture destroyed by the Nazis) fail because they naturalize the events, they bring them under a narrative paradigm or "plot," and lull the reader into thinking that she understands the events of the Holocaust. On such a criterion, the conclusion to Dawidowicz's chapter on the concentration of Jews in ghettos, particularly the Warsaw ghetto ("Who Shall Live, Who Shall Die"), is all prelude to the following chapter ("For Your Freedom and Ours") on the partisans and the uprisings in the Warsaw ghetto; it attends far too much to agents (in "Who Shall Live," the Nazi state apparatus; in "For Your Freedom," the Jewish resisters) and patients (the Jewish inhabitants of Warsaw; the surprised officers and soldiers of the German army and their national allies). It is, in other words, unsuccessful because it insists far too much upon its own verisimilitude.

But White overestimates, we think, the ability of any writer to establish verisimilitude, and this is due in part to misunderstanding what it
means, in Geoff Bennington and Robert Young's words, for "language [to
be] the origin of history" (9). One way to think of verisimilitude is in
terms of the rhetorical or poetical figure. Traditionally, metaphor is understood as a system of substitution: in Aristotle's example, "there stands
the ship," the term "anchored" is substituted for the term "stands," and
through the difference between the spoken word and the unspoken (but
intuited) one, our attention is focused not only upon the closeness of one
set of experiences (which we may recognize) and another (which we may
not); it is also focused upon its dependence on language. Depending on
the number of terms substituted in the silence of the analogy (and in Aristotle's understanding of poiesis, the skilled speaker could hold four terms
in a relation of similarity in a single figure) the reader or listener's ability to
individuate the terms in use becomes jarring as the distance between them
in the analogy grows. In an extreme circumstance—*kenosis*, in which a set
of terms is so far removed, in terms of similarity, from another that it begins to systematically undo their claim to order—metaphor "breaks up a
totality into discontinous fragments" (De Man 275), disordering our illusion of the coherence of the real supplied by figure, and forcing upon us
the realization that the chain of signification (founded upon metonymy, a
relation of contiguity rather than substitution) is just that, a chain that is
unhitched from the world of the real.

White's assumption, of course, is that the metonymic relation—in
which the terms substituted for one another are so closely related that they
repeat themselves endlessly—is that upon which "normal" discourse (or,
perhaps, historical discourse) is founded. In an essay on figurative language,
Thomas McLaughlin says of metonymy that it "accomplishes its transfer of
meaning on the basis of associations that develop out of specific contexts,"
and "that it relies on connections that build up over time and the associations of usage" (83, 84). For White, the importance of metonymy is that the
terms placed in relation ("sail," "ship") are assumed to be related in the
given context, and because of what he calls this extrinsic relation (that there
must be some order of reality outside the discursive situation that provides
the context in which these terms may be related), the reader is able to understand more clearly the aspects of the reality the metonymic figure is
meant to distinguish (see *Metahistory* 34–6). In other words, metonymy,
through a repetition of different aspects of the same reality, offers the reader
a clearer, more direct understanding of the nature of the reality being described. With metonymy, cause-effect relationships are so well established

that we are lulled into believing that what we are being given is a description of the real under a paradigm. Metaphor distances us from our ability to regularize our assumptions about the reality purportedly being described. Metonymy is transitive, whereas metaphor is—or at least has the capacity to be—intransitive (see White, *Metahistory* 37–8); metonymy assumes that history (the context presumed to be exterior to discourse) is the origin or language, whereas metaphor assumes that language is the origin of the historical real.

One of the difficulties of Abraham Lewin's account of his ordeal in the Warsaw ghetto, as with other such accounts, is that it is often metonymic rather than metaphoric. Though he sometimes makes comparisons between objects or events from radically different paradigms (as he does when he compares the liquidation to the worst ordeals of the Jews in the land of Mitzrayim), he more often simply makes lists of events, often tiresomely, gruesomely similar events, and names appear after names. On White's accounting, these lists should lull the reader into understanding that what is being repeated is simply sameness: "Today the Germans have surrounded the following streets: Gesia, Smocza, Pawia, Lubiecka, and took away all the occupants. Yesterday the following were taken away: Khanowicz, Rusak, and Jehoszua Zegal's whole family" (Lewin 146). It takes a footnote by the editor to make the reader understand that Jehoszua Zegal was the grandfather of Lewin's wife Luba, and no notes establish the context for the names of the streets that were surrounded, and what events took their toll upon the inhabitants of the houses on those streets bordering the Jewish cemetery on the western side of the ghetto. It is the effect of repetition—of the "transitivity" of metonym, the figure that lulls one into thinking that "I know this," and that allows us to forget that "I was not there"—that seems to work against White's claims for transitive writing. Our point, though, is not that intransitive writing does not have the effect White (and with him, Lang) suggests that it has. It is that there is a certain intransitivity that occurs even metonymically—even in language that on the face of it seems to regularize the narrative, *vraisemblable* historical world—that rends the apparently historical order and confronts the reader with the disaster.

This is true, in part, because of an aspect of metonym that White doesn't account for. By focusing on the effectiveness of the historical narrative in favor of the narrative's ability to convey a state of affairs exterior (or anterior) to it, White finds it necessary to examine and catalogue the "tropics"—the figural dimension—of those historical representations, and thereby insists on the priority of language: language no longer represents the world, it is the world. But what he ignores, we fear, is the distance between the effect of metonymy (or of metaphor) and the cause of that discursive effect. If metaphor is a word-for-word exchange, whereby terms and their contexts are substituted for one another, metonymy is a contiguous chain of signification, a word-to-word exchange, whereby the context is presumed and the *displacement* of one term by another defers understanding (or closure of the historical hermeneutic). While it is true that metaphor is a displacement of meaning because it draws our attention not just to the similarities between terms but also to their radical difference, and forces the reader to imagine (and, as a result, always to *misname*) the relation between them, it is also true that metonym forces a disjunction between a term and its substitute, but a disjunction of a different kind. The displacement of metonymy, because it does not allow a reader outside the chain of signification (because it presumes the context inside of which the substitution takes place), is potentially more disruptive, more anxious: in Françoise Meltzer's terms, "in spite of its apparent difference of meaning in each case, each signifier in this chain has in fact the same meaning as the one before it: the lack which spells desire" (160). It forces the reader's attention, in other words, not on that which appears familiar—the different aspects of the same—but upon the the impossible relation between all of the different attributes of the object or event and the singular, palpable sense of the object or event itself.

In a different context, Saul Friedlander makes the connection between repetition—the sheer volume of the sequence of sign, after sign, after sign; the sense that the repetitive nature of the trope reduces the object of discourse to something inanimate—and the *unheimlichkeit*, the uncanny.[1] Through repetition "we are confronted with [an uncertainty brought on by the representation] of human beings of the most ordinary kind approaching the state of automata by eliminating any feelings of humanness and of moral sense. . . . Our sense of *Unheimlichkeit* is indeed triggered by this deep uncertainty as to the 'true nature'" of the referent of the narrative itself (Friedlander 30). The repetition of the names of the dead, the streets surrounded by German soldiers, and of the impossible options left to the survivors of the liquidations ("7 zloty for white bread, 1,80 for potatoes") is a sign that what we had once recognized as the *heimlichkeit*, the homely or familiar, is actually made up of the shards of its attributes, but that they are attributes that cannot possibly be the sum total of the familiar. Language truly is the origin of history, but through the uncanniness brought on by the rupture of the homely or familiar in the repetition of the metonymic, we catch a glimpse of the terror, and of the weight, of the occurrence itself, the cause or the underside of language.

To return to White's argument with Berel Lang, it becomes more
clear that their disagreement is the result of a misunderstanding of Lang's
prohibition of the "aestheticization" of the events of the Shoah. White
cites a long passage from Lang's *Act and Idea in the Nazi Genocide* that
reads, in part, "imaginative representation would personalize even events
that are impersonal and corporate; it would dehistoricize and generalize
events that occur specifically and contingently. And the unavoidable dissonance here is evident" (144; qtd. in White, "Historical Emplotment"
45). He goes on to note that Lang seems to suggest that to provide an
individual point of view for "characters" whose individuality was stripped
bare by their treatment (as "corporate entities" or automatons) by the
Nazi Final Solution misrepresents this depersonalization, an element essential in understanding the Holocaust and its effects. And to a certain extent, we are just as uncomfortable with Lang's apparent willingness to
make distinctions between the figural and the historical, a distinction
that—as we've tried to argue here—does not bear up under the weight
of contemporary historiography, or even of historical evidence itself. But
Lang's assertion of a dissonance—between, in his terms, figural and historical representation; in our terms, between the transitive and the intransitive, or (more radically) between the occurrence of an event and its
experience or its "utterance"—is not limited to "aestheticized" versions
of historical events, but to the records themselves. In a section of Lang's
book that White does not cite, he argues that the privileged status of the
diary resides in its closeness to the historical events themselves: "since the
diary is written at the same time that the events of which it takes note
occur, it combines an unmediated connection to those events with the individual and expressive point of view of the author" (Lang 128). The
diary "is a representation of the diarist's experience." It doesn't take
much to note the dissonance here between the experience and its representation, even in writing that occurs simultaneously with the event.

White has missed Lang's point in this section of the book: it isn't as
important to note that Lang is trying to make distinctions between historical and aesthetic representations that don't bear up under the weight of
scrutiny as it is to note that Lang is attempting to show that there is a certain uncanniness even in "historical" documents—like diaries—that needs
to be accounted for. (For Lang, this uncanniness is evidence of a certain
moral force that should not be lost in representations of the events of the
Shoah; this is a point to which we will return in subsequent chapters.) In
other words, Lang's point is that we ought to resist the notion that stories—of any kind—will allow us to "understand" the Shoah.

Speaking of revisionism, Pierre Vidal-Naquet explains that "a historical discourse is a network of explications that can give way to 'another ex-
plication' if the latter is judged to take better account of the facts," but
"events are not things, even if an irreducible opacity of the real exists"
(318).[2] The opacity of the real, however, is not available in the "absolute
negativity" of the kind Vidal-Naquet attributes to Adorno—who suggests
that the historical narratives of revisionism do not raise "another explica-
tion" but radically exterminate the idea meant to be explicated—but in the
distance between occurrence of an event and our ability to place ourselves,
as speaking subjects, into their midst. It is in the distance between the individual sign and the next sign in the metonymic figure, where we realize that
in this accumulation of discourse—in the repetition of the same—that we
are radically disconnected from the object to which we'd hoped to have access, that we understand "radical negativity" as the distance between
thought and experience, between the extremity and the concept, the litany
of names lost to Abraham Lewin in the Warsaw ghetto and the occurrences
that—taken together but never knowable—combine to form the lives of
the named. In paraphrasing Merleau-Ponty's *Phenomenology of Perception*,
Louis Mink argues that "the unique problem of history is not the explanation of *events* but the understanding of *advents*" (115), and it is these advents that make their way to the surface of the inadequate historical
narratives that historians—or, before them, the agents of history in the
form of the individuals who find themselves living in the midsts of events—
cannot avoid writing. It is language that provides the medium of repetition,
the frightening, sublime feeling that comes at the recognition that the
image provided through figure—metaphor, metonymy, or anything else—
and the events themselves are dissonant.

III. *The Disaster as Object of History*

It remains to be seen what alternative there is to the impasse between
functionalists and intentionalists on the one hand, and objectivists and
subjectivists on the other hand. Events like the liquidation of the Warsaw
ghetto make their way up through the surface of discourse and leave a
trace upon utterance, and those traces effectively explode historical narrative while at the same time providing a sense of the *unheimlichkeit* of
events themselves. This sense leads us back to consider what Walter Benjamin called a redemptive view of history, or what Gershom Scholem
called, in another context, a counterhistory (see Biale 10–12, 189–205, for

a discussion). Counterhistory—or redemptive history—takes as its point of departure the kind of historiographic assumptions White makes about the impossibility of recovering the event, and further suggests that there is a textual aspect to the historical object—in White's terms, a narrative component—that traditional historical work tends to ignore. For Scholem, the counterhistorical tradition is founded in the kabbala, in the mystical understanding that in the world of appearances there is a divine aspect: in Scholem's terms, "there is something of the *sitra ahra*, from the other side entirely, that emerges" from the historical method of his predecessors (qtd. in Biale 10). "The true history lies in a subterranean tradition that must be brought to light, much as the apocalyptic thinker decodes an ancient prophecy or as Walter Benjamin spoke of 'brushing history against the grain'" (Biale 11). Like the mystical tradition and Benjamin's interpolation of it, a reading of history has to assume that in any given historical moment—in any occurrence—there is an element of the unreadable, the unthinkable, and that this element—call it the counterrational, the destructive, the *unheimlichkeit*—makes itself apparent to the reader, forces itself upon him, and forces him to confront the limit of reason, the limit of the language in which history is written, and ultimately of history itself.

The experience of displacement—of the uncanny—in redemptive history is what Maurice Blanchot calls "the disaster," and it is the disaster of history, the disaster of the unsayable, that Lewin's diary brings to the surface of the narrative, and, we would argue, any attempt to render an occurrence that beggars the imagination. We want to briefly lay out Blanchot's notion of the disaster, because it clearly recognizes the unsayable aspect of history, and takes account of the difficulty of writing or understanding the events of the Shoah, even for those who were there. In all of this, we want to be very clear about two things: we're not implying that the Holocaust, as a series of events, is inaccessible to history, and we do not stop at the conclusion that history's competing narratives yield a composite narrative of the events and the events' contiguity with the contemporary moment. We are interested in understanding the extent to which the traces of the events that remain embedded in the narratives themselves—simply by dint of the nature of narrative, a different order of reality from the events they represent—unwrite, "de-scribe" in Blanchot's terms, the narrative and provide a sense of the destructive (and redemptive) nature of the events.

Experience, Blanchot tells us, is a state of being that requires knowledge. The occurrence of the event, in which a person is implicated and sees herself as such, precedes experience. The occurrence is immediate: "not only [does it] rule out all mediation; it is the infiniteness of a presence such that it can no longer be spoken of" (24). Whether the event implicates other individuals, or whether it happens to a single person in isolation, it is nonetheless an experience of "otherness," particularly in the case of events that, like the Holocaust, seem to disobey the rules of logic or order and appear instead to embody a horrifying chaos. There is, in the immediacy of the event, a contradiction. In the moment of the event's occurrence, the individual is "expose[d] to unity": in order to render the occurrence as an experience at all the individual becomes defined as a subject. She becomes an "I" over against which the event can also be identified, given attributes, and finally named. At the moment the individual recognizes the occurrence of the event as an experience, and herself as the subject of experience, the event "falls in its turn outside being" (24). The experience, recognized by the witness and named, is nonetheless haunted by its status as event, and "the names [for it are] ravaged by the absence that preceded them"—the event now lost to memory except as a name—and "seem remainders, each one, of another language, both disappeared and never yet pronounced, a language we cannot even attempt to restore without reintroducing these names back into the world" (58).

Blanchot begins the book with something like the following question: How is it possible to write the events that occurred under the name of Auschwitz? The imperative of history is to write, and the chilling thing is that we write without being chilled, that we write and in writing we have "written it away." Blanchot's text is an attempt to trouble history's ability to name the event—to embed it in a narrative—and in so doing to "say it away," to speak things as though they did not have an effect. Ann Smock, Blanchot's translator, notes the transitivity of the words before and after the "of" of the title: the writing of the disaster, the disaster of the writing. Blanchot's aim—like Benjamin's and like that of the redemptive tradition of Luria and the other kabbalists—is to explain both the promise of the historical venture—of providing a text in which we may have a coherent understanding of events—and the risks involved in such coherence. In effect, Blanchot's discussion in *The Writing of the Disaster* is characterized by the double edge of redemption—in the writing of history, there is inevitably released a divine, unspeakable and unreadable element that both reveals a trace of the extrahistorical moment and also destroys the coherence such writing purports to provide. In writing the events that comprise the liquidation of the Warsaw ghetto in the summer of 1942, a man like Abraham Lewin regularizes the events so they become narrative, but in so doing he makes apparent the uncanny, the destructive and redemptive aspect of the events that cannot be written, but can nonetheless be glimpsed in writing.

In terms of history, the documents and remnants of history—the detritus of the event—don't so much speak as resist speaking. They need to be inserted into the historical series, as the reports of those losing children to the transports to Treblinka, and the work cards never to be used by those waiting in the Umschlagplatz to be herded onto trains, need to be understood by creating a narrative in which those documents may be written and read so that they render individual voices, individual names, to an historian and to the readers of history. The events, however, of which these documents and records are the remains, are irretrievably past—they have already been passed by the narrative that has been written to speak in their place—and between the events themselves and the narratives that speak them, there is silence. It is the job of historians to bridge this unbridgeable gap. Blanchot's point, however, is that in attempting to bridge it—in expressing the difficulty, and the obligation, of writing into history this irretrievable series of moments—writing itself will inevitably leave a trace of the event, as a mar on the face of the narrative. The immediacy of the moment, which makes itself felt in the silences between the event and its narrative—between the phrases written by Lewin on August 8, 1942—becomes apparent, as does the realization that the relation between word and word, phrase and phrase, is endlessly repeatable and that at no point will the phrases be joined by the events themselves. "What Luba recounted of the children (150) and the women teachers during the blockade. Their packages in their hands, ready to set off—to their deaths. Kon said yesterday, 'I am writing a testament about the events.' Chmielewski's parents were taken away yesterday and he comes to the factory and is still on his feet" (Lewin 150). Any intention that would drive the historian to provide a causal connection between those phrases would be refused by what Blanchot calls the silence of suffering, the destructive element of the event, the element that puts the lie to the name.

But naming is impossible to avoid: speaking is the human imperative. Even in silence, Blanchot suggests, there is a telling. But there is a difference between the language or the speaking that assumes it is coincident with the object of language—the event—and a speaking that understands itself as also a not-speaking. This is, again, the paradox of Blanchot's purpose: to describe the impossibility of speaking of an object while also describing the imperative of speaking; the impossibility of speaking the immediacy of the experience while acknowledging that speaking the experience is what constitutes it.

Writing makes present the intention of naming—of knowing—at the same time that it makes clear just how impossible it is to name. When you see words on the page, or when you try to write words on the page, implies Blanchot, what your attention is drawn to is the relation among the words as much as to the presumed relation between words and events, words and things. There is this entry in Lewin's diary, written on the day after his wife of fourteen years is transported:

> Eclipse of the sun, universal blackness. My Luba was taken away during a blockade on 30 Gesia Street. There is still a glimmer of hope in front of me. Perhaps she will be saved. And if, God forbid, she is not? My journey to the Umschlagplatz—the appearance of the streets—fills me with dread. To my anguish there is no prospect of rescuing her. It looks like she was taken directly to the train. Her fate is to be a victim of the Nazi bestiality, along with hundreds of thousands of Jews. I have no words to describe my desolation. I ought to go after her, to die. But I have no strength to take such a step. Ora—her calamity. A child who was so tied to her mother, and how she loved her.
>
> The "action" goes on in the town at full throttle. All the streets are being emptied of their occupants. Total chaos. Each German factory will be closed off in its block and the people will be locked in their own building. Terror and blackness. And over all this disaster hangs my own private anguish. (Lewin 153–4)

Writing, here, obeys the obligation to name: Lewin names himself ("my own private anguish," "my desolation") and he tries to imagine the other individuals and events that form the context for his writing ("the people will be locked in their building," "God forbid, if she is not [saved]?"). Yet he can neither fix the one or the other, nor can he fix the experience he intends. But at the moment of writing, Lewin displaces both the "I" and the "other" from which, and to whom, he writes as well as the historical event of the disaster. It is this moment of displacement, the moment of writing and of loss, that produces a violence, "the rupture, . . . the break, the splitting, the tearing of the shred—acute singularity, single point" (Blanchot 46). It is here that events—Luba's deportation, the terror of their daughter at being made motherless, the mechanical and awful willingness to continue to speak in the face of all this—are *omitted* from the langauge of the writing but are made present in the absence of the writing. The intention to write is shattered by the event's ability to elude writing. What we're left with, on the page, is the figural representation of the moment the vessels—the experience—are shattered.

Events obliterate history. "The disaster is related to forgetfulness—forgetfulness without memory, the motionless retreat of what has not been treated—the immemorial, perhaps. To remember forgetfully: again, the outside" (3). If the immediacy of the experience hurtles inevitably into the past, into narrative, once we name it (once we speak it, once we know it), then we cannot remember it. Between the moment of intention and the naming that takes place before it and after it is a disjunction. We remember names and knowledge, but the experience itself is, in Blanchot's terms, "immemorial." To "remember" such moments of immediacy, we have to "remember forgetfully:" they are recalled not in the narrative with which we have carefully regularized ourselves, but come to us outside of memory, as traumatic traces of the events themselves, traces that disrupt and destroy the carefully regulated history in which we insert our selves.

The language Blanchot uses to describe the contradiction between the occurrence of the event and the experience of the event—a contradiction that resides in the transition from seeing to recognizing—is similar to that which has been used to describe the language of eyewitness testimonies, particularly testimonies of the Shoah. It is only in the writing—in the testimony—of the disaster that the events themselves are made available. They're not available as content, but as effect. "The language of writing momentarily, in the extenuatedness it presupposes—in its repetitive difference . . .—opens or offers itself in the direction of the other," of the event as it precedes knowledge (79). The disaster can't be remembered, exactly, but it can be seen in the attempts to recover it. The disaster is "a remainder which would bar with invisibility and illegibility all that shows and is said" (40).

Remembering forgetfully can be likened to that "passive demand that neither welcomes nor withdraws the past, but, designating there what has never taken place (just as it indicates in the yet to come that which will never be able to find its place in any present), refers us to non-historical forms of time, to the other of all tenses, to their eternal or eternally provisional indecision, bereft of destiny, without presence" (85). Remembering forgetfully designates the moment in the past that "didn't take place"—it isn't recordable in historical time—but that leaves a fragmentary trace in its undoing of historical system or coherence. The immediacy of relation—the disaster of immediacy that can't be recorded as identity—can only be remembered as something that takes place out of time. "Forgetfulness designates what is beyond possibility, the unforgettable Other; it indicates that which, past or future, it does not circumscribe" (117).

It is at this point that we can return to Benjamin, in order to see the sense in which history's other—the disaster—may be called redemptive. For Blanchot, at least, it appears that the disaster—what Benjamin would call "crisis time"—is unredemptive, because the disaster is at once the defining moment for human action and the impossibly elusive moment, outside of experience, outside of memory, and destructive of any historical narrative that an individual might attempt to construct for it. But for Benjamin's mentor Scholem, and in the kabbalistic tradition that the latter studied, redemption is precisely such a moment: it can only be brought about through human activity in the world of the profane, and it can only become apparent in the rupture of human activity—in a burst of divinity—amidst the ruins of historical time. In her book on Benjamin, Scholem, and Levinas, Susan Handelman points to the Angel of History, a thematic strand that weaves its way through Benjamin's work from the 1920s onward, and suggests that it is this angel—caught in the winds of the storm of the catastrophe, looking backward to the ruins of the past, with its wings outstretched not in flight but in the panicked realization that it cannot prevent itself from being blown into an uncertain future—that most clearly marks the redemptive aspect of a critical history, and of the disaster. Adorno asked of this angel whether "it proclaims complete disaster or the rescue hidden within it" ("Commitment" 94), and Benjamin might answer "both." As Handelman puts it in an essay on Karl Kraus, Benjamin associated the angel

> with the evanescence of the beings described in the Talmud; their song of praise, their truth, was of the moment—a full present but a transient one. The voices raised in lament, hope, horror, chastisement were those of beings living in a precarious instant and soon to vanish into nothing, yet also to be followed by the instantaneous creation of another angelic horde. (168)

Like the disaster, the historical event (the full and present moment) and the human actions and utterances taking place that bring it to consciousness (voices raised in lament, horror, and chastisement) take place out of historical time, not in the utterances themselves, but in the moment between the occurrence and the utterance. Each moment, preceding historical time, is "the strait gate through which the Messiah might enter" (Benjamin, "Theses" 264).

And like the disaster, the moment's redemptive potential is simultaneously its catastrophic potential. "The Messiah," Benjamin makes clear,

"comes not only as the redeemer, he comes as the subduer of the an-
tichrist," and as such the moment of redemption is also the moment of destruction. If the task of the historian is truly to blast the moment of the
now out of the continuum of history (261), in the hopes of releasing from
"'the time of the now'[,] which is shot through with chips of Messianic
time" (263), those divine sparks, not the historical narrative but the remains of the occurrence of the historical events themselves, then the task
is a dangerous one. It is dangerous—or maybe a better word is terrifying—
because it comes with the knowledge that it has been preceded by the shattering of the divine, and that it must be followed by the redemptive
moment's reinsertion into the historical series, the narrative into which it
will be lost once more, only to require further violence, further redemption. Blanchot puts it this way:

> [I]f it happens that to the question "When will you come?" the Mes-
> siah answers, "Today," the answer is certainly impressive: so, it is
> today! It is now and always now. There is no need to wait, although
> to wait is an obligation. And when is it now? When is the now which
> does not belong to ordinary time, which necessarily overturns it,
> does not maintain but destabilizes it? (142)

The response is that it is always now, but the moment of time is irretrievable to history, it is only retrievable to memory—not traditional Jewish
memory, relying on the repetition of the historical series, that guards
against the forgetfulness that leads to distortion (see Handelman 171)—a
forgetful memory, a memory "that is seized only as an image which flashes
up at the instant when it can be recognized and is never seen again" (Benjamin, "Theses" 255). While Benjamin had a difficult time reconciling the
role of memory in Jewish thought with memory's role in the deadening
historical method against which he was working, the memory that is truly
redemptive is one that works against the historical memory that acts as
continuum, and it is a memory that wrecks the names of history, the
names of the historian, and the coherence with which we comfort ourselves about the naturalness of our language, of metaphor, and the world
it describes.

It is the disaster in Abraham Lewin's diary—the events unnamed, and
perhaps unnameable, by history—that redeems (in both its ameliorative and
in its catastrophic aspect) the narrative of the liquidation of the Warsaw
ghetto and the deportations to Treblinka. Knowing as we do the historical
context of the General Government's task, and knowing the parts played by

the functionaries of the government and of the ghetto, we're able to construct a narrative—in White's terms, a narrative comprising metonymically the component parts inside the exoteric parameters of what has come to be known as the Shoah—into which we may drop Lewin's diary, and the diary then becomes evidence, or an artifact, that explains and can be explained by—granted a name through—the exoteric context itself. The hermeneutic circle is closed if we grant the diary a status as evidence, and the name of the disaster is spoken: Abraham Lewin, member of Oneg Shabbas and recorder of the anguish of the ghetto, rounded up and transported to Treblinka and undoubtedly gassed sometime after the last entry of his diary, dated January 16, 1943. If, however, we take the language of the diary as the writing of the disaster, and we see in its writing the traces of the time of the now, "shot through with chips of Messianic time," and read the repetitive, mesmerizing, and extremely discomfiting words and phrases as attempts to inscribe a moment so utterly alien and yet so utterly natural that they jar the writer and the reader out of the narrative of history—the chronology of dates, the feeling that we know this moment, though we were not there at all and though this is clearly not a memory of our own—then Lewin's language is redemptive. It is redemptive because it makes visible not the world of Warsaw in 1942 and 1943, or a life or series of lives of those who died at the hands of the Nazis, but because it forces open those worlds we might imagine, and through that opening comes a confrontation with what the human mind can and cannot do. Lewin's diary does not describe the world of one who was there, for even those who are there cannot possibly describe the disaster: it is long past even at the moment of writing the words in the diary. But it is redemptive in the sense that in what it cannot say—in what is de-scribed, unwritten, in the words and the images incanted by them—we see the disaster as it affects us individually, as it destroys the narratives and the memories we have created to contain both our "selves" and the name of the Shoah, and as it fleetingly and irretrievably connects Lewin, and the event, and us, to the uncanniness of the divine.

Notes

1. The uncanny is distinct from the "incomprehensible," which—for Dan Magurshak—is an untidy and imprecise term that is often used as a justification for avoiding an analysis of the historical record left in the wake of the Holocaust. See his essay, "The 'Incomprehensibility' of the Holocaust: Tightening up Some Loose Usage."

2. Jeffrey Mehlman's translation of this essay, in *Assassins of Memory*—which collects a number of Vidal-Naquet's musings on revisionism in France and the United States—is slightly different. His account reads: "Events are not things, even if reality possesses an irreducible opaqueness. A historical discourse is a web of explanations that may give way to another explanation if the latter is deemed to account for diversity in a more satisfactory manner" (97). Mehlman, it seems, is more wary of "facts" than the translator in Furet's collection.

3

The Epistemology of Witness:
Survivor Narratives
and the Holocaust

The disaster is related to forgetfulness—forgetfulness without memory, the motionless retreat of what has not been treated. . . . To write . . . is to be in relation, through words in their absence, with what one cannot remember.

Blanchot

When you're hungry, it gets to a point where you don't mind stealing from your own sister, from your own father. . . . Now I—you would never picture me, and I can't even imagine myself doing that now. But it happened.

Testimony of Leon W.

In the last several years, a number of groups and individuals have made an effort to record the memories of those who survived, in one way or another, the utter burn of history. Two of the most notable are the Fortunoff Video Archive for Holocaust Testimonies at Yale University, established in 1982,[1] and the Survivors of the Shoah Foundation, established with the help of Steven Spielberg in 1994. In addition to recorded oral testimonies, we have those gathered much earlier, recorded with paper and ink: Primo Levi began writing *If This is a Man* (which, in its later printing, became *Survival in Auschwitz*) in 1948, less than four years after the liberation of Auschwitz, and countless others have committed to language the memories that haunted them and the realities that confronted them as they were starved, beaten, and left to watch one another be killed or die. In the case of both written and oral testimonies, in spite of the prima facie differences between them, it becomes clear that the distance between what has been witnessed and what can be committed to testi-

49

mony—what was seen and what can be said—is often wide, but always palpable. And it is palpable not only in the witness's statements but in the
shrugged shoulders, the winces, the tears, and the silences that punctuate
the oral testimonies and that are aestheticized but not domesticated in the
written language of figure. Nathan A.'s description of an *aktion*, in which
Jewish villagers are asked to dig a ditch and then line up at its edge to be
shot, along with, later, all of their neighbors, proceeds this way:

> They used to throw the earth on the top, and the earth used to go
> up and down because they are living people: One—the son bury his
> mother; the mother was still alive: "Moyshe, ikh lebh; bagrub mikh
> nish leberdikerheyt" ["Moyshe, I'm alive; don't bury me while I'm
> alive"]. . . . But Moyshe had no choice, because the Germans no give
> him the choice. And he bury alive.
>   [Interviewer:] He buried his mother alive?

At that, Nathan shrugs his shoulders without any facial expression (FVA
tape T-113). The shrug of the shoulders and the lack of apparent emotion
in this account, as much as the incongruous connection of the pleading of
a mother to her son and the statement bereft of anything but description
that concludes the episode ("and he bury alive"), mark a point between
witness and testimony that can be seen as a moment of trauma, a moment
in which the historical real and the memory of it as demanded by the imperative to testify to it disintegrate and present for both the witness and the
interviewer (as well as those who are present to view or listen to the testimony) a break. This moment, this break, is neither a site of historical fac-
ticity, a kernel of "truth," nor the recovery, for the witness, of the moment
by way of memory. It is, in Cathy Caruth's words, a moment in which the
object—in this case, the moment not of the son burying his mother, but of
Nathan A.'s witnessing of the acts he attempts to describe—is "grasped
only in the very inaccessibility of its occurrence" (Caruth, "Unclaimed Experience" 187) in which the object is denoted not by the words but is
borne by the shrug, the connective "and," and the impassive face of Nathan
A. as he confronts the interviewer.

In Binjamin Wilkomirski's *Fragments: Memories of a Wartime Childhood*, there are equally devastating moments in which the writer presents
his reader with incomprehensibly painful and quite literally unbelievable
moments of cruelty. In one, the boy Binjamin—perhaps a pseudonym for
a Jewish child who in 1944 is no more than five or six, and who finds himself separated from his brothers and transported to Majdanek—recalls

what happens to two young boys who are caught soiling their already fouled bunks:

> They were forbidden to come back into the barracks. They were meant to be a warning for the rest of us. Huddled over, crying constantly, they knelt in the filth. I stared horrified at their trousers, which were all spotted with red.
> The older children explained:
> . . . As punishment, [the block wardens had] taken little sticks and pushed them up into the boys' penises as far as they'd go. Then the block wardens had hit their penises, making the sticks break off. The wardens had laughed a lot and had a good time.
> "Now all they'll do is pee blood," said one of them.
> When evening came they were still whimpering. Then people came and took them away. (Wilkomirski 60–61)

The Wilkomirski text is an especially vexed narrative because its status as "authentic" testimony has been questioned repeatedly in the two last years.[2] Both Elena Lappin and Philip Gourevitch, after months of research, have concluded along with Daniel Ganzfried that the events described in Wilkomirski's book are not his own memories, and that they may be compilations of narratives and testimonies the author had read and made his own through nearly thirty years of reading and viewing Holocaust histories and memoirs. Unlike Ganzfried, though, both Gourevitch and Lappin also conclude that though Wilkomirski may or may not have witnessed the events he describes in his memoir, he has nonetheless experienced some trauma, the "evidence" of which is visible in the text of *Fragments*: though the distance between witness and testimony is here perhaps far greater than that in other testimonies of trauma, particularly the trauma experienced by survivors of the Shoah, that distance is characteristic of the rupture of history that we see in other testimonies by other survivors. Regardless of its status as historical document, as testimony it does not include language that might be considered "literary," and displays, as much as Nathan A.'s testimony, the hesitation that results from the incommensurability between what can be told and what has been seen. What marks the memory here is an absence: of a language that omits more than it reveals, and in the absence of the two boys who are taken away never to be seen again except in the spare language of the testimony and—far and away exceeding that language—in the memory of the witness.

It is this gap, this distance between witness and testimony, that we will explore in this chapter. We do so in part because it is a distance that no one writing on the testimonies of Holocaust survivors has been able to make consistently, including the most interesting and prescient in the field, Shoshana Felman and Dori Laub (in *Testimony*). The distance is that between trauma and the *language* of trauma, between—in Caruth's terms—history as event and history as trauma or forgetting, a connection that we will make clear below. The distance between the seen and the told functions in much the same way as the distance between, in Walter Benjamin's formulation, one language and another in translation, in which neither language by itself makes clear the object of reference but where the impasse between the two reveals the sublimity of the object, if only fleetingly. In addition, we want to make clear that the structure of witnessing—the structure of a break or an interval between the seen and the (mis)recognized, between the act as it plays itself out in the presence of the witness and the imprint on the witness that can be recalled but perhaps not told—is present in both oral and written testimonies, examples of which we will cite here. Our thesis is that representations of witnessing—testimony—make present a series of breaks, of stutters, in which the act of witnessing itself becomes apparent *only* at points of trauma, traumas that prevent the construction of a universal ethics, one that would let us say where to go from here. It is only through the radically particular ethics suggested by the epistemology of witness we'll lay out below that we are able to redeem the horror of the Shoah.

I. Oral Testimony

Lawrence Langer's *Holocaust Testimonies* is a rich and disturbing collection of the anguished memories of Holocaust survivors and at the same time a meditation on the difficulty of finding a paradigm on which to understand these testimonies as a record of human behavior recognizable outside the context of the camps and the ghettoes. In the preface to his book, Langer tells us that one of the first tapes he watched in the Fortunoff Archive was of a Mr. and Mrs. B., who tell their stories in sequence. Afterwards, the interviewer asks one of their daughters, who was born after the Shoah, one of the same questions she'd asked the couple, and immediately after that response—in which the daughter tells of her connection to Judaism through the experiences of her parents—the tape abruptly stops, leaving Langer, expecting to see more, to think, "'Wait a minute! Something's wrong here! Either someone's not listening, or someone's not telling the truth!" (x). The horrific stories told by the parents, and the tale of strength and connection told by the daughter just don't seem to add up. Langer confesses that this was a "naive response," and concludes that the division instanced here—a division between the witness's presence in the historical circumstances which she tries to narrate, and the moment of testimony itself—is a distance between an historical present that is, in Blanchot's terms, "inexperienced" or outside of our ability to understand it as experience at all, and the witness's struggle to narrate that present in an historical moment (apparently) completely divorced from it.

Langer goes on to draw a number of conclusions from his viewing of the testimonies in the Fortunoff Archive, two of which are worth reconsidering. One is that the two "selves" involved in all of the narratives of survival and life after the Shoah—the one which, in Cynthia Ozick's terms, comprises the lives "before" and "after," the normal rhythms of lives not destroyed by the extremity that eludes the concept of the Shoah; and the life "during" the extremity itself—vie for prominence in the narratives (see Ozick, "Rosa" 58). This is a conclusion that Langer sometimes adheres to and sometimes does not, as when he says later, in the chapter on "deep memory," that "the two kinds of memory [of the pre-camp and post-camp selves] intrude on each other, disrupting the smooth flow of their narratives" (Langer 6). The other conclusion is that the testimonies of these witnesses are disrupted because they are oral, unvarnished and unrehearsed, and that it is oral testimony that confirms the "vast imaginative space separating what he or she has endured from our capacity to absorb it," while written testimonies and memoirs "eas[e] us into their unfamiliar world through familiar (and hence comforting?) literary devices. The impulse [in written testimonies] is to *portray*" reality (19). We intend to question both these conclusions based on the premise that the epistemology of witness does not involve a competition between two different worldviews, each of which has a coherence incompatible with the other, but instead involves an incommensurability between witness and testimony, an incommensurability made palpable in its most extreme form by the enormity of the event of the Shoah itself. Because this incommensurability, this incompatibility, of witness and testimony is a structural one, it is available in written testimonies as much as it is in oral ones.

We want to turn now to some examples from recorded oral testimonies, some of which Langer uses to prove his point but which could serve equally well to call it into question. We do so not to argue with Langer, whose work on oral testimony is pathbreaking, but to push his points beyond where he has taken them in order to further explore the epistemology of witness and to seriously examine the disjunction between witness and testimony. The case of William R. offers an example of the difficulty of finding coherence between the act of witness and the testimony that presumably opens that act up for another to understand. Langer uses it as an example of the heroic act turning tragic, a turn that the witness must attempt to come to terms with, but which makes no sense in either the logic of the present or of "Hitler." The testimony follows:

> I'll never forgive myself. Even if I want it, I can't. I had a brother, he was 16 or 17 years old. He was taller than I, he was bigger than I, and I said to him, "Son, brother, you haven't got no working papers, and I am afraid that you will not be able to survive. Come on, take a chance with me, let's go together." Why did I take him with me? Because I had the working papers, and I thought maybe because I gonna go to the right, I knew people who had their working papers, they gonna go to the right, because the Germans need people in the ghetto, to finish the job, whatever they had to do. He agreed with me. At the same time I said he is built tall, then maybe he gonna have a chance.
>
> When I came to the gate where the selection was, then the Gestapo said to me (I showed him my papers), "You go to the right." I said, "This is my brother." He whipped me over my head, he said: "He goes to the left." And from this time I didn't see any more my brother. . . . I know it's not my fault, but my conscience is bothering me. I have nightmares, and I think all the time, that the young man, maybe he wouldn't go with me, maybe he would survive. It's a terrible thing: it's almost forty years, and it's still bothering me. I still got my brother on my conscience. God forgive me! (FVA tape T-9)

In Langer's terms (following Charlotte Delbo's), there are two selves and two memories at work here, and they do battle for control over the narrative, and over control of William G.'s ability to know—to understand—both his actions during the war and his survival forty years later. Here you have a "self who 'does' and [a] self who is 'done to'" but these selves cannot be reconciled by the narrative (47). The two selves "interact and intersect continually" (7). But what Langer fails to do is understand the terrain on which this battle takes place. There is no historical moment, available to either the witness or to the viewer/reader of the testimony, that can be gleaned from the passage above, and neither is there an historical moment in the present, caught on the videotape, against which the moment in the past—the horrible moment when William's calculation cost him his brother—can be juxtaposed. That moment has already plunged into the abyss; William G. recognizes this fact full well—"I'll never forgive myself. Even if I want it I can't."

The language of the testimony is evidence enough of the inaccessibility of the historical moment of witnessing and the rupture of the testimony in the face of the moment's absence. What, precisely, is the act witnessed here by the survivor: the moment of his separation from his brother? The moment of his decision to take his brother with him, in spite (or because) of his failure to have papers that might otherwise have kept him alive a little longer? Neither of these historical circumstances is made available by the testimony, though both of these moments are part of the narrative, told without words—"And from this time I didn't see any more my brother." The decision to take his brother with him is provided as litany: "Because I thought I had the working papers, and I thought maybe because I gonna go to the right, I knew people who had their working papers, they gonna go to the right. . . ." This is a language reporting not so much a series of events but a language that instantiates a rupture of the normal sequence of events—in this case, the historical circumstances of William G.'s separation from his brother and the forty years of anxiety that it has caused. This language indicates the *absence* of the event witnessed rather than the event itself. William's conclusion—"I still got my brother on my conscience. God forgive me!"—is not so much an appeal to the divine in the moment of the present (the moment of the interview) but a recognition of the failure of his testimony to recover, and certainly its failure to purge or even work through, the palpable existence, even now, of his unnamed seventeen-year-old brother. Far from marking a conclusion to the war of selves or of memories here—the moments of separation and, later, of horrible guilt—in favor of the present circumstances of the survivor, William G.'s exclamation provides a glimpse of the absence that marks the act of witness and the failure of language to contain it.

What Langer calls an "inner coherence" of these testimonies is only coherent insofar as it provides a vehicle for the space of absence or trauma, of a sublimity that is made present not in the recovery of the historical moment but in the structure of witnesses' ability to see what is no longer (or perhaps what was never) there. Listen to the description—really a dialogue/monologue—of Moses S., whose childhood memory rings eerily similar to the "memory" of the young Binjamin Wilkomirski:

Two boys having one bunk. One said to the other, "Will you watch after my piece of bread? I'm going to the bathroom." He said, "OK." When he come back, was no bread. Where was the bread?

"I'm sorry. I ate it up."

So he reported to the Kapo. Kapo comes along, he said, "What happened?"

"Look, I ask him to look after my piece of bread, and he ate it up."

The Kapo said, "You took away his life, right?"

He said, "Well, I'll give it back this afternoon, the ration."

He said, "No, come outside." He took the fellow outside. "Lie on the floor." He put a piece of *brett* [board] on his neck, and with his boots—bang! On his neck. *Fertig* [finished]! (FVA tape T-511)

What is perhaps most chilling about this tape is not the content of the story—of the memory—itself, but of what cannot be placed into the narrative: the cracking of the board against the child's neck, the quick, almost frantic walk outside the barracks to the yard, the look of panic in the boy's eyes just before the Kapo sentences him to death. They find no place in the language of narrative, but they do have a place in the testimony of Moses S.: in his gestures. Here, in the no-place of the narrative, is the gaping, open wound, the trauma experienced by Moses S. (who may be the other boy; we never find out) and that is witnessed only in terms of the ending—*fertig!*—or the ending or the absence of Moses's own place in the historical circumstances he narrates. In Langer's terms, the self caught up in the time during the killing—"'This was Hitler'" (Ozick, "Rosa" 58)—wins the battle over the present, so sickening the interviewer and Moses's wife that they both urge him to call it quits. We would argue that the witness is making present an absence that so disrupts his present that they become absolutely inseparable, so much so that Moses's language becomes submerged by his gestures, and he actually, with a motion of his hands and his feet, becomes the Kapo and finishes the memory with the violence that killed the little thief forty-five years earlier.

Absence is a structural part of witness. Cathy Caruth makes the point that history and trauma bear an indissoluble connection with one another, with trauma functioning as the cause of history ("Unclaimed Experience", 181–2; see also *Unclaimed Experience*, 1–9). With regard to Holocaust testimony, it is the traumatic event that marks the point of witnessing—it is that event that the witness "sees" but that precedes the witness's experience. For we do not remember trauma so much as we forget it—take leave of it—in much the same way that the survivors in the Fortunoff archive do not so much recall their past selves in the present of the interviews but instead mark an absence in their narrative—of their lives, of their coherence as selves—that is only available as a (mis)remembered, a (mis)recognized history. What Langer takes for an antinomy of selves is in fact an absence that marks the origin of the survivor's history.

Caruth's argument is founded on Freud's pioneering treatises on trauma, particularly *Moses and Monotheism*. There, Freud reimagines the narrative of diaspora and return as the divided narrative of two individuals named Moses with two different belief systems, divided by an event—the murder of the first and his replacement by another—that qualifies as a rupture in history. The return of the Jews to Israel is not so much the logical consequence or completion of the diaspora as it is a departure: a departure from Egypt but also a departure from the first to the second Moses, from one belief system to another, and from the deed (the murder) that in its violence is repressed, forgotten, and paved over through the Mosaic narrative.

The point Caruth makes here is that "captivity and return, while the beginning of the history of the Jews" according to Freud, "is precisely available to them only through the experience of trauma. It is the trauma, the forgetting (and return) of the deeds of Moses, that constitutes the link uniting the old with the new god" ("Unclaimed Experience" 185). The point we are trying to make here about a witness's relation to testimony is the same: it is not the traumatic act—the death of the child in the barrack or the moment when one brother realizes his calculation has caused the death of his sibling—that is visible in the testimonies of Holocaust survivors. What is visible is the structure of trauma that is made apparent in these painful narratives that try but fail to muster a language capable of making the viewer, the interviewer, see. Rather than understanding Holocaust testimonies as a glimpse at a pre-camp and post-camp self trying to reconcile irreconcilable worlds with one another, as Langer tries to suggest, those selves, those histories, are replaced by an absence: there is no self, properly understood, at all in these testimonies. The point Langer makes about Moses S., that he "reenacts," relives, the horrible memory of the child's death under the boot of a Kapo, is more to the point than he may realize: he is enacting not a return to the moment of trauma, but an instance of forgetting, an instance whereby the testimony he provides is a testament to what cannot be seen, what could not be seen—and understood conceptually—but what could only be "experienced" as excessive and as impossible to narrate.

Freud's discussion of trauma, which follows the odd reconsideration of Moses' place in Jewish history, takes the following turn:

> It may happen that someone gets away, apparently unharmed, from the spot where he has suffered a shocking accident, for instance a train collision. In the course of the following weeks, however, he develops a series of grave psychical and motor symptoms, which can be ascribed only to his shock or whatever else happened at the time of the accident. . . . [T]he problem of the traumatic neurosis and that of Jewish monotheism, [corresponds] in one point. It is the feature which one might term latency. (Freud 67–8)

At least as important as the period of latency or forgetting that insinuates itself between the moment of trauma or witness, and the moment in which the "psychical" symptoms of trauma are made visible in the wrenching, broken testimonies of witnesses, is the fact that the "victim of the crash was never fully conscious during the accident itself: the person gets away, Freud says, 'apparently unharmed'" (Caruth, "Unclaimed Experience" 187). Caruth goes on to make this point about trauma's link to history: "The historical power of trauma is not just that the experience is repeated after its forgetting, but that it is only in and through its inherent forgetting" (or, perhaps better, its in-experience) "that it is first experienced at all" (187). The act of witness is only available in another place and in another time: the time of the nightmare and—in testimony—the time of the writing or of the speaking to the interviewer. Witness can only be accessible to the extent that it is not fully perceived or experienced as it occurs, and it can only be grasped in the very inaccessibility of its occurrence.

Thus the significance of the gaps, the inability to speak, the hesitations, in the Holocaust testimonies: they are points at which the act of witnessing makes itself fully apparent to the witness himself, but which can only be glimpsed, through those gaps, by the interviewer or reader. In the late winter and early spring of 1997, a pair of interviews were conducted with a Holocaust survivor, Mary L., who lives in St. Louis and acts as a docent in that city's Holocaust Museum. The interviews are significant because of Mary's work with the museum, where her job is, in part, to testify to the events that she witnessed during her childhood in Lodz and later in the women's barracks in Auschwitz. What becomes clear during parts of her interview is that she has become accustomed to providing a narrative of the events of the Holocaust as she herself was connected to them. But this narrative is very different from a testimony of events to which she bears witness. As she puts it, her work at the Museum is not easy because what she says day after day "may be similar, [but] it's not learned by heart stuff; after all I can only tell my particular story, I can't tell you anything else . . ." (Stanovick 2). Like those whose video testimonies were recorded for the Fortunoff archive, there is in this survivor's case a sense that the experiences to which she bears witness are only available to her, and that whatever she manages to get across can only pale in comparison to the horrors of watching her mother die in the ghetto, or of four years in displaced persons camps. But as Caruth explains of trauma, in this case Mary herself cannot recall those experiences because as they are witnessed, they are not remembered and they are not conceptualized *as* experiences.

As they make their way through the St. Louis museum during their first meeting, the interviewer asks some initial questions, and as she points to a railway car she asks about Mary's transport from Lodz.

Interviewer: You were there with your mother and father?

Mary R.: Just my father. My mother died in the ghetto.

I: Of starvation?

M: [hesitation] She became sick. [Hesitation] And that combination, I guess. . . . [Silence]

I: Was she living with you?

M: Oh, of course, we were in that one little room together, but she had hepatitis and she had pneumonia, there weren't enough medications, she was a fragile person. [Silence]

I: How was taking care of her?

M: Very difficult. I don't even like to think about it. In all, eleven million civilian people killed in the concentration camps and otherwise by Germans. Out of that were six million Jewish people, and out of that were a million and a half children. (Stanovick 1997, 1–2)

The silences and hesitations that appear throughout this section of Mary R.'s interview mark spaces in which the experience of her mother's death cannot be narrated at all, but which haunt her, events whose traces cannot be effaced but which appear as disruptions, as departures. Like the period of latency between the Egyptian Moses's murder and the Hebrew Moses's elevation as leader of the Jews, in which the act of murder marks a departure from one monotheistic religion to another, in Mary R.'s testimony the gaps mark a separation between the traumatic occurrence witnessed prior to experience and its return as a disturbance in the narrative of the testimony. And, as in Freud's text, the mother's death returns in the context of the death of eleven million during the Shoah—the particular act of witnessing becomes embedded in another, more generalizable and historically understood event that is (though problematically so) conceptualizable at the universal level. "Very difficult. I don't even like to think about it. In all eleven million civilian people killed." The act of witness makes itself apparent only in the gap between the particular event and the conceptual, historical narrative of the Shoah, a testimony that is so troubled by the traumatic occurrence that it falls apart before our eyes. As when Mary R. hands the interviewer stories she has written for various local, sometimes Jewish, publications in St. Louis on her experiences in the camps, at the moment of witness—at the moment when the occurrence makes its return, as rupture, in the mind of the survivor—the reversion to the language of history well understood by her intended audience signals the return of the repressed moment of trauma. Mary R.'s repeated insistence that she has managed, all things considered, to live an assimilated, American life after her emigration to the United States is a chilling reminder that she is able to understand her experiences as one, in Freud's language, "apparently unharmed," while her testimony betrays that things are otherwise.

II. Written "Testimony"

Langer's point that there is a significant difference between oral testimonies and written ones also bears some scrutiny, on the same hypothesis: the structure of witness/testimony is the same, whether in oral or written narratives of the events. The difference between oral and written testimonies according to Langer is this: "[When] a witness in an oral testimony leans forward toward the camera . . . that witness confirms the vast imaginative space separating what he or she has endured from our capacity to absorb it. Written memoirs . . . strive to narrow this space, easing us into their unfamiliar world through familiar (hence comforting?) literary devices" (19). As the writer experiences the abyss "separating words from the events they seek to animate[, t]he writer strives to narrow that abyss. At a more fundamental level, driven by anguished memory, witnesses in oral testimonies plunge deeper into it even as they venture to escape" (42). Langer then points to the middle chapter of Primo Levi's *Survival in Auschwitz*, in which the author tells the story of his encounter with Jean, the Pikolo of the "chemical command," a young French man who spoke no Italian, though he was fluent in German and French. As they carry water, Levi tries desperately to find a lingua franca through which they may communicate, and what flashes through Levi's mind is Dante's *Divine Comedy*: if he can only teach Jean phrases from this work, then they may be able to engage in a connection that was actively prohibited by the SS, the kapos, and the convoluted logic of dehumanization that characterized the Final Solution. Langer points to Levi's hesitation, his inability to re-call the Italian, and says "it is not Auschwitz he is forgetting; it is literature, Dante, poetry, the *Commedia*." He goes on:

> I think the irony of this passage, whose content [i.e., lines from the "Canto of Ulysses"] contrasts so visibly with the setting and the scene, is explicit. For a moment, both Levi and Jean, under the com-pelling sway of Dante's art, forget who and where they are. And this is precisely the point: when literary form, allusion, and style intrude on the surviving victim's account, we risk forgetting where we are and imagine deceptive continuities. It is a dramatic interval in Levi's own text, as Dante's lines seize him with a fervor and transport him for an instant into the literary reality of the poem. . . . But his fervor quickly abates and . . . he escapes unscathed from the confusion of genres. (Langer, *Holocaust Testimonies* 45)

Without pausing to examine the tantalizing similarity between Langer's as-sertion that Levi escapes unscathed and Freud's remark about the trauma victim getting away "apparently unharmed," we want to suggest, instead, that this passage demonstrates quite clearly that the structure of witness is founded upon the *inability* to escape the (un)experienced traumatic mo-ment, and that it is precisely the "confusion of genres," the hesitations and aporias in the narrative of the witness's testimony, that mark his inability to communicate in conventional terms the traumatic occurrence. Whether this happens in written or oral language matters little: the trauma of the (un)experienced event registers in either case, and in either case what is im-portant is the extent to which the hesitation—as the mark of the traumatic moment—can be said to mark the point of witness, the moment between the occurrence of the event and one's ability to translate it into testimony.

This section of Levi's story is in fact highly self-conscious about translation, the difficulty if not the utter impossibility of passing from one language into another without doing damage to either of the languages and to the object of language itself.

Here, listen Pikolo, open your ears and your mind, you have to understand, for my sake: 'Think of your breed; for brutish igno-
rance/Your mettle was not made; you were made men,/to follow
after knowledge and excellence.' As if I was hearing it for the first
time: like the blast of a trumpet, like the voice of God. For a moment I forget who I am and where I am. (Levi 113)

In a book that is at best ambivalent about the line that separates "the facts"
of the camps from "documentation . . . of certain aspects of the human
mind" (10, 9), the urgency of bearing witness—of making sure that the
registers of the language provide the reader access to its object—is notable,
because it suggests that at base Levi's purpose is to provide a translation of
the events in Auschwitz to readers who were not there and who have no
point of departure or set of experiences to which they can refer in order to
do so. This conflict is similar to the one faced by the translator: he knows
that no language can do justice to the original, the language of the camps,
the *univers concentrationnaire* in which only a certain kind of sense was allowed and which left an impression but made no sense at all; and he also
knows nonetheless that beyond the language of the camps as well as the
language into which he must translate it, there lies something perhaps inaccessible, the abyss of the event as it precedes experience and discourse,
an abyss that Walter Benjamin says is "vouchsafed to Holy Writ alone," by
the language of the divine (Benjamin, *Illuminations* 82). No more or less
so than oral testimonies, written testimonies like Levi's attest to the difficulties—if not the impossibility—of recuperating in language those events
that precede language. What written testimonies *may* provide—indeed
must provide—is a written record of the hesitations involved when bridging the gap between witness and testimony that in oral testimonies registers as silence, the shrug, and the retreat into the litany of numbers—
"eleven million . . . six million . . . one and a half million."

Binjamin Wilkomirski's *Fragments*, like Levi's story of the Pikolo, is
painfully self-conscious about its status as testimony and as translation, in
part because its author is—consciously or not—translating one trauma in
terms of another. He begins the book this way:

I have no mother tongue, no father tongue either. My language has
its roots in the Yiddish of my eldest brother Mordecai, overlaid with
the Babel-babble of an assortment of children's barracks in the Nazis'
death camps in Poland. . . . [T]he languages I learned later on were
never mine, at bottom. They were only imitations of other people's
speech. (3–4)

The writer here is almost dismissive of the possibility that he may find a way to match the contours of the language that "has its roots" in Yiddish but that is not itself Yiddish, and the language of the camps, and a language that follows "the ordering logic of grown-ups" (4). His aim, instead, is to fit together "shards of memory with hard knife-sharp edges, which still cut the flesh if touched today. . . . I'm not a poet or writer. I can only try to use words to draw as exactly as possible what happened . . . with no benefit of perspective or vanishing point" (4–5). The author is looking for a way to bring to the surface of text a sense of the un-remembered event itself, in all of its destructive capacity, to the point of destroying the language (and perhaps the idea of history) through which it is built. And yet it is not clear at all, given the vexed structure of testimony outlined by Caruth and others, whether what's brought to the surface—the trace of the event—bears any historical relation at all to the narrative itself.

After spending some months in an orphanage in Switzerland immediately after the war, Wilkomirski is told he will be transported to the home of a foster family outside of the city. The boy, whose childhood experiences were formed by Bergen-Belsen, Majdanek, and the inconceivable brutality of survival, understands the term "transport" in the only conceptual scheme he has available to him: a two-day journey by boxcar without food or water to a death camp where the only terminus is murder. Upon hearing the word, the boy flies into a wordless panic and attempts to flee:

> "No, no transport, no—I won't go on any transport," I screamed despairingly. "I want to go home, let me go home. Not the transport, please!"
>
> Lots of people talked to me but I didn't understand what they said—I didn't want to understand anything. (120)

Only later does he come to learn that the paradigm in which his understanding of the term—a paradigm founded upon an experience not shared by his interlocutor or his reader—was wrong.

The important thing to notice here, more important than the miscommunication between the woman from the orphanage and the young boy, is the fact that the incommensurability of the paradigms themselves speaks to a third object beyond either of them. For the woman whose aim is to bring Binjamin to a foster home, the significance of the term, probably spoken in German—a language which, though in its most brutal form, he probably has come to know—is as an everyday method of conveyance. But for the boy, the term's significance, unspoken by the writer though it

is written into the language of the narrative in terms of the action that follows its utterance, exceeds these two meanings of the term. The author explains that the meaning of transport was gathered from other children
who, when asked about their brothers or sisters, responded that they had
been put on a transport—"and that always meant that they'd gone forever" (120). But whatever may have occurred in the lived life of the author, and whatever the untranslatable, prior meaning of the terror in the
child's response, they come not from the phenomena that the writer could
have described, the "manifestations of life," but from a trace of the moment that founds them (Benjamin, *Illuminations* 71), a moment beyond
the speaker's capacity to know—or remember—them at all.

Earlier, in Majdan Lublin, a woman in a grey uniform called Binjamin by his name, a name he barely recognized as his own. She asks him,
"You're . . . ?" and Binjamin nods.

> "Today you can see your mother, but — only dahle."
> I didn't understand what she was saying. What did "dahle"
> mean? I still have no idea today. She pronounced it with a very long,
> broad aah. And what did "mother" mean?
> I couldn't remember.
> I had certainly heard other children using the word "mother"
> from time to time. I'd heard some of them crying, and calling out
> for mama. . . . All I understood was that a mother, whether you had
> one or not, must be something immensely important, something
> that was worth fighting for, the way you fought over food. (46–7)

After he is led over to a cot where, under a blanket, lay a pale and thin
woman, he stands there dumbfounded, not knowing what to do. The
woman gropes under her blanket for something, and she hands it up to
Binjamin.

> I took the object, clutched it tight against me, and went toward the
> door, which now stood wide open, silhouetting the dark waiting
> shape of the gray uniform . . .
> "What is this?" I asked the gray uniform as we reached my
> barracks.
> "That's bread." (50)

The narrative describes an event as understood by a child of five or
six, but it makes reference to not only what occurred to Binjamin
Wilkomirski in late 1941 but to that instant at which some other traumatic

event returns to the author Bruno Doesseker and breaks upon him without warning. Like the moment at which the child understands the significance of the word "mother" without recognizing that he indeed had one or that the woman lying before him may be the person who secreted him and his brothers out of Riga in the winter of 1939, the words written here by the author do not refer either to the one or to the other moment because they cannot be mapped onto one another, cannot be translated. But between them, and by recognizing both as fragments of a moment that exceeds them, both become "recognizable as fragments of a greater language, just as fragments are part of a vessel" (Benjamin, *Illuminations* 78). We catch a glimpse not of the woman on the cot or of Binjamin wrestling to comprehend whether "dahle" and "mother" are the same thing, but of a moment outside of history and memory that interrupts historical time and language. Wilkomirski has not translated these moments into literary language—he has not made clear a fifty-year-old memory. Instead, through the (in this case vast) distance between witness and testimony, he has brought into being what Walter Benjamin calls an impossible memory unforgotten (70), or, in Blanchot's terms, "immemorial," the void of silence that can only be made available in language (3, 8).

It is the disaster in Primo Levi's book, *Survival in Auschwitz*—the events unnamed, and perhaps unnameable, by history—that we see in his utterances. Knowing as we do the historical context of the events taking place in Auschwitz in 1944–45, and knowing the parts played by the SS, and the kapos, and the *haeftlinge*, we're able to construct a narrative into which we may drop Levi's story, and it then becomes understandable as an episode in a life lived in unbearable circumstances, an episode that perhaps brought a moment of clarity: "I must tell [the pikolo]," he says, "something gigantic that I myself have only just seen, in a flash of intuition, perhaps the reason for our fate, for our being here today . . ." (Levi 115). The hermeneutic circle is closed if we grant this flash of memory the status of knowledge—that somehow Levi's intuition has matched the shattered pieces of memory, and the name of the disaster is spoken: Primo Levi, *haeftlinge* number 174517, chronicler of the *univers concentrationnaire*, rounded up in Italy and transported to Auschwitz in 1944, and freed by the Red Army at the end of January 1945. If, however, we take the language of the book as the writing of the disaster, and read the urgent, fragmented, and out-of-place words and phrases as attempts to describe a moment so utterly alien that they jar the writer and the reader out of the narrative of history, then we can see it as providing access to the trauma of witness. This language—like the anguished testimonies of Moses S. or Mary R.—makes visible not the world of Auschwitz in 1944, or a life or series of lives of those who lived and died at the hands of the Nazis, but forces open those worlds we simply cannot know, and through that opening comes a confrontation with what the human mind can and cannot do. Levi's account, Wilkomirski's "memoir," and the testimonies in the Fortunoff and other archives do not describe the world of one who was there, for even those who are there cannot possibly describe the disaster: it is long past at the moment of writing the words, and it is, in spite of the flashes of clarity, nonetheless comprised of babel. Levi's chapter ends not with understanding, but this way:

> We are now in the soup queue, among the sordid, ragged crowd of soup-carriers from other kommandos. Those just arrived press at our backs. "Kraut und Ruben? Kraut und Ruben. [Cabbage and turnips? Cabbage and turnips.] . . . Choux et navets. Kaposzta es repak."
> "And above our heads the hollow seas closed up." (115)

This is no description of the event, but "meaning that plunges from abyss to abyss until it threatens to become lost in the bottomless depths of language" (Benjamin, *Illuminations* 82). But in what it cannot say we glimpse the traumatic event as it affects individuals, as it destroys the narratives we have created to contain both our "selves" and the name of the Shoah.

III. Witness and Ethics

As a testimonial document, Art Spiegelman's two-volume *Maus: A Survivor's Tale* is a hybrid text: it is at once the testimony of Vladek Spiegelman, Art's father, whose family was deported from the cities of Czestochowa and Sosnowiec in Poland and destroyed at Auschwitz and other death camps, and the testimony of Artie, the son conceived after the war who is haunted by the memories of his father, his mother's suicide, and the evanescent but always palpable sense that he cannot take the place of Vladek's son Richieu, who died during the war. But it is hybrid in another sense: it is an historical document, comprised by the tape-recorded testimonies of Vladek in the presence of Artie, a second-generation memoir of Artie's efforts to recover the history of his family and of his distinctly troubled relationship to his father and his family, and a metafictional analysis of the problems of representing any historical occurrence—whether it must be recovered from the annals of the past or memory, or whether it is taking place in the lived, present moment—by means of a language or a medium that simply cannot meet it halfway. But what is uncanny about this text is that in its failure to reconcile the anguished memory of the son to the tortured memories of the father—to decide, on Langer's terms, the extent to which oral testimony or literary testimony bears the weight of the act of witnessing most adequately—it nonetheless makes clear, in the interstices of the text and its images, the epistemology of what we might call the "real," the structure of trauma to which witness can be borne but not testified, that is at the heart of the survivor's confrontation with the events of the Shoah.

Spiegelman's text is problematic for those who believe that the Holocaust can only be discerned or represented in completely historical terms. Some find its chief representation of Jews as mice and Nazis as cats offensive, or its comic book form disrespectful of the material that it attempts to show. It is this problem of reception—a problem of context and meaning—that makes *Maus* important for us when considering what the Holocaust tells us about representation, about the way in which any particular trauma—Blanchot's "utter-burn"—is re-presented or re-written. James Young investigates this very problem of narrating the Holocaust in *Writing and Rewriting the Holocaust* (and, more recently, in an essay on *Maus* in *Critical Inquiry*), focusing explicitly on the effects narration has on history, interpretation, and memory. Following Young's consideration of the nature of narrative, we will consider the relationship between the demand for historically accurate and meaningful recordings of experience and the often contrary demands of narrative itself, focusing on Spiegelman's *Maus* and the impasse between knowing the historically accurate and knowing the significance of the event itself—its meaning as memory. What makes *Maus* so important—as a record of the impasse between witness and testimony, and as a document that makes available in that impasse a sense of the immemorial traumatic occurrence—is the way in which it combines an historical contextualization with something that its narrative form, its fictional structure, can only supply: a symptomatic juxtaposition of the past and present that allows something real to be introduced into the historical, something of the impasse between the particular representation of experience and the universal understanding of such an experience. In *Maus*, Spiegelman offers evidence for the "utter-burn" that forms the center of any knowledge of the Holocaust.

To explain how, we need first to address how knowledge itself is a function of discourse, where there is what Lacan would call an underside to representation that carries meaning beyond epistemology. To say that knowledge functions relative to or separate from discourse would mean that a given knowledge is sufficient to itself as it enters different discourses, that knowledge and meaning are the same and are independent of the discursive structure in which they are signified. We have tried to suggest, though, that the Holocaust shows that some discourses are in fact completely unable to localize trauma or allow meaning to oscillate rather than be erased by elision with knowledge: "eleven million . . . six million . . . one and a half million." The Holocaust as a trauma—as evidence for something real—resists signification, points specifically to such an impasse between historical/epistemological reality and the reality of specific instances of discourse. The Holocaust, then, resists such significations, leaving unveiled the kernel of the event (its cause, perhaps).

In *Writing the Disaster*, Maurice Blanchot points at just such a limit in representing trauma, where one attempt at formulating a whole of the disaster, of the Holocaust, leads to deconstruction of the particular, an event that he also describes as disaster:

> Fragmentation, the mark of a coherence all the firmer in that it has to come undone in order to be reached, and reached not through a dispersed system, or through dispersion as a system, for fragmentation is the pulling to pieces (the tearing) of that which never has preexisted (really or ideally) as a whole, nor can it ever by reassembled in any future presence whatever. (60)

Blanchot finds the response to the inadequacies of representation to be the beginning of an ethics, that the disaster occurs when one's particular is held up as everyone's universal, producing a knowledge of the whole in contrast to the impasse itself. More recently, Berel Lang, in "The Representation of Limits," has similarly discussed a relation between language and discourse, focusing on Nazi rhetoric for describing by not describing the Final Solution, seeing a rhetoric of genocide in the workings of language. Both Blanchot and Lang point at an ethics—and thus a pedagogy—of considering the Holocaust that privileges the gap or impasse between the representation and represented, seeing response to such incongruities as a way of knowing and teaching that keeps horror itself recognizable.

An important effect of the horror of cutting off meaning from knowledge is the problem of representing particulars in relation to universals, of constructing knowledge from particular narratives: of binding testimony to acts of witness. Particular representations of the Holocaust do not construct adequate universals in and of themselves. Rather, particular representations present a limit to such universal constructions, pointing towards the necessarily impossible nature of a universal knowledge within a universal discourse, an epistemological foundation on which academic discourse is grounded. Such a position marks the very impossibility of transmitting real knowledge, of offering a singular or even pluralistic way of achieving recognition of an event. One may arrive at an understanding—a universalized position—but cause itself is left suspended and not recognizable. It is to this problem—the problem of understanding that Primo Levi recognizes in the preface to *Survival in Auschwitz*—that purely historical accountings of the Holocaust fall prey, where the trauma of the event is covered over by principles of accounting. Like Levi's nonhistorical motivation for writing *Survival at Auschwitz*, Spiegelman's *Maus* is a text that not only defines an historical moment but also questions the localization of such a moment qua moment. In this sense, *Maus* transcends any attempt at constructing academic knowledge, subjectifying the very limit that academic discourse must by definition foreclose.

In Spiegelman's account, the impact of the initial act of witness into the present and any attempts to testify to that act, the retroactive effect of the present on a knowledge of the past, show a deeply particular instance of a "meaning" of the Holocaust. As testimony, Spiegelman's account of his father's experience defines the author's own struggle with knowledge and understanding, ultimately re-presenting the very possibility of transmitting a recognition of the Holocaust as a real knowledge. This does not mean that *Maus* is "realer" or more genuine than other attempts to provide a record of the events of the Shoah from a survivor's perspective. Rather, what makes *Maus* distinctive is the way in which the narrative itself focuses on the problems of knowing meaning by problematically overlapping present and past narratives, defining a structure at work in all representations of the Holocaust. Spiegelman presents us with a means of defining witnessing in terms of a movement of meaning that resists knowing—a recognition of the swallowing up of the knowable, a recognition that is itself recognizable.

In *Maus*, Spiegelman balances the telling of his father's witnessing with witnessing itself, moving back and forth between what his father is telling of the past and his own reception of his father's experience. This interaction is highlighted several times by the actions of his father, Vladek, in the present relative to what has just been narrated about his experience. The very opening sequence in *Maus* (v. I) sets up this type of interaction, showing a memory of Artie's childhood and the reaction of Vladek when Artie comes to him after being teased by friends: "Friends? Your friends? . . . If you lock them together in a room with no food for a week . . . then you see what it is friends!" (5–6). Similarly, chapter three begins with an argument at dinner over Artie not eating his food, followed by Vladek's recollection of Artie doing the same as a child (40–45). This frame sequence is immediately followed by Vladek continuing his narrative of serving in the Polish army when the Germans invaded. Overlapping the dinner and the recollection is Vladek's continuing disagreement with his wife Mala, an argument from which Artie tries desperately to distance himself. It is through the overlapping of the frame story with the remembered event—the insertion of Vladek's past into Artie's present—that Spiegelman points at the disaster, not in an attempt at defining the Holocaust, but rather as a means of pointing at its presence in the lives of his family.

We can see this overlapping most clearly in a moment when Vladek is telling of being separated from his family:

(*Maus* I 63)

In this scene we see the past and present connected into one larger image, where the memory of Vladek's recuperation is visually tied to his telling of his story. Here the narration in the present of Vladek's family sending food to friends is punctuated by the resting Vladek in the past, where "finished" is emphasized in both moments. Similarly, we see the same juxtaposition later when he tells of the decision to keep his son, Richieu, in Poland.

(*Maus* I 81)

Terrence Des Pres cites this particular caption as a way of showing the interaction between the present and the past, where Vladek's cycling is set to the rhythm of the narrative frames above. De Pres concludes that: "the agony of the earlier predicament, and Vladek's pain as he remembers, yield a pathos that would be excessive except for the iconography though which suffering is displaced" (229). The iconography, however, does more than displace pathos. The images themselves bring together visual markers for the continued intrusion of the past on the present, the continued layering of history with narrative. Later in his essay, Des Pres more precisely concludes:

> In *Maus* the spectacle of pathos is complete, a seamless world of pain except for the comic energies at work. . . . At the heart of *Maus* is the family romance, replete with guilt and unresolved complexities caused by the hold of the past upon the present, a kind of knowledge-as-suffering that cannot be dismissed, but only shared in the "survivors tale" before us (230–31).

And it is the form of the work—the overlapping of images and text—that is structured around a "knowledge-as-suffering," where the kernel of the real pierces language. Thus, *Maus* shows that although we cannot know the "utter-burn" of the Holocaust, its effect of suffering is transmissible.

Perhaps the clearest instance of the transmission of suffering occurs when we see Artie's comic book on his mother's death in chapter five of volume I, and the self-examination of Artie in chapter three of volume II. In both of these sequences we see the effects of Vladek's life—his narrative that is the center of both books—on Artie's day-to-day survival, where the definition of Holocaust survivor is blurred between father and son. In the *Maus* II example, we see how the absence of his father has left Artie masked, with only the tape-recorded sessions to hold his attention.

(*Maus* II 47)

This sequence offers a present for Artie where all pasts overlap: the past of his father's life in Auschwitz, the tortured relationship he had with his father, and the moments of attempting to reconcile these pasts into a coherent narrative. The sequence captures the subjectifying tensions of the Holocaust as a field of meaning rather than a field of knowledge. Artie's sigh in the final caption functions to heighten the irresolvability of these narratives, marking the space from which meaning itself is recognizable.

Similarly, the scenes with Artie's "shrink" continue to blur the father and son together, showing the effects of the father's past on his son.

(*Maus* II 44)

As the "real survivor," Artie marks a locus of meaning, a moment where the sadness continues and is recognizable. In this sense, Blanchot's "utter-burn" is not something that is resolvable or knowable. But it is transmissible; we can recognize—bear witness to—the horrors within representation itself, the underside of Artie's more knowable retracing of his father's past in his own present. The Holocaust as presence/present brings us closer to understanding an epistemology of the real, a knowledge based on a recognition of trauma in relation to particularity. The moments of Vladek's memory intrude into Artie's present. And although Artie and Vladek may not recognize the intrusion, Spiegelman's juxtaposition of the two moments offer us a recognition of history as effect and affect rather than as factual or experiential.

Noting the differences between oral and written testimonies, Lawrence Langer tells us that, in listening to the former, "we unearth a mosaic of evidence that constantly vanishes, like Thomas Mann's well of the past, into bottomless layers of incompletion" (21). The trajectory of incompletion is understandable if we acknowledge, as Caruth has of trauma, that the occurrence of the event, and our implication in it, is no more accessible to memory than is the *ursprache*, the source of divinity, in the difficult work of the historian or translator. While oral testimonies, which grapple with the void that is the Shoah as the witness plunges forward, word by word, mark the distance between the occurrence of the event and its experience in memory, "[m]ost written survivor narratives, on the other hand, end where they have been leading—the arrival of the Allies, and the corresponding 'freedom' of the victims" (57). While Levi's *Survival in Auschwitz* does end with the Soviet occupation of the camp, Wilkomirski and—notably—Spiegelman end, in their narratives, elsewhere. In *Frag-ments*, the writer ends not with Binjamin's rescue and adoption by a Swiss family after the war, though the difficulties of making his way in Swiss cul-ture and in particular in a Swiss school, are the subject of much of the book. He ends instead with a recollection of visits to a teacher.

> He was an old man, and a wise one. The last surviving member of a centuries-old family of Romanian Rabbis, he had studied, among other things, music, physics, mathematics, philosophy, and medicine. He was my guide and mentor, the kind of father I would have wished for myself.
>
> He was the only person with whom I could be open. He was the only person back then who understood if all I could dare do was hint at past events.
>
> He understood what I was really saying. (152)

As if to turn full circle on his story, the author here makes plain the distance between what he is able to call up—to (mis)remember—of the occurrences in the years between 1939 and the early 1950s, whose understanding was greater because of the imperfect and partial narrative testimony he was pro-vided by witnesses to the destruction of the Shoah. The descriptiveness, the brutality, of the images called up by Doesseker's prose, if they are more com-plete than the hints of past events provided to his teacher, nonetheless can only be understood as the traces of events. But they may be taken, by their incompleteness, as a rupture of chronology, of sense, and of memory of the events created in the language of testimony.

"Asked to describe how he felt at the moment of liberation, one sur-viving victim declared, 'Then I knew my troubles were *really* about to begin,' inverting the order of conflict and resolution that we have learned to expect of traditional historical narrative" (Langer 67). It's as if this sur-vivor recognized that, in the gap between the traumatic experience—and its forgetting—that constitutes witness, and the creation of a narrative that may be said to move the victim forward that constitutes testimony, there ex-ists the underside of knowledge, what troubles knowledge and insists upon disrupting its language, which, like the disaster, destroys everything. Art Spiegelman's subtitle for the second volume of *Maus* is "And here my trou-bles began." One is almost tempted to ask, "Where?" It makes more sense to think of the troubles beginning in 1933, or at the point when Vladek's textile business was appropriated by the Polish General Government, or at any number of other temporal locations in the Spiegelman family history. But perhaps the troubles begin where the testimony, finally, ends: the point at which Artie, the son whose recordings of the story of his father's testimony must finally be borne witness to, in the closing words of his father, not—we assume—recorded on tape but indelibly upon the (second-generation) witness himself. In the last panels of the book, Vladek's final illness is getting the best of him, and his son knows that he is racing time to allow his father to finish his story. Earlier, Vladek had pulled out a box of photos, many of relatives who survived the war, but a few left from before the maelstrom, including one or two of Vladek, his wife Anja, and their son Richieu.

Vladek welcomes his son into his room, and he continues with the story. Barely noticeable, above Vladek's bed, is a portrait of Richieu, the only surviving photo of his first son, in overalls and a white shirt, and at the conclusion of his narrative, Vladek rolls over, and asks Artie if it's all right to stop for now.

(136)

This error, this mistake of identities, is at the core of the trauma not only of Vladek's narrative, but also Artie's: every caricature he has drawn of the Spiegelman family before the war that includes Richieu, at whatever age— even as an infant—is drawn exactly the same: dark overalls and a white shirt.

If trauma is the paradigm through which we understand the impasse between witness and testimony, then the break here—where both Vladek and Art Spiegelman's troubles began—is that which takes place at the moment of the destruction of the family, of Richieu, and eventually of his wife Anja as well, the specific instance(s) of destruction that we cannot know through the universal narrative of the Holocaust, or through a recitation of the events of a life, or of a series of lives ("eleven million . . . six million . . . one and a half million") but only through the experience, for the first time, of the recitation of the break. Spiegelman's story, like Freud's in *Moses and Monotheism*, is the story of a trauma borne witness to, "a history whose traces cannot be effaced, which haunts Freud [as well as Spiegelman] like a ghost, and finally emerges in [his work] involving extensive repetition" (Caruth, "Unclaimed Experience" 189), in this case, the repetition of the ghost in the imaginative figure of Richieu. For in the dedication page of *Maus*, volume II, appears that photo, the one that is repeated again and again in the

FOR RICHIEU

AND FOR NADJA

pages of both volumes of his story, in dark overalls and white shirt, the ghost that represents the break, but which does not tell its story.

When we argue that the Holocaust is particular, that it is unlike other traumas, other genocides, we are invoking a different epistemological focus than simply saying it's unique. Rather, as Spiegelman's *Maus* shows, we are saying that the Holocaust shows us something about epistemology itself, laying bare the underside of an understanding that tends to speak only in universal terms. For Spiegelman's story of his family's past and his own relationship to this past we only have a particular rendering, a layering of images that shows the inadequacies of universal contents. The Holocaust, then, teaches something about the limits of epistemology, the foreclosure of recognition that is necessary for understanding. The Holocaust requires an epistemology based on the intrusion of the real rather than its foreclosure, pointing towards an ethics that forces us beyond reducing the Holocaust to a simply symbolic system. This is not to suggest that we should be silent in the face of the Final Solution, a position Berel Lang clearly attacks at the end of his "The Representation of Limits," as does Peter Haidu in "The Dialectics of Unspeakability." But rather than solely listening for the possibility that speaks symbolically, the historical academic discourse, I would suggest we listen to the impossible that speaks loudest, the horror, the "utter-burn" that cannot exist as the possible but rather as its underside, its structure. It is only from considering the particularity of a witness's voice that we are then able to listen, if not to its meaning, then to the trauma that destroys it.

Notes

1. Fortunoff Video Archive for Holocaust Testimonies, Yale University, tape T-2. Testimony of Leon W. Further references to testimonies from this archive will appear parenthetically in the text abbreviated FVA.

2. During the early fall of 1998, a Swiss writer named Daniel Ganzfried published two articles in *Weltwoche* (Zurich) that claimed that the individual named Binjamin Wilkomirski is a fiction, and that the account published in *Fragments* was written by Bruno Doesseker, a child adopted in Switzerland in the years after the war. Elena Lappin, for *Granta*, and Philip Gourevitch, for *The New Yorker*, each investigated the matter, and reported their findings in the early summer of 1999. Even those who most clearly question the veracity of the Wilkomirski narrative have little doubt that Doesseker experienced some trauma, either at the hands of the Nazis or at the hands of the Swiss authorities. Lappin suggests that Doesseker's Swiss mother may have been herself subject to abuse as an indentured laborer, and that she may have given him up for adoption because of her own, and her child's, experiences as such. See Lappin, "The Man with Two Heads," and Gourevitch, "The Memory Thief." Bernard-Donals has laid out the consistency of the Wilkomirski "memoir" with the dynamic of memory and forgetting in narratives of trauma in "Beyond the Question of Authenticity: Witness and Testimony in the *Fragments* Controversy" (*PMLA*, forthcoming). In addition, there is a significant body of literature on the validity of witness accounts in Jewish legal writing: see two having to do with the Holocaust—Carlo Ginzburg's "Just one Witness," and Martin Jay's "Of Plots, Witnesses, and Judgments," both in Saul Friedlander's collection, *Probing the Limits of Representation*. We will have more to say about the controversy in the book's conclusion.

4

Literatures of Presence and Absence: Borowski, Appelfeld, Ozick

Perhaps the most sublime passage in the Jewish Law is the commandment: Thou shalt not make unto thee any graven image, or any likeness of any thing that is in the heaven or on earth . . .

Kant, *Critique of Judgment*

Aharon Appelfeld, responding once in conversation to a comment on the obliqueness of his novels' representations of the horrors of the Holocaust, commented that "one does not look directly at the sun." . . . "M'ken nisht," literally Yiddish for "one cannot." . . . But [this way of speaking] conveys a certain ambiguity, as if the m'ken nisht *had a way of becoming* m'tur nisht, *"one must not," so that an acknowledgment of limit might serve as a warning of the forbidden.*

Lang, *Writing and the Holocaust*

It is the numbers, the facts of the Shoah that should speak for the event, not fiction representing it: "Keep literature out of the fire zone," is a phrase that Aharon Appelfeld recites as the imperative for writers of fiction. This imperative seems to be imposed most clearly upon those writers of fiction whose generation did not know, firsthand, the experience of the Holocaust—the Nuremburg laws, the confiscations, the humiliation of concentration, and the indignity of death in the ghettos or camps. James Young argues that there is something legitimate about survivors' desire to tell their stories—though their accounts could not possibly be uncorrupted by political, religious, or private motivation—because suffering requires the expiation that comes with the anguished utterance. Conversely, there must be something illegitimate, we feel, about those who tell stories about an event that they could not know firsthand. They are committing the cardinal sin in the post-Auschwitz world: singing in the face of the disaster, or perhaps more to Adorno's point, allowing those within earshot of the song to derive pleasure from the deaths of millions. Young suggests that in order to fend off this criticism, novelists historically removed from the event make use of the trope of the document, they mimic the eyewitness account in all of its fallibility, its corruption by motives beyond objectivity, and—in theory at least—recreate the horror for those to whom they bear (false) witness.

But the witness, as often as not, finds herself unable to speak in the face of the memories of events that seem to defy any kind of discursive logic—or any kind of logic at all. If there is a ring of fire surrounding the events of the Shoah that provokes a respectful or, more likely, fearful silence, that silence would seem to put an end to representation, and confounds Young's sense that fiction would replicate the language of the eyewitness. If that language is at least partly a language of silence—stutters, the inability to speak, the desire to speak knowing that any language is inappropriate or inadequate—then how, precisely, does that language replicate the horror of the event itself? If what we want is fiction that replicates the documentary presence of history, or chronicle, or diary—a language of presence—then we need to closely examine just what that language looks like, and how (or perhaps if) it provides readers with an immediate sense of the event, if not a representation of it. To do so we need now to examine what such representations look like, and just what effect they have, story by story (see Bernstein 52–5). In this chapter we'll examine the responses of three canonical writers of fiction of the Holocaust to the injunction to keep literature out of the fire zone or, in Appelfeld's phrase, to avoid looking directly upon the catastrophe itself. Aharon Appelfeld has, in his stories and short novels, obeyed his own injunction by writing about the effects of the Holocaust on both survivors (*The Immortal Bartfuss*) and bystanders (*Katerina*), and upon those who will die by gas and fire (*Badenheim 1939*, *To the Land of the Cattails*) and those who escape, apparently unharmed (*Age of Wonders*). More to the point, his prose is metonymic, placing sign next to similar sign to seal off what Alan Mintz has dubbed the "Appelfeld world" from the context that would deign to make sense of it. By contrast, Tadeusz Borowski, whose stories of the camps were collected as *This Way for the Gas, Ladies and Gentlemen*, seems obsessed by the horrible details of the *univers concentrationnaire*, and for that reason looks directly at it. His prose is almost cruel in its willingness to show atrocity in the context of the everyday world that exists just outside the gates of the camps. It is metaphoric, constantly holding up the events to which he attempts to bear witness in a language that follows the patterns and rhythms of the western tradition. It is the gap that resides between the language of the normal and the impossible horror through which the reader faces the abyss of reason that Borowski and others like him endured in Auschwitz. Cynthia Ozick, a writer who was not there, places the languages of presence and absence into a relentless dialectic and, in the novella *The Shawl*, provides us with a complicated representation of the Holocaust (see Wirth-Neser 315), one that rests on a dialectic of presence and absence, metaphor and metonymy. In "The Shawl," Ozick both presents and withdraws from presenting the event that forms the story's core, the murder of a child, essentially presenting a void of memory at the center of the tale; in the second story, "Rosa," she makes clear that the void has had an effect: not a silence but a torrent of language, though it is a language that calls up a negative image of that which it tries to represent. What the three authors suggest, taken together, is that the trope of history cannot be depended upon to provide a sense of the horror of the events of the Shoah—to let the numbers speak for themselves, and to keep literature, or language, out of the fire zone. In fact, the trope of the documentary may be the least able to provide the immediacy of the event; it may well be that the language of fiction—with its ability to confound history, and with it our deperate need to name the events that comprise it in the name of reason—is the best means that we have to approximate the heat of the fire itself.

I. Absence and Presence (Appelfeld, Borowski)

It has become a commonplace of Holocaust literature that novelist Aharon Appelfeld confronts the Shoah not directly but indirectly, perhaps for fear of the blindness that would result from looking directly on the horrible events themselves, but also perhaps—as is intimated by Berel Lang—to avoid granting his characters (or to the reader's capacity to imagine) an individuality, the capacity not only to imagine but to act, that those individuals, destroyed during the Holocaust, could not possibly have had (*Act and Idea* 154–5). It has equally become a commonplace that the Polish writer Tadeusz Borowski, in the veiled fiction of *This Way for the Gas*, the stories written after his release from Auschwitz, is relentless in his direct confrontation with the details of camp life, of its brutality. Unafraid to look directly into the sun, "Borowski's style conveys the rhythm of a hammering factuality. . . . [The stories'] authenticity makes us, I would say, all but indifferent to their status as art" (Howe 192). Borowski, having become blinded by gazing directly into the glare of the Shoah, committed suicide in 1951. Both commonplaces suggest something about the fear of the negative that writers on the subject of the ultimate negation, in Adorno's terms, show in their willingness to forge into figure those details of destruction. But both commonplaces also ignore precisely the work's status as art, and the fact that both are openly negotiating—and quite successfully we might add—with not only the impossible object of representation, but also with what lies beyond it.

Perhaps the most stunning example of Appelfeld's refusal to confront directly the events of the Holocaust is *To the Land of the Cattails*, written six years after *Badenheim 1939*, the novel that brought Appelfeld to the attention of the English-speaking reading public. (Up until 1980, when the earlier book was published, Appelfeld—who writes in Hebrew—was mainly known in Israel.) Like *Badenheim 1939*, *To the Land of the Cattails* focuses its attention upon events in the years leading immediately up to the concentration and transportation of Jews in eastern Europe in the late 1930s; like the earlier novel, its characters are only vaguely aware of the events that form the backdrop of their actions, and attend to the details of everyday life while each day the catastrophe approaches. But unlike *Badenheim 1939*, in which the characters have an inkling of the coming disaster (they speak openly of their resettlement in the eastern territories, and their dislike of the *ostjuden*), the characters in *To the Land of the Cattails* are ignorant enough of their circumstances that they are travelling away from the relative safety of Vienna in the late summer of 1938 and toward the source of the Bug River in Ruthenia which would, in the two years covered in the novel, be emptied of all its Jewish population, first by transport and later more violently by the *einsatzgruppen*.

Like all of Appelfeld's other work set in the years prior to the Holocaust, there are hints dropped throughout the novel of a language that will forever be changed in the years after 1945. As they begin their travel by carriage, Toni—a single mother who travelled from her parents' home on the Czech-Hungarian border to Vienna in the 1920s—tries to explain her background to her son Rudi, who senses that he is Jewish but whose immediate concerns have more to do with the discomfort of travel and his leaving the gymnasium and his studies in the city. Toni is not a well-educated person, and she is only dimly able to communicate the importance of her commitment to Judaism and her need to return home in the face of catastrophe. In one confrontation, Rudi "ambushes" her (Appelfeld's word) with questions and what amounts to an accusation:

"You are a believer." For a moment, she would lower her head, but, recovering quickly, say, "Certainly I am a believer. No one will take away the faith I received from my father and mother."

"But you . . . How should I put it?" he would jab.

"That does not matter. I am ready to die for my faith."(8)

This utterance, placed as it is here as a response from a mother trying to persuade her son of the depth of her beliefs, might be read as a cliche, a commonplace, derived from the martyrologies of Christianity more than Judaism perhaps, but a commonplace that registers a steadfastness rather than a death wish, a profession of faith and strength rather than a statement of fact about the immediate future. But the utterance cuts another way: Toni and Rudi are marching eastward into the maw of a rural anti-Semitism and—as readers of fiction we recognize the locus of history and of geography—the killing fields of the eastern front and the launching point of *Einsatzgruppe* IV. There is an impossible connection between this mother's profession and the historical circumstances she cannot know: that millions will die for their faith, not as a voluntary act of martyrdom but as murder. Speaking of a Ruthenian woman's enthusiasm for Jews as Toni and Rudi make their way through the town of Ozrin, she explains to her son that such enthusiasm is ill placed in the countryside: "the Jews mixed them up a little, spoiled them a little, but in a year or two they will forget the Jews" (17).

This is a language of absence, though it hardly avoids the Holocaust. Appelfeld's descriptions, and the historical context of the novel's setting, do not account for the destruction of the Jews of Europe as historical reality. His language works metonymically rather than metaphorically, refusing to signify outside of its immediate context. It "demand[s] that the reader provide a supporting ground and literary frame of fact and expression—detailing the face and aura of horror—that more usually . . . the writer himself would accept responsibility for enacting" (*Act and Idea* 106). In the face of the historical reality of "forgetting the Jews," Appelfeld's imagined conversation between a mother and her son on the subject of a peasant woman's fondness for Jewish culture and learning, for example, becomes impossible: the abyss between the one and the other, between the commonplace of the conversation and the horror of utter destruction, is too broad. Instead, the absence of such a ground that would breach it does not compel the reader to provide it; phrases like the ones noted here (and others invoking smoke and fire, rail transportation, and concentration in *Badenheim 1939* and *The Age of Wonders*, to call up only a few examples) function as symbols, language that acts not as an indicator of a context exterior to the immediate one—conversations while waiting for coffee to boil, the petty arguments of a mother and her son—but as a negation of that exterior context. That context—the Shoah, as it is prefigured in Rudi's and his companions' patient wait for the train that will "scrupulously gather up the remainder" at the end of the novel (148)—is palpably absent. The phrases that call up this absence, this abyss, are not meant to bridge it (to connect the Shoah with the conversation between mother and son, the impending historical fact of the relocation of the Jews of Ruthenia and the Carpathian Alps with the pair of travellers eventually separated by chance) but to point to their own status as that which exceeds both event (Shoah) and event (the imagined conversation), and to act, themselves, as a remainder, a product of the clash of figure/commonplace and the event that defies it.

James Hatley writes that Appelfeld is attempting to represent the collapse of memory: the hermetic universe in which the characters exist, and in which the intimation of horror isn't understood because history remains unrevealed, isolates them from others who would know their fate and mourn their loss. "Their memory is impoverished, a merely literal memory, a memory of words written and read by we who know what happened to these others and who empathize with their plight but fail to have any access to that plight beyond poiesis" (Hatley 448). But Hatley goes on to argue that it is through the poetic, figural excess of the metonymic repetition of the everyday acts of life, that the dead and what they cannot foresee are remembered, though as an absence, by those on whom they leave a trace. It is a trace that functions like the beyond of representation: it is "an exteriority beyond what can be remembered palpably, . . . [what] Levinas speaks of [as] the 'alterity' of the other as transcending one's own being with a finality that resists all mediation" (Hatley 452).

As if to make a case for the language of excess as the by-product of trauma, Appelfeld's characters (in *Cattails* as well as in his other novels, most notably *The Immortal Bartfuss*) seem unable to speak at all, and yet speak they do in utterances that seem to make sense only to themselves. As with the case of a local police officer who tries to explain to Rudi that his mother may have been wrongfully placed on a transport to the east, characters seem to "pile up their words" (*Cattails* 118), to accumulate word after word with the effect of producing something that looks less like discourse and more like the incomprehensible terms on a list. After a first difficult winter travelling eastward, Rudi tries to convince his mother to make her way with the carriage toward an inn. As they do so, Appelfeld writes,

A kind of surprise was written on her face, as if some wonder had seized her and would not release her.

"Rudi, isn't it strange?" Toni said in a surprised tone.

"What?"

"To return home."

"Mother, forget your grandiose ideas for a moment. I see a grocery store."

. . . About an hour later, Toni had already spread a cloth on the ground, her looks had come back to her, and she said: "Nature is truly splendid here." That was one of her cliches, for she had no words of her own. (65)

There is no necessary connection between utterance and utterance, no context that draws the urgency of finding food to the wonder and the strangeness of the return. It is not so much that these are cliches, as Appelfeld's Rudi suggests, but "a language with no words, a language that was all eavesdropping, alert senses, and impressions" (*The Immortal Bartfuss* 21). Like the absurdities uttered at the novel's end—about the "superlative coffee" offered at the train depot as Rudi, his companion, and a passel of displaced Jews wait for transport; about the beauty of the surrounding countryside amid the squalor of the refugees; a quarrel between women whose conclusion is punctuated with a third woman striking her young son and growling "Now do you understand?"—these are words and phrases that are a residue of the impossible connection between moments of the imagined lives of individuals lost on their way between one place and another, and those historical moments we find impossible to render discursively and which nonetheless present themselves to us in flashes—in "eavesdropping," "senses," and "impressions." That they refer to no particular thing suggests not that they are the product of a writer trying to avoid the events or objects that impel them (or, on the other hand, trying to represent them directly). Rather, like the mute surprise Rudi registers when, in speaking of coffee, he is reminded of his mother, they are symbols that register the distance between what can be spoken and what can be known, between what may be thought and what can be imagined, of events that conclude with the most commonplace and yet most horrifying of endings: a journey by train.

Alan Mintz, in comparing Aharon Appelfeld's short fiction to the poetry of Uri Greenberg, says of Greenberg that "although [for him] the event may engulf the self and the self may incorporate the event or integrate aspects of it, the apartness remains as a distance to be crossed" (203).

But for Appelfeld, who did not escape to Palestine as Greenberg had but who survived the Holocaust in central Europe and only came to Palestine in 1946 from DP camps in Italy, the Shoah is inseparable from the self. The difficulty is not to connect the life prior to the Shoah to the *univers concentrationnaire*, or to sever a connection from it; the difficulty is to find language that will render that universe itself without destroying the writer. Appelfeld's strategy, then, is a strategy of repetition that avoids the metaphorical connection between the everyday world prior to the catastrophe and the catastrophe itself—Borowski's strategy, in which the horror he describes is all the more horrible because it is connected to commonplaces (mothers and children, trains, cordwood and corpses) with which we deal everyday. "Before, after, parallel to—yes; anything but the thing itself" (Mintz 206). Appelfeld "is so confident of [his] reader's familiarity with descriptions of Nazi bestialities that [he] never needs to mention them at all in order to have their specter loom in the interstices of every scene and dialogue." His strategy instead, suggests Michael Andre Bernstein, is to focus on the characters' "limited self-awareness" of the catastrophe going on around them, a catastrophe about which his readers are fully aware, and that myopic focus itself becomes an object of horror.[1] Appelfeld's strategy is to write in a language that discloses the burning light of the sun of the Shoah through what it refuses to disclose, what can be only glimpsed through the excessive repetition of the same.

Tadeusz Borowski's method is the direct opposite of Aharon Appelfeld's. Where the second intimates, the first lays out in stark detail; where the second presents the void of the events of the Shoah by rendering the mundane details and utterances of lives barely cognizant of it, the first unflinchingly presents details and utterances heavy with the connotations we have learned only too well since 1945. At first, in the title story of his collection, it appears as though with Borowski we are in the same place as we were with Appelfeld: "A cheerful little station, very much like any other provincial railway stop: a small square framed by tall chestnuts and paved with yellow gravel. Not far off, beside the road, squats a tiny wooden shed, uglier and more flimsy than the ugliest and flimsiest railway shack" ("This Way for the Gas" 33). This language doesn't describe the atrocity in ways we are used to seeing in print, the atrocities at Birkenau of the gas and the beatings and the suffering. But as the passage goes on, the ground becomes more familiar:

> farther along lie stacks of old rails, heaps of wooden beams, barracks parts, bricks, paving stones. This is where they load freight for Birke-

nau: supplies for the construction of the camp, and people for the gas chambers. Trucks drive around, load up lumber, cement, people—a regular daily routine. (33–4)

Presented here as equivalents are the railroad station, like any other railroad station, and the freight of lumber, bricks, and people for the gas chambers like any and all freight transported on railway lines. These are images of the Shoah to which we have become perversely accustomed: as Jay Cantor says, in another context, this is a language that destroys the commonplace—Aharon Appelfeld's small conversations about coffee, a mother's absentminded remarks about the beauty of a stream, a boy's memory of his family's housekeeper—by producing equivalences (freight=humans=death; railway station=unloading station for the gas chamber=death) that are as perverse as they are insistent. "This is like that: metaphor, the trope which gives value, that makes a world, here destroys it by yoking our present with the kingdom of death. Through metaphor our world is unmade; replaced by another" (Cantor 182). Lawrence Langer said years ago, in *The Holocaust and the Literary Imagination*, of Borowski's stories that their relentlessness lay in their ability to allow the reader to understand the minutiae and the detail of common life and the minutiae and detail of the uncommon and horrifying life of the camps as one and the same. For Langer, this was the presentation of the *univers concentrationnaire* par excellence, in which the reader is lulled into believing, if only for an instant, that there is in fact a ring of fire around the events being described but that in that instant it was possible for him to be transported into it in such a way that the description of it would make perfect sense in its own proper context (see 89–91).

Borowski's language is one that cannot escape comparing the world prior to the camps to the unspeakable illogic he finds in them. "The heavy condemnation of European civilization contained in his stories does not strike us as a detached theoretical statement. Apart from extreme bitterness, it also expresses the writer's longing for a different order of things" (Kihiwczak 402). It is the destruction of values, according to Andrej Wirth, characterized by the comparison of the atrocities of the camps to the commonplace, garden-variety world just outside the fence, the comparison of objects and events and turns of phrase so unlike one another that they create an impossible equation. He felt, as Wirth tells us, as though he had no other choice: "'[W]ho in the world will believe a writer using an unknown language? It's like trying to persuade trees or stones" (quoted in Wirth, 52). Borowski's strategy is to engage in comparisons so absurd, and yet also so familiar, that they at once fracture the context in which they could be understood, thereby also destroying reason's capacity to comfort itself in the acknowledgment that at least we have the capacity to do so.

Borowski breaks down the notion that behind the field of phenomena lies some inaccessible yet positive, substantial thing—an event, or a set of events, that may be made equivalent to the irrational and incomprehensible circumstances of the Shoah. By introducing the figure that points to a circumstance wholly outside either the one or the other, Borowski demonstrates that phenomena and what lies outside them are not to be conceived as two positive but separate domains. Instead of allowing the reader finally to agree to such a condition ("Yes, this perversity did indeed exist, but it's wholly separate from what I know"), the pattern of the *univers concentrationnaire* is broken by the word or figure that lets us know the pattern is just a ruse, that in creating a knowledge we have also to contend with the excessive word that indicates what lies beyond representation.

The breaks in the pattern of the *univers concentrationnaire* are as evident in "This Way for the Gas" and "A Day at Harmenz" as they are in Appelfeld's novels, but they are written differently. As we've tried to suggest, what makes Borowski's stories so tantalizing—so misleading, in that they tempt the reader into understanding the sublime object as somehow commonplace, as part of the scenery of atrocity—is their repetitiveness. "The morbid procession streams on and on—trucks growl like mad dogs. I shut my eyes tight," says Borowski's narrator Tadek, "but I can still see corpses dragged from the train, trampled infants, cripples piled on top of the dead, wave after wave . . . Freight cars roll in," and the horrible litany continues. Tadek as a character is often seen as despicable and pitiful in equal measures because he bears the task of the Kanada, the endless mopping up after the debarkation from the boxcars on the Auschwitz ramp, and bears it often with an air of impassivity. Borowski provides through the mouth of Tadek simple description. And yet the pattern is broken occasionally, and it is this break in the pattern that reestablishes the horrifying sense that what we're seeing is not something we should see, though see it we do.

One train has been unloaded, and another rolls in, preventing the Kanada squad from taking a rest. The description of this second train could easily be, word for word, the same as the description of the first. But we then have this:

Here is a woman—she walks quickly, but tries to appear calm. A small child with a pink cherub's face runs after her and, unable to keep up, stretches out his little arms and cries:

"Mama! Mama!"

"Pick up your child, woman!"

"It's not mine, sir, not mine!" she shouts hysterically and runs on, covering her face with her hands.(43)

A Russian prisoner, disgusted, hits her, knocking her down, picks her up with one hand, throws her on the truck taking the unloaded Jews to the gas, and throws the child onto the truck at her feet. The description ends this way:

> From under a pile of rags [Andrei, the Russian] pulls out a canteen, unscrews the cork, takes a few deep swallows, passes it to me. The strong vodka burns the throat. My head swims, my legs are shaky, again I feel like throwing up. (43)

There are no metaphors here, except for the one lonely description of the child's face, and Tadek's common turn of phrase to describe his dizziness, which could be caused as easily by vodka on an empty stomach as it could by the sight he has just witnessed.

But we have witnessed it too, and it looks—even to readers who may well be used to atrocities contextualized as "Holocaust literature," or "accounts of genocide"—both very much like what we have read in the endless descriptions of burning sun, lifeless corpses, and brutality, and very unalike. No one dies here—there is no violence in this passage except for the beating of the woman and the fate we well know is coming—but what we get instead is the direct opposite of what we find in Appelfeld's novels: a human action unrecognizable as human (a mother denying her child) told in a language so recognizable that we know precisely the shape of the action. This passage—and others like it in Borowski's stories—seems almost to remind us that the self-enclosed world of the concentration camp, with what passes for logic, cannot be circumscribed by logic at all, and that there is something outside of our capacity to describe that world, that universe, which also limits our ability to reason those things that we would otherwise believe or hope to be so.

II. The Ambivalent Language of Separation (Ozick)

If Borowski's language of fiction relies on the figural excess represented by presence, in which his readers are forced to look directly into the fire of the Shoah through the repetitive figures of metonymy, and if Aharon Appelfeld's language relies on the excess produced by absence, by the chasm between sign and sign found in metaphor, Cynthia Ozick's fiction of the Holocaust is highly ambivalent. Torn between her distaste for the idolatry of the image that stands in for the object itself, and her desire to understand the Holocaust as an event whose presence stands full force in the way of language or knowledge at all, she is at an impasse. Standing between the two dicta of Holocaust fiction, to present an image of the suffering and the horrors of the Final Solution as a memorial that guards against historical and cultural amnesia, and to respectfully remain silent in the face of the experiences that only survivors can speak of (and only then in a broken language that fails to bear the weight of the event), Ozick is faced with the impossible choice described by Michael Andre Bernstein: speak for the survivors, and risk substituting her voice for theirs, or allow the survivors to speak for themselves, risking the silence that comes with reticence, or trauma, or the death of the remainder (see *Foregone Conclusions* 42–52).

In her essays, Ozick has often spoken of sanctification, the separation that comes with holiness. Rather than redeem the six million, her response is that they, and the remainder, should be sanctified:

> When you approach Yad Vashem, the Holocaust memorial in Jerusalem, . . . you see, when you enter, a sign that gives a name to the murdered: *kidush hashem*, those who sanctified the Name [of God] in their martyrdom. The word *kidush* is related to *kadosh*, which means "holy"; but it also means "separate," because holiness is what separates itself from the things and places that are unclean. . . . (quoted in Lang, *Writing* 283)

Such a separation, or sanctification—such holiness, if you prefer—is not a positive but a negative separation. Like the injunction in the Second Commandment, it demands that a space be reserved for God: not to be filled by idols that would offer to depict God, but by those representations that voice the void, that manage to utter the "no" of the Commandment itself.[2] Such a space is the precinct beyond representation that presents to human understanding the traumatic underside of representation itself: the forgotten, immemorial event.

In her novella, *The Shawl*, the event is the murder of a child, witnessed by her mother. Like the traumatic occurrence seen but not recalled by the witness (see Caruth; Freud), the occurrence itself is separated from the witness's recollection, not because she can't remember, but because as an event it stands full force in the way of knowledge or the language through which it could be represented, either to herself or to others. As a witness, the character Rosa is left with the same choices Ozick herself is left with: the silence of witness, in which the one who got away, apparently unharmed, is left to re-see the event in memory without finding a way to bring it into language or knowledge; or the sound and language of repetition, in which the event, the murder of the child Magda, is constantly lost in the babel of testimony, a narrative that displaces the act, names it, and consigns it to the territory of history, history as written, not history as occurrence. Ozick's emphasis on sanctification, on the separation of event from experience, the event as it happened *to* the victims from the event as it occurred *in* them, leads her to focus on how language itself makes the event present, but as a dissonance, a disturbance, that forever separates us from the event and from those who were there. To do so, to make present the event that defies knowledge and language, she needs to find a way to show how language offers silence, how absence offers presence, and how "silence and darkness . . . offer a chance for survival" (Kauvar 182), redemption, and sanctification.

She does so by putting the two parts of her novella—"The Shawl," in which the act of murder is presented to the reader as if the author is forcing her to gaze directly into the light of the sun; and "Rosa," in which the absent act leaves an indelible mark on both the character, Rosa, and the reader whose memory also contains the imprint of the earlier story—into an impossible pairing. "The Shawl," like Borowski's stories, relies at least in part on the language of presence, a language that repeats, in image after image, the act of speech that leads to Magda's death and Rosa's narrative, whereas "Rosa" relies, like Aharon Appelfeld's, on a language of absence that refers constantly to acts and events that, no matter the language used to call them up, can only be understood as a trace or a void. The relationship between the two stories has been noted before. Hana Wirth-Neser, for example, notes that the passage from silence to speech that marks Magda for death in "The Shawl" is complicated and redeemed by the profusion of language that issues from Rosa (and Ozick) in the later story—Yiddish, English, Polish, and in the epigram from Celan, German—and by the distinctions Rosa is at pains to make between her unique experience as a human being and as a mother who has lost her child, and those who would categorize her as "survivor," or "emigre," or simply "Jew." Joseph Alkana goes further, suggesting that "Rosa" is a *midrash*, a commentary and complication of the original story, "The Shawl," one that, like all *midrashim*, refuses closure and proliferates meaning rather than provides "aesthetic gratification." We want to extend and complicate these points about the relation between the two stories that comprise *The Shawl*: the relation between the stories is a discursive one, a dialectical relation between the negative presentation of the event through the excess of meaning and figure—a repetition funded upon metonymy—and the effect of that presentation upon memory, history, and humans' capacities to provide a narrative representation of the event that escapes understanding. Ozick isn't exactly confounding Jewish-American attempts to accommodate the Holocaust into a theology of remembrance—in Alkana's words, to show that "the failure to assimilate Holocaust experiences into the everyday serves as a defense against Adorno's challenge to a post-Holocaust literary aesthetic" (980). Her project seems more positive: it is an attempt to show that the only possible response to the bludgeon of the Holocaust and its devastating effect upon both a culture and upon individual witnesses is through the repeated insistence upon negative presentation—"My Warsaw was not your Warsaw"—and the amalgam of languages and narratives it proliferates. Like Borowski, she stares directly into the sun of the event, but having had the negative image of it burned upon her eyes, she has no recourse but, like Appelfeld, to refer not to the sun, the event, but to the void it has left.

Ozick's story, "The Shawl," and the story that follows it ("Rosa," published together, after their separate appearance in *The New Yorker*, as *The Shawl*), work to suggest not only the presence of the unspeakable and our capacity to confront its presence in fiction but—more importantly—its presentation as negation. Presence and absence in the narratives are inextricably bound together, and the figures employed to describe the actions and the imaginings of the characters move back and forth between metonymy and metaphor, between pure description and what could only be called poetry, in the same sentence, in the same line. In "The Shawl," as with Appelfeld's novels, the immediate historical context of the narrative is not clear, though we could make—as we do with Appelfeld's novels— some intelligent guesses. Unlike the details in Appelfeld, however, which render significance only to themselves and occasionally outside of themselves to a sense deformed by the Shoah, and unlike those in Borowski, which are always heavy with the presence of the atrocity, Ozick's cut both ways—they provide a sense of the historical real while they simultaneously cut against them.

The first descriptive passage in Ozick's story is a depiction of the infant Magda nestled inside her mother's shawl as they and Rosa's niece march to an unnamed camp:

> a squirrel in a nest, safe, no one could reach her inside the little house of the shawl's windings. The face, very round, a pocket mirror of a

face: but it was not Rosa's bleak complexion, dark like cholera, it was another kind of face altogether, eyes blue as air, smooth feathers of hair nearly as yellow as the Star sewn into Rosa's coat. You could think she was one of *their* babies. (4)

The volume of figure in this passage is worth noting: the shawl is described not only for its ability to safeguard the child but also for its duty as a winding-cloth, a shroud. The child's face is itself both a mirror and not a mirror, for she stares back at the face of her mother—a look no parent can say that they do not recognize—but also a face wholly alien to her, alien because of her blond hair, her blue eyes, her Aryan features. But the child cannot be Aryan at all because she is marked by the stain of the star sewn onto her mother's coat in the ghetto (and we learn, in "Rosa," that it was in Warsaw) as non-Aryan, as Jewish, as other. What this description provides is a glimpse of the impossible contradictions that mark the identity of the characters involved in this story, and most notably the character whose presence figures most prominently (the child Magda) and whose absence is the abyss above which the following story, "Rosa," is suspended. And it makes the figure of Magda not a sign—she is more cipher than sign, a figure so laden with meaning as to be meaningless, at once the innocent child lost as well as the tiger of retribution that so vituperatively springs from the older Rosa's mouth in the later story, the Aryan/Jew, the everyone/nobody. She is a symbol. As symbol, Magda's multiple significance focuses attention upon the fact that Ozick is here writing, and that she is writing about an event that, even in the imaginings of a writer or a reader, can barely be glimpsed. As a symbol, the child Magda here and elsewhere in "The Shawl" becomes the visible space of the negative of language in the face of the event, the projection of what is beyond the limits of human understanding.

The pivot on which the story turns is a change from figures of sight—and the focus early on is Magda's eyes—to figures of sound: it is the point in the story when Magda, mute from the point at which her mother could produce no more milk, finds her voice.

[E]very day Magda was silent, and so she did not die. Rosa saw that today Magda was going to die, and at the same time a fearful joy ran in Rosa's two palms, her fingers were on fire, she was astonished, febrile: Magda, in the sunlight, swaying on her pencil legs, was howling. (7)

It is a pivot not only because of the conscious shift in the sensory detail but also because of the furiousness with which Rosa responds to her daughter's speech. It is another impossible contradiction—it is with not only fear but also joy that she reacts to her daughter's long howls. If silence is what provides individuals the opportunity for life, and it is sound that nonetheless brings a kind of dangerous joy to her mother, then the astonishment with which she hears her daughter's scream is also the pronouncement of the death sentence intimated earlier in the story. It is with this mixture of the possible and the impossible, the imagined and the apparently real, that the story moves to its conclusion. Realizing that it is because the child is missing her shawl that she has begun to scream, and that her niece has taken it for warmth, "Rosa tore the shawl free and flew—she could fly, she was only air—into the arena. The sunheat murmured another life, of butterflies in summer. The light was placid, mellow. On the other side of the steel fence, far away, there were green meadows speckled with dandelions . . ." (8). Rosa cannot fly—this is a conceit—and yet those suffering from severe malnutrition, as Ozick clearly imagines her character suffering, feel light as ghosts, and so perhaps she could truly imagine herself flying toward her daughter. The heat—as the electric fence further on—here murmurs. Of course the heat does not murmur, but clearly the electrified fence does, and yet it is not with the hum we have become accustomed to, but with "grainy, sad voices. The farther she was from the fence, the more clearly the voices crowded at her. The lamenting voices strummed so convincingly, so passionately, it was impossible to suspect them of being phantoms" (9). As the SS guard raises the child on his shoulder and runs toward the fence, "the electric voices began to chatter wildly. 'Maamaa, maaamaaa,' they all hummed together" (9).

Only after the commotion of figure—"the steel voices [going] mad in their growling," Magda "swimming through the air" in "loftiness," "like a butterfly touching a silver vine"—yields to the inevitable narrative end, does the language of poetry also yield to the language of description: "Magda had fallen from her flight against the electrified fence" (10). It is only here that Ozick reverts to Borowski's language—the stark language of memory, of history apparently unfettered by figure—and we are left with the fact of the narrative's conclusion: one of the six million, a blond blue-eyed Jewish child, has been murdered by a soldier who one can imagine "under the [sparkling] helmet [and] black body like a domino and a pair of black boots" looks much like her. This conclusion, which ends in forced silence, makes clear that the object of representation in "The Shawl" is not the Holocaust or the suffering of the three characters, but the relation between them, in thought, word, and deed. The relation between presence and absence—object and language—is complexly drawn: we are not seeing the

event of the Holocaust (or its absence, in the sense that the fiction illumi-
nates a relation rather than an event) but the intricacies—and the separate,
individual instance—of lives it affected. And it does so by weaving impossible contradictions and impossible figures together that confront the reader
with something in the narrative that he sees but cannot recognize as ordered by sense or mutability.

"Rosa" is set in Miami Beach nearly thirty-five years after the events
depicted in "The Shawl," but the cast of characters is the same. Rosa has
destroyed her secondhand store in New York and has moved to a one-
room apartment, while her niece, now a doctor living in the suburbs, takes
care to send her money and the occasional letter. Magda is Rosa's interlocutor in long, eloquently lucid letters in Polish, and it is to Magda whom
Rosa explains the fact of her life, a life she insists was stolen, as an urban
Jew raised in the progressive Haskalah tradition of much of urban Europe
before the war. After the war, her secondhand store provided the opportunity to explain to her customers, "to tell our story," of her life in Warsaw,
of her concentration in the ghetto. Rosa finds herself a refugee: she has
been given a story, that of a Holocaust survivor and an amorphous European Jew, one that works against the particularities of her life—a woman
trained in chemistry, whose life was filled with her father's books and her
mother's poetry in Polish, not Yiddish; a woman disdainful of the super-
stitions of the hasidim and rural Jewish culture more generally and proud
of her father's position in the financial world of a very modern Warsaw. In
effect, Rosa is cut off from everything that was her life in Poland before
the war, but more painfully she seems cut off from the language that
would allow her to create a narrative of her self that is understandable to
others. She is only able to begin to do so to Magda in her letters:

> What a curiosity it is to hold a pen—nothing but a small pointed
> stick, after all, oozing its hieroglyphic puddles: a pen that speaks,
> miraculously, Polish. A lock removed from the tongue. Otherwise the
> tongue is chained to the teeth and the palate. An immersion into the
> living language: all at once this cleanliness, this capacity, this power
> to make a history, to tell, to explain. To retrieve, to reprieve!
> To lie. ("Rosa" 44)

Even the language in which Rosa feels most familiar is essentially a lie: her
imprecations to shoppers in her New York store could not render her anything but an "immigrant," nondescript, anonymous, unmarked by her particular circumstances, and, like her daughter, mute. What Rosa has available

to her is only the mark of the Shoah itself. There is "the life before, the life during, and the life after. . . . The life after is now. The life before is our real life, at home where we was born." "And during?" asks her suitor Persky. Rosa replies "This was Hitler." She goes on: "Before is a dream. After is a joke. Only during stays. And to call it a life is a lie" (58).

In the language Ozick has used before, Rosa is separate, apart, and the descriptions she is able to provide for herself are nondescriptions: my Warsaw isn't your Warsaw. The only place she can reside—with her daughter—is not a location, either spatially or temporally, at all, and so she resides in a language that she suspects (or is it Ozick?) mangles the reality of even a written location. Of Persky, Rosa thinks, "The Americans couldn't tell her apart from this fellow with his false teeth and his dewlaps and his rakehell reddish toupee bought God knows when and where—Delancey Street, the Lower East Side. A dandy." Rosa is at pains to distinguish herself from this parody of the immigrant Jew, and says "Warsaw! What did he know? In school she had read Tuwim: such delicacy, such loftiness, such Polishness" (Ozick 20). But the irony in Rosa's attempt at distinction here is undercut by Tuwim's own acknowledgement that he identified himself as a Polish Jew, an amalgam, and that the Tuwim of her beautiful image of the Polish language himself became "the Manifesto of assimilated Jewry throughout Europe" (Kauvar 186). The image that haunts Rosa toward the end of the story is that of the bridge that separated two sections of the Warsaw ghetto, and the idea that Poles in the trolley underneath it could look up at her, a woman who was physically no different from them and certainly more highly educated, and see her as a composite, a Jew. The hint near the end of the narrative that she may finally return to New York to live with her niece Stella comes to nothing. Though the conclusion offers some hope that Rosa may in the end yield to the interests of others—may yield to the life "after," the joke—the story's final words are these: "Magda was not there. Shy, she ran from Persky. Magda was away" (70).

What is telling, suggests Hana Wirth-Neser, is that the distinctions Rosa makes are distinctions based upon a void, upon an absence, upon experiences that she has not had, and can only imagine, experiences that she desperately puts in the place of the one she cannot shake: the murder of her daughter. "Rosa seeks protection in languages that are never represented mimetically in the text . . . [that] represent oases of cultivation" (318). She writes her daughter, who has in her imagination survived and has become a professor of classical Greek and Latin at Columbia, letters "in the most excellent literary Polish" (Ozick 14): "A pleasure, the deepest pleasure, home bliss, to speak in our own language. Only to you" (Ozick 40). Those letters "are conveyed in apostrophe, which always 'calls up and animates the absent, the lost, and the dead' (Johnson 198)" (Wirth-Neser 318). The language in which she calls up the image of her daughter points to another absence, a moment in which the future that cannot possibly be called up is overlaid upon the horrifying moment of her death, a moment that Rosa is desperate to forget but cannot, imagining her as the butterfly, the image she calls up as the child flies, unstoppably, toward the electric fence: "Butterfly, I am not ashamed of your presence; only come to me, come to me again, if no longer now, then later, always come" (Ozick 69). Rosa is sanctified in that the language she has at her disposal, and the distinctions that she relies upon to keep from being assimilated into the woman the Americans see as crazy and self-destructive, is a language based upon an absence. Latin, Greek, literary Polish: they are all dead languages, and her differences from Persky are invisible to those around her. What keeps her separate, though, is not her life as an anachronism but the void of memory—the death of her daughter—that compels her to speech, that compels her to fill that void with language, but in this case it is language that is the negative image of the language of presence. It is a language of the impossible. But it is not the language of the Holocaust, Borowski's relentless metaphorical comparisons of object to object, corpse to cordwood. It is impossible because it can only indicate what for Rosa is so clear and yet so unnameable—that she is alone in her experience and bereft of a language with which to make her connection to others possible.

This is a sanctification based on suffering that simply cannot be written—in Polish, in descriptions of a stolen life or of the life of a refugee both from language and from location—and which is nonetheless written into the language of this pair of stories. Rosa is sanctified because she is forever divided from the event: though she lives it as it occurs, afterwards the event only survives as what disrupts language and knowledge. The event is absent, but it is evocable. It can't be represented—something that Ozick shows in the first story, in which the murder is told in terms of silence and noise, the break between them signalling the death of Magda—but only presented by means of the failure of the image, of the historical language that would try to make present the event itself (see Kauvar on sound and silence, esp. 181–4). Victor Strandberg suggests that Rosa brings the memory of Magda alive through a retreat into fantasy; we'd suggest that her memories of Magda are not memories so much as tapestries of language woven around an absent middle—the murder of the child—and that they are not retreats into fantasy so much as they are repeated attempts to invent a language that presents the horror of the absence, a kind of incantation. The object of representation here is not the Shoah. The language of this story, as it does to a different degree in those of Borowski and the novels of Appelfeld, presents a relation between the unspeakable and the voice, of what can be imagined and what can only be thought as a negative. Ozick's narrative forces the reader to recognize a location beyond the event of the Holocaust itself, a location that has as much to do with her own ability to understand the events as it does with the event's enormity.

III. Conclusion

It is the moments when the historical/commonplace is fixed in the same figure with the figural/unreal that the most direct representation is possible in Holocaust fiction. This isn't, however, the same thing as mimesis. The writers we've examined here move from that which is impossible to represent, the thing which they wish to draw upon, the Shoah, to a narrative location beyond representation by forcing the impossible image from language—in Ozick, the whiff of almond in the shawl, the crafty silence of Magda, the deathly yell of the child coupled with the roar of the electrified fence—that likewise forces the reader or viewer out of all connection with the logical and into contact with what surpasses it. The historical real is simply not a crucial issue.[3] Whether or not a writer was there, the writer's responsibility is to make use of images that have a place in poetry and place them into an historical situation—albeit not a narrative that is drawn directly from a situation that she herself witnessed—to dislodge from both of them the kernel of the irrational and horrifying irregularity of the event. It is through this—not the historical real, the incorrigible repetition of the language of the rational—that fiction could be said to be redemptive: it releases from the rational that which surpasses the rational and which contains both the positive, divine sense—there is in the capacity of the human mind the ability to come into contact with and make real this event in narrative—and the dangerous, disruptive sense of terror—in the uncanny idea that the irrational feeling potentially annihilates reason and that it did, historically, annihilate two-thirds of the Jews of Europe.

In an essay entitled "Metaphor and Memory" written in 1985 and published in *Harper's* a year later, Ozick argues that metaphor is the connection between the aesthetic and the historical, or maybe better, between "inspiration" and "obligation." We have traditionally understood art—inspiration—to have a moral dimension (or, for our purposes in the chapter, a redemptive one), and we go back to the Greeks for our warrant. We've always understood that the oracular visions of the priests and the cathartic nature of the dramas of Aeschylus and others were at least partly intended to bring about a stability to the state by providing a vent for the illogical and chaotic in human life. Ozick suggests that we have it wrong: the Greeks understood the *interpretive* act that followed the acts of the seers or the representations of the plays as having a political or moral function. But the works themselves—the auguries, the spectacles represented in the dramas—are effectively separate from the rational, logical sphere into which the Greeks were hard pressed to integrate them.

Ozick's point seems to be that the injunction that a poem must not mean but *be* is a tacit link to the Greek understanding of the irrational aspect of art, but that this irrational aspect always was and always will be unconnected to morality, the human predicament. "Inspiration," she says, "is spontaneity" (*Metaphor and Memory* 276); if there is a moral lesson to be learned from the examples of the oracles, "it is either that the bravery of the gods should be emulated; or else that it is hubris to suppose the bravery of the gods can be emulated" (275). Representation either forges the connection once and for all between the illogical and the logical, or it points to the painful fact that there is no possible connection whatsoever. This view of aesthetics is a view of art as idol, in Ozick's view, and this view of aesthetics may be connected to the logic of Holocaust representation that you see in the argument over whether the event can or should be represented. If the event is absolutely inimical to logic or to sensible precepts of human ethics or morality, then any representation of it must be one of two things. Either it is an idol (that is, it must have a presence all its own, unconnected to the event itself, and must serve as a symbolic entrance into the event but not a representation of the event itself; this is what critics have said of Appelfeld's work); or it must be a moral or cautionary tale whose lesson may be learned relatively easily through form or content or both by following the traditional recipes for their interpretation.

What Ozick calls metaphor, however, is the connection between the aesthetic—the illogical or chaotic moment in which one glimpses something one has never glimpsed before—and the historical; it is the connection between our experience and an experience wholly other. Ozick sees the inception of metaphor in the Jewish world, and sees its paradigm in the biblical injunction to treat the stranger as one would be treated himself. For the Greeks, that which was unspeakable—that which was unexplainable in terms of the logic of the priests or the law—was wholly other, and was represented as such. The Levitical line (19.34) reads:

> The stranger that sojourneth with you shall be unto you as the
> homeborn among you, and you shall love him as yourself; because
> you were strangers in the land of Egypt.

It is a line that connects figure with the moral precept. It joins figurally
(with the connector "as") the stranger and the homeborn, the stranger as
the self, with the moral in a single line. The impossible equation becomes
possible—the other is the same, that which had heretofore been unspeakable or wholly outside that which is familiar, must be forced together with
the imaginable—through the strength of history: "because you were
strangers in the land of Egypt." What Ozick is at pains to point out here—
and earlier in an essay entitled "Toward a New Yiddish"—is that metaphor
forces the unfamiliar to be spoken in terms of that which we know, and in
doing so provides the impossible with a moral force: we are forced to make
a connection that is nonetheless impossible to make, and we must do so
because this is the predicament of the human condition. Ozick puts it this
way in "Metaphor and Memory:"

> Inspiration calls for possession and increases strangeness. Metaphor
> uses what we already possess and reduces strangeness. . . . Inspiration
> attaches to the mysterious temples of anti-language. Metaphor over-
> whelmingly attaches to the house of language. (281)

The suggestion, then, is that in order for art to have a moral function, it must be understood metaphorically (or, as Ozick puts it in the earlier essay, liturgically) rather than as inspiration or aesthetically. That is, in
order for representation to have the means to present that which lies beyond representation—the narrative—itself (if not the object of representation), it needs to bind together the strange and the everyday and to
suggest not that the horrible or the beautiful cannot be put into narrative
form—that the poem or the narrative must stand in for the world since
neither can do justice to the other—but that the impossible glimpse into
the horrible or the beautiful can only be seen by means of the media to
which we are chained in this world.

The injunction against representation—of the things under the heavens or earth, of the events comprising the Shoah—is precisely an injunction
against *idols*, a kind of poetry or narrative that insinuates itself as either the
same as the moral lesson that the writer wishes to derive from it or as completely devoid of history or moral import at all. Idol is the assumption that

the repetition of image after image, event after event, releases the narrative or the representation from the connection with history, with the familiar, with things that we might recognize or events with which we have had contact. Idol assumes that the representation becomes an object unto itself separate from the event. In Ozick's words, however, "when man [or narrative] is turned into a piece of god he [and it] is freed from any covenant with God" ("Toward a New Yiddish" 163). When the event that evades logic or our ability to comprehend it is put into a category apart from logic or language or comprehension, it is elevated to the status of God, and this is the height of Second Commandment idolatry. "The German Final Solution was an aesthetic solution," says Ozick in an echo of Adorno's point from *Negative Dialectics*, "it was a job of editing, it was the artist's finger removing a smudge, it simply annihilated what was considered not harmonious" (165). Understanding sublimity as the limit or end of representation in this sense—there are those objects or events that simply defy representation, that simply cannot or should not be represented because any attempt to do so will inevitably fail—succumbs to the idolatry invoked in the Commandment. It ignores Leviticus—the need to understand the link between the other and the same as that which is historically our lot. To understand the sublime as the event or object whose effect we cannot have access to outside of the (failure of) representation—of narrative or of language—is to engage in the metaphorical act par excellence.

Ozick uses the image of shofar, the ram's horn blown on Rosh Hashanah and on Yom Kippur, the Jewish days of awe, to illustrate the liturgical (and we would suggest sublime and redemptive) aspect of narrative. "You give your strength to the inch-hole and the splendor spreads wide" (174–5). Anyone who has experienced blowing the shofar on the bimah understands this metaphor: the horn is notoriously difficult to blow, and the notes can sound sweetly or, when in unpracticed hands, shrill. She concludes by saying that to blow into the wider part of the shofar is to take the easy way out, to avoid the perils of representation altogether in exchange for not being heard at all. To blow into the narrow end is to be unable "to avoid the dark side of the earth, the knife of irony; [. . .] it will be Aggadic, utterly freed to invention, discourse, parable, experiment . . ." (175). To confront the Shoah in terms of figure, by acknowledging its sublime aspect not through whether it can or cannot be represented but by endeavoring to force together the possible with the impossible, is not to show us what it was like but to confront us with its effects as we are startled by recognizing what we have no business recognizing at all: that which is beyond representation.

Notes

  1. That myopia is what Bernstein finally criticizes Appelfeld for most bitterly. In their lack of awareness of the circumstances that surrounded them, Appelfeld's assimilated Jews are open to the charge, as is the author, that Jews were at least partly responsible for their own slaughter. See *Foregone Conclusions* 53–73.

  2. See Ozick's remarks on the terseness of the commandments in the Torah, in Lang 280: "The ornamental elegance of the King James Version gives us the Ten Commandments with rather a baroque thrill to them—all those thou Shalt Not's. But if you listen to the Commandments in Hebrew, you will hear a no-nonsense abruptness, a rapidity and a terseness. They begin with *Lo*, the Hebrew word for No. *Lo tignov*, Do not steal. *Punkt*. The Torah the Jews carry stands for No. . . ."

  3. This point is open to debate. See Norman Finkelstein's chapter on Ozick in *The Ritual of New Creation*, particularly 64–70.

5

Film and the Shoah:
The Limits of Seeing

We are made aware of our silent and detached glance as spectators, removed in time and place. Neither the creator of this film nor his viewers can assert, like the chorus in the Oresteia: "What happened next I saw not, neither speak it."

Hartman, "The Cinema Animal"

In the winter of 1993–4, on the release of *Schindler's List*, Steven Spielberg offered the film free to any school that wanted to use it for the purposes of Holocaust education. He did so in the midsts of a firestorm of controversy over the film. In its most simplified form, that controversy revolved round the film's use of realist techniques—black-and-white film, the painstaking accuracy of the sets, the desire to film on location in Poland—and the question that was usually asked was whether the film was finally able to offer a representation that once and for all could "stand in" for the Holocaust itself. In effect, the debate surrounding the release of *Schindler's List* was a debate over how well the film was able to produce a knowledge of the Holocaust that was adequate to the event. And for most critics, the answer was that no, the film was not adequate to the event, nor could it be, given its shameless use of voyeurism, gratuitous violence, and sex, not to mention Spielberg's encyclopedic use of Hollywood conventions—as if the Final Solution was not rife with voyeurism, violence, sex, and an obsessive use of convention. (For what we think of as the best response to these criticisms, see Hansen.) But most survivors (who needless to say did not speak with a single voice) suggested that they were pleased that Spielberg was able to represent on film the images that had haunted them since the events themselves. Though the film was not adequate to the event, they seemed to be saying, it was close enough.

103

Three of the four films under consideration here take the imperative of knowledge seriously: Alain Resnais, Claude Lanzmann, and Steven Spielberg see their role in whole or in part to lay the events of the Holocaust bare enough so that no one can say that they did not occur. In fact, Resnais and Lanzmann were explicit about that purpose well before their films were shown: Resnais in the 1950s was working against a tide of silence and the active reconstruction of a French past that had little to do with the extermination of Jewish Europe; Lanzmann was battling the rising tide of French anti-Semitism of the late 1970s. Though they were responding to local political situations, the French filmmakers could be seen as reacting to Wiesel's imperative of "never shall I forget," the imperative to bring every viewer to the conclusion that the events of the Shoah were so horrible that we should endeavor never to let them occur again. Spielberg, working during the peak of what Yosefa Lishitsky calls "the Holocaust boom," may have believed that if he could only show a fragment of what the Holocaust was like, then the threat of hatreds like those that supposedly gave rise to the Final Solution could be ameliorated, if not avoided. Certainly his offer of the film as a pedagogical tool suggests he is aware of its value in the production of knowledge of the events it depicts. It is unclear whether Roberto Benigni, whose *Life is Beautiful* has aroused far greater controversy than Spielberg's film, had Wiesel or the imperative to know in mind when making his movie in Italy. Certainly critics have taken him to task for not recognizing more clearly the stakes involved in producing a fantasy about the Shoah. But much of the discourse surrounding these films has missed the question of *how* these films obey the imperative of knowledge, and whether, in fact, any of them managed to do so. More to the point, very few writers and critics have asked whether, in the movies' failures to adequately represent the events of the Shoah, the films have presented something other than knowledge.

Part of the problem results from seeing these films as attempts to produce testimonial evidence of the Holocaust. Certainly Lanzmann's film is only the most obvious example of filmed testimony. But if we see testimony as an attempt to render in language that which we know—if we see testimony as a narrative account of the occurrence of events, events we have experienced by bringing them to knowledge ourselves—then Resnais', Spielberg's, and Benigni's films all function as testimony. They all function, at some level, as an attempt to testify to the events of the Shoah, to bring the events to knowledge for the viewers of the film. But as we've tried to suggest throughout this project, while you can arrive at knowledge —a universal position that can be understood by every speaking subject—

something is lost from it: the encounter with the object is itself not recognizable in knowledge. The trauma of the event is covered over by the language that endeavors to speak it. What we'll argue in this chapter is that all four of the films under discussion—though sometimes in apparently different ways—avoid this problem (either in whole or in part) because they haven't been seen as vehicles for this kind of universal position. Instead, they present a limit to universal constructions—to knowledge—pointing instead to the necessarily impossible nature of a universal language (one that communicates without misunderstanding, or loss of meaning). They do so by differentiating witness and testimony, the seen and the said. If witnessing involves the recognition of the event that occurs prior to knowledge and speech, then the problem of film involves placing the viewer in the position of witness: how does the film allow the viewer to see what precedes knowledge, and how do the juxtaposition of sound and visual image, of convention and its opposite, of the familiar and the shockingly alien, work to produce the effect of witnessing?

Alain Resnais' 1956 documentary *Night and Fog* offers one of the most celebrated depictions of the Shoah. In it, Resnais brings together black-and-white file footage documenting the evolution of the Final Solution with contemporary color film surveying the ruins of the death camps as they fell into decay at the time of his filming. The movement back and forth between the black-and-white and color film, between the past and the present, traces an imperative of memory between the events of the Final Solution and the vantage of just over a decade later. This movement between the violent black-and-white past and the more subdued, almost serene color of the present creates a narrative tension the film goes on to explore: how do the actions of the past, captured on grainy documentary footage, intrude into the ruins of the present? How do these decaying symbols of horror intrude backwards into a past that already seems distant, a black-and-white past that cannot be well integrated with the color of the present? Although Resnais and the writer of the narration, Jean Cayrol, never once mention the death camps as a tool for the annihilation of the Jews—referring instead to all victims of the death camps as "deportees"—the film's juxtaposition of past and present, present and past still makes an important statement about the Shoah. In a work made so close to the time of its object—just eleven years after the liberation of Auschwitz—Resnais' film already points to the chasm that irrevocably separates the present from the trauma of this past. In addition, the juxtaposition subjectifies our own looking backwards, implicating our vision by seeing the Shoah both as a looking backwards as well as a reading in the present.

Early in the film, the camera establishes the movement back in time by following the now overgrown rails toward a concentration camp. The camera moves slowly along the tracks while the narrator explicitly speaks of the presence of the Shoah as it intrudes on the present, as more than just a relation to the past.

> Today, along the same track, the sun shines. Go slowly along it, look-
> ing for . . . what? For a trace of the corpses that fell out of the cars
> when the doors were opened? Or the footprints of those first arrivals,
> driven toward camp at gunpoint while dogs barked, searchlights
> wheeled, and the incinerator flamed in the distance in one of those
> nocturnal settings so beloved by the Nazis?[1]

Night and Fog makes it clear that we look in the present towards the past and that what we construct of it, what we see, comes not only from the material remains but from the position of the viewer, from our wish to see and know to what these traces refer. Although the film does not return to emphasize the way our vision and our desire implicate the historical re-claiming of the trauma of the events themselves, it does consistently leave us with images that cannot bear witness to what happened there. In fact, one of the remarkable facets of the film is that it does not rely on the po-sition of the eyewitness at all. No one speaks either for the living or the dead. No one leads us back through memory to reconstruct the horrors of the past, evidence of which the film presents the viewer like hammer blows. Instead, as if through an archive, Resnais leads us among the evi-dence, reminding us that we are the ones who are burdened to construct what happened there, follow "the same track." In so doing he reminds us that in such an act of construction, from the color of the present, that past to which that evidence came becomes irretrievably lost, and the narrative we built to take its place becomes irrevocably, troublingly, our own.

Resnais' insistence is not just an effect of the stylistic system of the film. *Night and Fog* makes explicit and precise reference to its own inabil-ity to construct a knowledge of the events it circumscribes even while it presses the viewer to see. As it challenges its viewers to be vigilant lest the horrors of the Shoah be repeated, Resnais' film makes it clear that the hor-rors themselves are beyond our reckoning, outside knowledge; we may fol-low the same tracks, and we may wonder about others who made their way over the same terrain in the past, but we cannot see their step as it leaves "the footprint" or hear the dogs or feel the beatings. As the camera makes its way into what remains of a barracks, the narrator wonders what it is that we can actually know from these leavings of trauma:

> What remains of the reality of these camps—despised by those who made them, incomprehensible to those who suffered here? These wooden barracks, these beds where three people slept, these burrows where people hid, where they furtively ate, and where sleep itself was perilous. No description, no picture can restore their true dimension: endless, uninterrupted fear. We would need the very mattress where scraps of food were hidden, the blanket that was fought over, the shouts and curses, the orders repeated in every tongue, the sudden appearance of the S.S., seized with desire for a spot check or for a practical joke. Of these threatened sleepers, we can only show you the shell, the shadow.

At first it seems that Resnais calls for even more documentation, the "very mattress," the "blanket," objects that hold some familiarity. But as the list grows longer the film invokes objects that are not material, objects that cannot be recovered: the languages and words spoken and the menacing "appearance of the S.S.," "endless, uninterrupted fear." Like his earlier invocation of sights and sounds, these are things that the camera cannot capture as it draws the viewer's gaze to what survives of the camps. The material remains present us only with the "shell" in which some kernel of the event is no longer present.

Resnais' sense that even the material evidence of the camps could not give us a sense of the events themselves is consistent with something Jay Cantor pointed out a decade ago: that as a filmmaker Resnais is acutely aware of the "constructedness" of the camps ("Death and the Image" 176–80). There is something ominous in the Nazi attempt to pave over the atrocity of annihilation by means of art: as Cantor points out, the film's title is derived from the phrase *Nacht und Nebel*, "a piece of Hitler's poetry" designed to provide a name, a representation, a beautiful ruse, for the disappearance of the Jews into another kind of vapor. But this perverse artisanship points toward a space beyond representation, a space beyond which the knowledge we have created of the events behind history and narrative cannot be easily contained by recognizable words or everyday objects. At one point, in what could pass for one of the film's lighter moments, Resnais shows us photos of guard towers at several of the camps, still aiming to suggest the camps' art:

A concentration camp is built like a grand hotel—you need contrac
tors, estimates . . .

The camps come in many styles [at which point the photos appear with each word]: Swiss; garage; Japanese; no style.

The references to styles comprise the shell, Hitler's beautiful poetry, and
Resnais here tries to make us spectators in what amounts to a realty auc-
tion, effectively making us complicit in the poetical act: we have seen
neighborhoods like these, mismatched architectural styles thrown together
in a simulacrum of internationalism, and in making the connection between the art of the camps and the familiar fake styles of homes, we have
made—in Cantor's terms—an equation. Art equals death.

But the equation doesn't work as simply as this, because Resnais has
pointed to something that the litany of art cannot bear. Not only does a
chalet seem out of place in a series with a garage; it seems profoundly out
of place as a guard tower on a death camp. As if the still photos of the towers themselves were not enough to trouble us, the phrase "no style" snaps
us out of our spectatorial slumber and jars us back to what cannot be contained by the metaphors of contractors and grand hotels. For what we are
shown in this photo is a thrown-together monstrosity with a corroguated
tin roof posed on stilts that only barely contains its weight. And once the
narrator intones "the leisurely architects plan the gates no one will enter
more than once," the deal has been broken and we are on terrain no
longer familiar. No style. The shadow. It becomes clear here that our
memories—of neighborhoods, of hotels and contractors, of art and the
place of Hitler's beautiful poetry—could not possibly be adequate to what
lies beyond the images, and that while we might imagine the artifice of the
guard towers and the bustle of contruction, we could hardly make our way
from the representation to knowledge of the individual horrors that took
place inside the camps.

It is through the contemporary footage that *Night and Fog* shows us
most clearly that the Shoah cannot be fully present within the remnants, or
the artifice, of the past; that the file footage might capture a moment of
something we might call the Holocaust, but given what we know now, and
see now, it is not enough to give form to, or a knowledge of, what happened. Thus, for Resnais, evidence—the detritus of history—cannot really
account for those who suffered, cannot represent the trauma of the event
except as an absent center—a "shell" or "shadow"—that the surroundings
once circumscribed. The contemporary visions of the material remains of
the Final Solution mark a place of memory, but the contents of such a

memory can only be hinted at by their absence. And in fact, the contents of that memory may cut two ways. Inasmuch as the contemporary footage of the gas chambers may afford the viewer in the present a sense of ethical urgency, they may also present the opportunity for voyeurism. The narrator tells us, over contemporary glimpses of the remains of the gas chambers, that "nothing distinguished [them] from an ordinary block. . . . The only sign—but you have to know—is the ceiling scored by fingernails." But over contemporary glimpses of crematoria, he tells us "an incinerator can be made to look like a picture postcard. Later—today—tourists have themselves photographed in them." The present is built of such knowledges: of what we must know, and of what we refuse to know. The comfortable, colorful present is our own to do with what we will; what any spectator builds in that present is not history, not the event. The present use of the past, history, can only offer up a place marker for which an event cannot be signified or contained. In this sense, history cannot bear witness nor be redemptive since it can only point away from the particular kernel that intrudes in the present.

Night and Fog does, however, present us with something that we might call redemptive, that offers up a moment of seeing between fragments of knowledge of both past and present. The juxtaposition of the black-and-white footage of the deportations and the camps with the color, contemporary images suggests a distinction between the present and the past that is effected in a dialectic, a dialectic that offers a superimposition of the event and the now of the modern viewer. The film begins with statements documenting the sources for the black-and-white images, setting up a factuality on which the film's structure depends. The implication is that without the images of the atrocities that took place in the concentration camps—without the facts that speak for the event—how would we read what we find there now? How could we know anything about that to which the remains themselves bear witness? The images of the present work, conversely, to bring the footage from the past into some form of accessibility, both as a narrative device and as an object on which to hang the past events. For example, the film presents the contemporary image of the camera following along the rails leading into Auschwitz along with film footage of deportees in boxcars. Likewise, the camera's movement along the line of bunks in one barracks connects to footage of haunting faces peering out from the wooden racks, including the now famous picture of Elie Wiesel staring at the camera from among the other men there with him in Buchenwald. Although, as the film's narrator makes clear, this linking of the remainders of the past with the experiences of the camps does not offer a concrete or coherent account of the individual traumas that these pieces of footage point toward, the juxtapositions do enact a distancing between what constitutes history, the "shell," and the impossible kernel that history covers over. Put another way, this juxtaposition points towards a different space altogether, an atemporal space that allows past and present to become commingled, if only fleetingly and perhaps not happily. This traumatic space, a kernel of the real that intrudes into the temporal moments represented, is presented by the juxtaposition of past and present, between black-and-white and color footage, even as the very distinction between past and present is troubled and affected by this real, traumatic ordering. *Night and Fog* makes it difficult to grasp what gives rise to trauma and history (Is history an effect of trauma or is trauma an effect of history?), but it does show that the two are inseparable. Although *Night and Fog* tells us that all we have access to is the shell of the Holocaust, its physical and epistemological remains, its temporal dimensions, it does maintain a certain connection between the shell and its kernel. That connection indicates that there is something, the events comprising the Shoah, inside the shell, what we call the Holocaust; the event is at the center of, and troubles, history. At the same time, the film affirms that we cannot retrieve the kernel that the shell once contained, that was once present but whose now broken and dispersed shards cannot be adequately brought together again. We do not have access to it.

Night and Fog offers no witness testimony per se, no particular individual representing camp experience (even Wiesel is not named in the image from Buchenwald). In effect, Resnais' film acts as a witness, forcing upon the viewer an opposition between a knowledge of the Holocaust—one we assume (or hope) is available through footage, evidence, history—while pointing toward the event's resistance to knowledge, how we simultaneously know and do not know the experiences of those who suffered by means of the Nazi machinery created to destroy the Jews. The film carves out a relationship between testimony and witnessing that follows along the same lines we have developed in our discussion of history and fiction: by offering up the very real dimension of the Shoah outside of purely historical terms, Resnais shows that there is a moment of/in history that we see or feel only in terms of remainders of the event that we neither know from memory nor encounter within the context of representation, or narrative, or history. *Night and Fog* situates the Shoah within what on the surface looks to be a fabric supported by what we can still see today. On the other hand, Resnais' film makes it clear that the Shoah does not reside in its historical remainders, that the trauma of the event exceeds the material remains. Put another way, *Night and Fog* is very aware of itself as a testimony of the Holocaust, one based on the masses of experiences rather than on a particular confrontation, an individual's traumatic renderings of those experiences. In this sense, the film subjectifies its own limits: it shows us what remains, tells us what happened here, while insisting that the real trauma of the event and the witnesses to particular atrocities are radically absent, that there is no ground on which a knowledge of the event can be laid. Although these are two paradoxical positions, two contrary notions of history and knowledge, Resnais' film holds both to be true simultaneously, that we must remember and cannot remember at the same time. These two ways of knowing become the final demand of *Night and Fog*, which became a major influence on how the Holocaust was represented in later years.

Films that attempt to portray the Holocaust, to represent either individual experiences or the larger historical context, similarly deploy themselves along the range marked by the epistemological limits set by *Night and Fog*: they can emphasize the historical material as a way towards knowing the event and they can emphasize the impossibility of ever really knowing what happened. But these are not two mutually exclusive acts, though they are in dialectical tension with one another. More importantly, even in a film that attempts to align itself with only one of these acts, the other still intrudes. And the ways in which a given film works within these two acts or possibly even ignores or hides the ends of its representation, lead to the many controversies surrounding the visual representation of the Shoah. We see this in two important, but radically different, films: Claude Lanzmann's *Shoah* and Steven Spielberg's *Schindler's List*. We clearly see the difficulties of these competing notions of history and representation when we try to bring together these two very different films. The passionate debates surrounding *Schindler's List*, a hugely successful and popular film, has polarized much of the thinking on Holocaust representation, especially when considered in conjunction with Lanzmann's more "historically" driven, more "factual" *Shoah*. But as we have seen, whether it's historical fiction or fictional history, neither film escapes the very real difficulties of narrative emplotment, just as the USHMM and Yad Vashem are equally implicated by the need for establishing a coherent identity.

❦

Claude Lanzmann's *Shoah*, considered by many to be the best film made about the Holocaust, apparently offers a "third way" to subjectify the

Shoah. Lanzmann himself has said that he did not want to use documentary footage, footage upon which *Night and Fog* relies. Nor did he want to tell a fictive narrative, a coherent story that might be elevated to the place of a singular rendition of the Holocaust, following the American television series *Holocaust*. As a way of charting what he considered a new genre, *Shoah* was to construct all new material, new evidence relying on witness testimony as the basis for a knowledge of the event. Beginning with Simon Srebnik's revisiting Chelmno, where as a young boy he sang folk songs to the Nazis, running errands for them as well as burning the remains of those gassed in vans, Lanzmann shows us the faces of the witnesses as they speak about what they saw. Often the most revealing moments have no words at all, just images of a survivor staring (Srebnik standing in the field where he exhumed bodies for burning), or a Pole sorrowfully thinking about lost friends, or an historian contemplating the medieval roots of Hitler's Final Solution. Lanzmann's camera captures the fullness of the recollection that he in turn punctuates through editing, connecting survivor recollections to Nazi officials describing the way a camp functioned or with testimony of Polish farmers who watched the deportation trains go by their fields. In linking these varied pieces together—the words and faces of survivors, bystanders, perpetrators—Lanzmann carves out a space similar to Resnais' *Night and Fog*; much like Resnais' use of juxtaposing past and present to get at glimpses of the horror, Lanzmann's survey of different kinds of witnesses also constructs a space that we would call a traumatic kernel, a space that is an effect of the same tension between the horror's presence in the present and its emanation back to the origin of its memory.

Lanzmann's construction of testimony follows a consistent logic, whether he interviews survivors, bystanders, or perpetrators. A given scene usually begins in the midst of a testimony, after Lanzmann has already started his questioning. Sometimes the speaker of the testimony is all we hear and see, while at other times Lanzmann prods the witness for more information. We see this form in particular when Lanzmann interviews Mrs. Michelsohn, a German wife of a Nazi schoolteacher at Chelmno. Lanzmann weaves together Mrs. Michelsohn's testimony with that of the Polish witnesses, and the two survivors of Chelmno, Simon Srebnik and Mordechai Podchlebnik. In the midst of his shifting from witness to witness, Lanzmann presents a scene where Michelsohn examines not only what she saw but her knowledge in the present of what she saw, points of her memory in conjunction with present imperatives to distance herself from those memories. This scene begins with Michelsohn detailing the arrival of Jews at Chelmno:

Mrs. Michelson: The Jews came in trucks, and later there was a narrow-gauge railway that they arrived on. They were packed tightly in the trucks, or in the cars [. . .] Lots of women and children. Men too, but most of them were old. The strongest were put in work details. They walked with chains on their legs. [. . .] These weren't killed right away. That was done later. I don't know what became of them. They didn't survive, anyway.

Lanzmann: Two of them did.

Mich: Only two.

Lanz: They were in chains?

Mich: On the legs. . . .

Lanz: Could people speak to them?

Mich: No, that was impossible. No one dared.

Lanz: No one dared. Why? Was it dangerous?

Mich: Yes, there were guards. Anyway, people wanted nothing to do with all that. Do you see? Gets on your nerves, seeing that every day. You can't force a whole village to watch such distress! When the Jews arrived, when they were pushed into the church or castle . . . And all the screams! It was frightful! Depressing. Day after day, the same spectacle! It was terrible. A sad sight. They screamed. They knew what was happening. At first the Jews thought they were going to be deloused. But they soon understood. Their screams grew wilder and wilder. Horrifying screams. Screams of terror! Because they knew what was happening to them.

Lanz: Do you know how many Jews were exterminated there?

Mich: Four something. Four hundred thousand, forty thousand.

Lanz: Four hundred thousand.

Mich: Four hundred thousand, yes. I knew it had a four in it. Sad, sad, sad! (Lanzmann 92–4)

Lanzmann's intrusion into Michelsohn's narrative, "Two of them did," referring to Srebnik and Podchlebnik, who we have seen just prior to this clip, tears apart the seamless fabric that her testimony attempts to create: Lanzmann reveals to her that there are two survivors, implicitly placing her story into the context of a present in which what she says might be questioned. From this interruption, Lanzmann pushes her to speak about the public nature of the treatment of Jews in Chelmno, drawing her into places where her narrative can't cohere: "there were guards. Anyway, people wanted nothing to do with all that. Do you see? Gets on your nerves, seeing that every day." Michelsohn's disjunction between not being allowed to speak to the work details ("No one dared") and not wanting to ("Gets on your nerves") offers a switch in discursive position, what Lyotard would call a shift in phrase regimens, Michelsohn's inability to recapture the tangible moment of trauma. At the same time, the tension between being present and seeing Jews marching through town chained ("Gets on your nerves, seeing that every day") and a disavowal of seeing ("No one dared") presents Lanzmann with the impossibility of grounding history securely in the story of this one witness, bringing back the need for circumscribing the event through the juxtaposition of witnesses.

Perhaps the most telling example of the impasse between seeing and saying comes in Lanzmann's secretly taped interview with Franz Suchomel, an SS Unterscharführer who guarded prisoners at Treblinka.

Lanzmann: Can you please describe, very precisely, your first impression of Treblinka? Very precisely. It's very important.

Suchomel: My first impression of Treblinka, and that of some of the other men, was catastrophic. For we had not been told how and what . . . that people were being killed there. They hadn't told us.

Lanz: You didn't know?

Such: No!

Lanz: Incredible!

Such: But true. I didn't want to go. That was proved at my trial. I was told: "Mr. Suchomel, there are big workshops there for tailors and shoemakers, and you'll be guarding them."

Lanz: But you knew it was a camp?

Such: Yes. We were told: "The Führer ordered a resettlement program. It's an order from the Führer." Understand?

Lanz: Resettlement program.

Such: Resettlement program. No one ever spoke of killing.

Lanz: I understand. Mr. Suchomel, we're not discussing you, only Treblinka. You are a very important eyewitness, and you can explain what Treblinka was.

Such: But don't use my name.

Lanz: No, I promised. All right, you arrived at Treblinka. (53–4)

The implicit deception in Lanzmann's move towards the end of this passage, "we're not discussing you, only Treblinka," concludes with the explicit deception of promising not to use Suchomel's name. This whole scene is filmed with a hidden camera with frequent cuts to technicians in the van outside Suchomel's apartment trying to maintain a clear signal. Lanzmann includes not just Suchomel's testimony, but also the lengths he goes through to get it. Like his interview with Mrs. Michelsohn, Lanzmann keeps the present/presence of the memory in question both in his own interrogations, and by subjectifying the process of testifying.

Perhaps the most controversial segment of Lanzmann's film is his interview with a survivor living in Tel Aviv. Abraham Bomba was moved to a work detail by the Nazis because he said he could cut hair. He was immediately placed inside the anteroom of one of Treblinka's gas chambers and, along with other barbers, removed the hair of those about to be gassed. In what some have called an act of cruelty, Lanzmann conducts the interview with Bomba in a Tel Aviv storefront barber shop, and as we see customers and barbers move about in the background, Bomba is cutting the hair of a middle-aged man. As the interview goes on, Lanzmann's questions become more and more aggressive, and Bomba—perhaps fending off the images that dart by his eyes—tries to divert Lanzmann's attention by talking about other, more abstract issues.

Lanzmann: But I asked you and you didn't answer. What was your impression the first time you saw these naked women arriving [in the gas chamber to be shaved] with their children? What did you feel?

Bomba: I tell you something. To have a feeling about that . . . [Pauses]. It was very hard to feel anything . . . A friend of mine worked as a barber—he was a good barber in my hometown—when his wife and his sister came into the gas chamber. . . . I can't. It's too horrible. Please.

Lanz: We have to do it. You know it.

Bomba: I won't be able to do it.

Lanz: You have to do it. I know it's very hard. I know and apologize.

Bomba: Don't make me go on please.

Lanz: Please. We must go on.

> *Bomba:* I told you today it's going to be very hard. They were taking that in bags and transporting it to Germany.
>
> *Lanz:* Okay, go ahead. What was his answer when his wife and sister came?
>
> *Bomba:* They tried to talk to him and the husband of his sister. They could not tell them this was the last time they stay alive, because behind them was the German Nazis, SS men, and they knew that if they said a word, not only the wife and the woman, who were dead already, but also they would share the same thing with them. In a way, they tried to do the best for them, with a second longer, a minute longer, just to hug them and kiss them, because they knew they would never see them again. (117)

This scene is punctuated by silences, as Bomba tries to collect himself in the face of what could only seem like torture. As customers come and go in the background, Lanzmann's persistence is matched only by Bomba's fortitude. In his construction of new acts of testimony, although not structurally different from his predecessors, Lanzmann gets at the traumatic space created by *Night and Fog*. But more important than this, Lanzmann does more than reconstruct the past through the words of its witnesses. He also shows how the event of the Shoah remains active in the lives of victim, bystander, and perpetrator alike. What you see in the ferocious battle over Bomba's memories in this section of the film is not the disintegration of the present in the face of the past, for it is only partly the horrifying memory of his friend's encounter with his sister and wife that brings the barber to fall apart. What is all the more horrifying here is the memory's disruption of the present: Bomba's present, and Lanzmann's, but perhaps more importantly, the viewer's. Like the impossible juxtaposition of past and present in *Night and Fog*, in which a space of trauma is opened neither on the ground of the past of the filmmaker's present but in the viewer's moment of seeing, here the disruption of Bomba's present through Lanzmann's ruthless interjection of the past is effected through the eye of the camera. It is the viewer who is horrified here. But what does the viewer see? Not the terrible scene that passed before the barber's eyes, or the eyes of his friend, but the persistence of the traumatic kernel whose object is lost: Bomba's insistence, "Don't make me go on. Please." Lanzmann shows how the events comprising the Shoah persist, how the feelings of the wife of a Nazi schoolteacher at Chelmno still reflect Nazi racial attitudes or how some Poles think their lives are better without Jews or the anxiety and fear a survivor feels upon coming back to Berlin. And they persist in the viewer's unease, at the end of the film's first part, when she realizes that the truck the camera has been following bears the insignia of the company whose vans were used to destroy the Jews of Chelmno. Though Lanzmann makes use of live eyewitness testimonies where Resnais did not, the result is chillingly similar: we do not glimpse history. Instead the language of the witnesses re-invokes the trauma into the now. Each of these individuals experiences—and sees—something in Lanzmann's interview, something that exceeds mere recollection; and as Lanzmann pursues his testimony, the viewer herself sees what lies beyond it.

There are times in *Shoah* when Lanzmann does violate his stated commitment to using only new testimony. When introducing the deportation of the Jews in Grabow to the camp at Chelmno, Lanzmann reads a letter written by the rabbi of the Grabow synagogue to friends in Lodz. Lanzmann stands in front of what remains of the synagogue at Grabow and reads the letter from Rabbi Jacob Schulmann explaining that he has just heard of the gassing and shooting of Jews being brought to Chelmno. Lanzmann concludes by telling us that three weeks after sending this letter Rabbi Schulmann and all the other Jews in Grabow were sent to Chelmno and immediately gassed. On the surface, the use of Schulmann's letter seems no different from the testimony of those who Lanzmann interviews. It is not file footage nor is it a third- or fourth-hand account. In addition, it is delivered by Lanzmann in the real time of the film, not as a document reproduced by the camera that we in turn read. It also exists in between Lanzmann's own interrogations: as in other interviews, the scene begins and ends with Lanzmann's presence. However, none of these points can dismiss the fact that these are words of a dead man, one, more importantly, who very shortly after was killed in the death camp about which he is warning his friends. As a way of constituting evidence, this is no different from Resnais' inclusion of the picture of Wiesel at Buchenwald. More precisely, Lanzmann's use of the words of witnesses does not offer more authenticity than the form that Resnais chose. Very soon, all of the interviewees will themselves be dead, and their recorded words and experience will have the same limits, the same distance from the event, that Schulmann's letter has. Put another way, at this moment in *Shoah* Lanzmann places himself in the position to offer testimony, where his own position as speaker enunciates the words of Rabbi Schulmann. We are not witnesses to Schulmann's testimony; what we see is Lanzmann's represention of Schulmann. This is not a criticism of Lanzmann's use of the letter; rather, we want to suggest that it shows the limits of offering up the position of the witness from which others might see. In fact, it shows how Lanzmann may have different priorities in what he includes in his film, but the same structure is at work as in *Night and Fog*: he works to produce a space that localizes the traumatic kernel of the event as an effect of the narrative and images.

It might seem odd to say that *Shoah* is not a film about testimony, but that's precisely what we're arguing here. What makes *Shoah* work as a film has nothing to do with questions of history, if we think of history as providing knowledge of events. *Shoah* opens a space beyond history, providing images and voices of people whose stories we hear and whose experiences we see in the hearing rather than in the image called up by their language. If *Shoah* is about anything, it is about "space," what Michel de Certeau distinguishes from place or location: while Lanzmann provides images and situations that are palpably present—the fields into which Simon Srebnik walks, or the pathways on which the gas vans travelled fifty years ago; the gas vans whose similarity to cigarette trucks in Israel gives Michael Podchlebnik barely a pause—they indicate a location that is impossible to find on any map of the camps. If space is "produced by the operations that orient it, situate it, . . . and make it function in polyvalent ways" by "actions of historical subjects" (de Certeau 117–8), then *Shoah* is saturated not so much by place (the fields, the forests, the interiors of buildings and the architecture of the camps and ghettos, and the constant, noisy presence of the trains) as it is by a no-place, a terrain of horrifying experience that even Lanzmann's most persistent questioning of witnesses—and even Lanzmann's testimonial position itself—can only indicate. Simon Srebnik's words punctuate the very beginning and end of the film's first half: he says, walking through the fields outside Chelmno where bodies were burned by the thousands,

> No one can recreate what happened here. Impossible. And no one can understand it. Even I, here, now. I can't believe I'm here. Always. When they burned two thousand people—Jews—every day, it was just as peaceful. No one shouted. Everyone went about his work. It was silent. Peaceful. Just as it is now. (6)

He concludes this way: "I dreamed that if I survive, I'll be the only one left in the world, not another soul. Just me. One. Only me left in the world if I get out of here" (103). This is a space traversed by a thousand locations, a thousand possible feelings. But what is represented to the viewer is merely testimony. What the viewer *sees* is a space of trauma. "Impossible. . . . Just me. One." Lanzmann's film is, finally, fictive. He has produced a film that implicates the viewer, that makes us a part of his own story to find out what happened, to see a survivor's return to Poland, to watch his face as he points to where the bodies were buried at Chelmno only to be later dug up and burned. To say that Lanzmann's film doesn't have the structure of fiction would be to say that it is extra-discursive, that, like the hair on display at Auschwitz, it is a physical remainder unmediated by its constructedness.

Even a film as generically different from *Shoah* and *Night and Fog* as Steven Spielberg's *Schindler's List* localizes a space for the trauma of the Shoah, the possibilities of witnessing, in the same way. Spielberg's film emphasizes a fictive rendering of that space while the others emphasize an historical, but equally fictive, representation. For both, it is the linking of an image in a sequence that cannot itself present the image as anything *but* image (as representation) that prioritizes witnessing over testimony. The viewer, as witness, is left unable to place the fictive image into the historical series—her memory (itself a narrative representation) of events that bear some resemblance to what she tries desperately to recognize—and is left instead with what resides inside (or beyond) the kernel.

Critics have attacked *Schindler's List* for the way it manipulates testimony to "please" its audience. Sara Horowitz argues that people's positive reaction to *Schindler's List* is tantamount to a disregard for the truth, that acclaim for *Schindler's List* is "an acceptance of the film's truth claims, indeed an acceptance of the film as a discourse of the real" (119). By linking historical fact with truth or with a "discourse of the real," Horowitz forces us out of the realm of representation permanently: film and literature—any rendering whatsoever of trauma—must be read and readable only at the level of a knowledge or testimony. Such a precise rendering of the Holocaust would in fact prevent even Lanzmann from constructing his film. The real of discourse is not simply a content of history or a series of reportings. The real of discourse situates the trauma that the historical fabric covers over. In this regard, what connects Lanzmann to Spielberg is their admitted attempt to situate the viewer in the place of seeing something beyond just documentation. Lanzmann edits his film for precisely this effect. He does not simply give the product of unedited filming. In fact, he refilms some sections years after he shot the original footage in order to give a coherence to his film, to give us something of the discourse of the real that an unedited recording could not do. So Horowitz's attack on *Schindler's List* for what it represents beyond the historical record must equally fall on *Shoah* as well as *Night and Fog*. Lanzmann's comments about *Schindler's List* ignore this fictive component to his own *Shoah* (see Hartman 130).

This is not to suggest that historical veracity is not important. But veracity is itself an historical privileging: to be history, any historical accounting of events (and the order it supposes) must place factuality in the position of truth, must elide the witness and what she sees but cannot account for with the testimony. Film, most especially, is about the problems of eliding these two poles. Witnessing and testifying can both be represented in film. And the pedagogical implications of the Holocaust as that which must be taught so it will not happen again, requires both poles to be present and effectively placed in relation with one another. History as history does not itself produce witnessing. But the aesthetic representation does, and it effectively gives witnessing priority of place over the testimony. *Maus* is an example of a text that has been attacked as testimony. But as we tried to suggest, *Maus* foregrounds witnessing—it subjectifies the witness— to examine the underside of history, the no-place of memory that resides at the heart of the shell of history and of testimony.

A moment in *Schindler's List* when this fictive rendering of witness (and the radical particularity of the act of witnessing) occurs is that at which Itzhak Stern recognizes that Schindler is buying each prisoner on the list from Amon Goeth. When Stern recognizes that Schindler is paying for each name, he pauses and says: "The list is an absolute good. The list is life. All around its margins lies the gulf." At this moment, Stern posits the problematic concern of the film as a whole: we are hearing the story of those who are named—those whose names have known referents—as distinguished from the structurally infinite list that surrounds the fixed one at the center. Put another way, the list compiled by Schindler and Stern identifies those for whom there is a narrative, those who will survive to testify to the gulf on the outer edges of the list, where the trauma of identification resides, where those who are not named reside. This moment in the film (one that figurally reverses the metaphor of kernel and husk, inside and outside) shows an awareness of the relation between the gulf and the list, a relation that defines the movement from witnessing to testimony, from being unnamed to being named. In such a reading, it is a mistake to consider the film solely in terms of the names on the list, as a group with definition in the face of the rest that lack definition. For *Schindler's List* is just as much, perhaps even more, about those who do not make the list, those who are not recorded or defined or known. And it is this making of the list that suggests a distinction between testimony and witnessing: whereas the list itself functions as testimony, as narratives that can be told, the gulf that surrounds it presents a locus of the witness, where there is no adequate narrative or knowledge.

Adorno's now overquoted and later revised comment that there can be no poetry after Auschwitz provokes a similar question to such moments in *Schindler's List*, a question about the nature of representation: Not just what should and should not be represented but rather what is represented within any representation, what is the "barbarity" that is included in any attempt at holding onto, defining, or even speaking about something that is beyond the possibility of language, that occupies the place of Lyotard's differend. It is in this context that Adorno defines the nature of what he terms negative dialectics:

> If negative dialectics calls for the self-reflection of thinking, the tangible implication is that if thinking is to be true—if it is to be true today, in any case—it must also be a thinking against itself. If thought is not measured by the extremity that eludes the concept, it is from the outset in the nature of the musical accompaniment with which the SS liked to drown out the screams of its victims. (Adorno, *Negative Dialectic* 365)

Adorno's negative dialectics show us something significant about what we might call an ethics of representation. To prioritize the "extremity that eludes the concept" offers more than simply a recognition of that which is outside knowledge, or that which lacks an idiom within discourse; Adorno ask us to consider a beyond knowledge that knowledge covers over or tries to drown out, a beyond that is the underside of representation. It is this beyond to epistemology—a beyond to consistency—that offers a way into representations of the Holocaust as more than narrative, as more than any given testimony can elicit.

One way of localizing this beyond to knowledge is, as we've suggested, in the relation between witnessing and testimony. By considering the position of witnessing over the position of testifying, we understand testimony as a means towards witnessing rather than as a means towards knowledge. This distinction between witnessing and testimony also offers a way into the debate on Spielberg's *Schindler's List*. The responses in the *Village Voice* a few years ago illustrate the difficulty that many have with the narrative of *Schindler's List*, its story that speaks from the position of an ambiguous Christian savior and a Nazi perpetrator as a way of constituting a notion of survivors. But what struck us most about this discussion was the insistence by some—Art Spiegelman and Ken Jacobs particularly—of considering the film solely in terms of testimony, as representing a knowledge of the Holocaust, and thus, more dangerously, as potentially *the* knowledge of the Holocaust. Now we agree that the knowledge that *Schindler's List* constructs about the events it depicts is ultimately limited, in the way that Saul Freidlander and others use this term, as a limit to the possibility of representing trauma. The narrative of the film marks a limit to what we can and can't know about the Holocaust, what we can and can't question. But *Schindler's List* is more than a film that only constructs a narrative that follows Schindler and Goeth, Stern and the 1100 Schindler Jews. While narrating this one story, the film is marked by moments that exceed the narrative, moments of the gulf that go beyond the limit of representation, moments where other stories—other endings—are evoked. To take the narrative as the primary vehicle of the film—something that Spielberg himself often does—is to miss the beyond of epistemology that the film more importantly invokes, is to focus on the music of the SS over the screams of their victims. In this sense, it is to miss the act of witnessing around which the very testimony of the film circles.

Perhaps the most obvious example of a moment of witnessing within the act of narration occurs when Schindler observes the purging of the Krakow ghetto. In this scene, Spielberg's camera focuses on a little girl as she makes her way through the rounding up and killing of Jewish families. The girl's coat is colorized a reddish pink until she hides under a bed and the color is gone and the camera shifts to a wider view of the destruction. This mark of color, a staining of the black-and-white diegesis, marks a cut in the narrative of the film, a moment of enunciation that in turn demands punctuation. Such a cinematic insertion places us square in the middle of the gaze by positioning the audience between Schindler's seeing and the coat while suspending understanding: at this moment neither Schindler nor the audience has a knowledge of the coat or the girl. The color itself marks an excess to what the narrative holds, marks a point outside of the diegesis and thus outside discourse. But this position of seeing—of being caught by the gaze while gazing, of being seen by the film itself—is invoked again when the film repeats the colorization of the girl's coat as her body is exhumed for burning as the Nazis attempt to erase the evidence of the ghetto's extermination. It is in the repetition of the colorization that the anamorphic image is completed, that we recognize what we see, what we saw as we recognize Schindler's recognition. But what precisely have we recognized? What story has the film told us? The film itself doesn't say at this point. It demands a testimony rather than offers one.

It is retroactive moments like the colorized coat that the narrative ruptures—a moment of the real—and that situates knowledge differently in *Schindler's List*. Even as the film tells its story, there are repeated in-

stances of that which is beyond the narrative. Another such moment occurs as the women are being reloaded onto the train in Auschwitz. In the
midst of their salvation, one woman looks back to see families being led
down into another shower facility. Her gaze moves to the smokestack at
the top of the building and the smoke billowing out. At this moment the
film posits those outside of the we of the "Schindler Jews," those who are
in the gulf outside of the list. In addition, the relation between those walking down into the gas chamber and the ashes moving out of the crematoria is punctuated by the earlier moment of the ash falling onto Krakow as
Goeth burns the victims of the ghetto's extermination. In such repetitions
there is a movement that exceeds the particular narrative substantiations,
where there can be no "we" or "I" to construct knowledge.

The film's conclusion—the much reviled sequence that begins with
Schindler's departure from the camp (filmed in black and white) and ends
with the placing of stones on Schindler's tombstone in a cemetery in
Jerusalem (filmed in color)—provides another instance of this problem.
Many critics take Spielberg to task for this scene because of its overindul-
gence (though there are exceptions; see Ken Jacobs in Hoberman) and because it brings narrative closure to a series of events that defy it (see Bartov).
Those who react positively to this scene suggest, among other things, that
seeing the surviving *Schindlerjuden* paired with the actors who portrayed
them gives viewers a way to identify historical events with their representation, effectively closing the gap of verisimilitude and linking forever what
they saw on the screen with historical truth. But this is just our point: the
film works against this impulse at closure, in part because it puts the viewer
in the position of seeing the remnant—what occupies the gulf and remains
unnamed—when what the viewer may want is a representation of the name
(be it Schindler, or Eretz Israel, or the descendants of *Schindlerjuden* living
in diaspora who outnumber the Jews who remain in Poland). The final
scene of the film, in fact, is not the laying of the rose upon Schindler's tomb
at all; it is a silent panning shot in black and white of fragments of tombstones laid as paving stones on the road leading from the Plaszow camp.
Though the film seems to end with testimony—the memory-making of the
survivors, and the seamless transition from Czechoslovakia in 1945 to independent Israel in the 1990s (with "Jerusalem the Golden" sung in Hebrew in the American cut of the film)—and the names that can be
connected to individual lives in a series, it in fact concludes with what cannot be named: the metonymic marker of those who did not survive, the
devastated trace of a European Jewish civilization that has literally been trod
underfoot. This is what the viewer sees to close the film, the sign of the remainder, and it has the effect of voiding the names we might provide for

the film in the name of memory by drawing our attention to that which exceeds the name: those whose names have been lost. Like the sigh of relief we feel as the women from Schindlers' factory have been snatched from the maw of Auschwitz at the last minute, it catches in our throats as the camera pulls away and briefly shows us the stream of those who have been unloaded from trains (probably from Hungary) and moved directly down into the gas chambers never to be seen again.

Returning to Adorno's comment about the music of the SS over the screams of their victims, we see the problems of defining a narrative—of making sense—of the impossibility of trauma, of screams. By reading the film solely in terms of its testimony, we miss the moments of seeing, the moments of witnessing. Such a perverse vision of the Holocaust—as a knowledge that we can see and know and speak and understand—rejects the real epistemological significance of a representation like *Schindler's List*, a representation that consistently points toward the inconsistency of knowledge itself. In this way, *Schindler's List* is founded on an epistemology of the impasse, on that which cannot be expressed by the historical or the factual since it is the impasse that must be narrated over as cause of knowledge, as cuts into the symbolic or historical, as responses to an irresolvable question of identity. *Schindler's List* places the viewer in the position of having to recognize the ends of knowledge itself, of seeing the misperception necessary for understanding and thus questions the very foundations from which testimony is spoken, not in terms of historical fact, but in terms of the inability to represent trauma as trauma.

Roberto Benigni's *Life is Beautiful*, even more than Speilberg's *Schindler's List*, calls into question the accepted relationship between witness and testimony. Like Spielberg's film, *Life is Beautiful*'s commercial success is only outdistanced by the varied and vehement critical responses to its "use" of the Holocaust, its testimony that Benigni himself has termed a fable. The most extreme responses consider the end to testimony to be a knowledge of the event, the "what" of Benigni's testimony. Where they disagree, however, is on what this "what" should be: those that consider the film uplifting and passionate, responses that appear in the majority of the popular press who see the film as triumphant; and those that find it an abominable misuse of history, best represented by David Denby, who in his two-installment review in *The New Yorker* labels the film a form of Holocaust denial. But *Life is Beautiful* presents us with a test case: here we have a film whose status as a representation of the Holocaust is under serious scrutiny, and whose narrative—the story of a father trying desperately to keep his child from seeing the horror of the camp by enacting a "game," the object of which is to survive—is so prominent as to divert viewers' and critics' attention from the ways in which the narrative's failure is due to the structure of the film's status as testimony. What we would argue is that the film does indeed fail. But it fails in the same way that Spielberg's (and Lanzmann's and Resnais') did: in creating a narrative space with which to contain the testimonies that build the historical matter of the film, Benigni has also (and in his case perhaps inadvertently) opened up a space through which the viewer herself witnesses the underside—in de Certeau's terms, the no-place—of history and of representation. Nearly all the critical readings of Benigni's film focus on the story it tells, and nearly all say something similar about the relation between witness and testimony and the pedagogical ends through which we connect them. In each case there's an insistence that witnessing and testimony are the same, that what we see is the trauma of the event: that to speak about trauma, to testify, is not an act of translation or representation but rather a tightly wound knot that makes the two points indistinguishable. The end of testimony becomes to witness, the end of witness is to testify. These readings of the film judge it based on how the critic feels about the kind of testimony it represents as an adequate or inadequate representation of the trauma.

This elision of witness and testimony is not surprising, since *Life is Beautiful* makes just such a claim in its framing of the movie's central story, a claim also embedded in survivor narratives like those of Primo Levi. But unlike Levi's testimony, it is unclear whose story we are hearing, whose witnessing we are being drawn into. At the very beginning of the American release, a narrator introduces what is to follow: "This is a simple story . . ./but not an easy one to tell./Like a fable, there is sorrow . . ./and, like a fable, it is full of wonder and happiness." The narrator's simile, that his story is "like a fable," a phrase he repeats in separating sorrow from happiness, gets at the difficulty of telling this "simple" story. However, the narrator returns one more time, at the very end of the film, where we find out that he is Giosué, and that what we have seen is his own story: "This is my story./This is the sacrifice my father made./This was his gift to me." In this final contextualization, the film solves the initial problem of telling the story: once we know the name of the speaker, the difficulty of the story disappears, witness and testimony are seemingly bound together by the narrative position of the child survivor. Benigni's addition of the final voice-over allows the film to rest upon what Giosué saw, in a similar way to Levi's own narrative representation. And it is this final position—that what we have seen is this boy's story and that it is a story of Holocaust survival—that irks Denby and that other critics find redemptive.

Life is Beautiful's final contextualization through the voice-over only suggests one end of reading witness and testimony, the end that Levi de-emphasizes in his own testimony. Ignoring for now the politics of Benigni's reediting of the film to include this voice-over, the film casts what resides in between the two voice-overs contradictorily: initially, in terms it acknowledges are inadequate, "This is a simple story . . ./but not an easy one to tell"; and finally as an equation between testimony and witness, "This is my story." In its own insistence on a particular rendering of trauma, Benigni's text tells us something about both pedagogical ends of traumatic representation by offering a confluence of seeing and knowing that the form of his text resists. It is, in effect, an insisted elision of witness and testimony that continually breaks down as his opening remarks prefigure: this is indeed "not an easy one to tell."

The initial voice-over's insistence that this is a difficult story to tell comes out in the comparison to a fable: "Like a fable, there is sorrow . . ./ and, like a fable, it is full of wonder and happiness." This "like" quality to the film—that there are some actions or some elements that take it out of the realm of the fabular, elements that have nothing to do with its happiness or its sorrow—suggests that what follows is inadequate to the experience, that the fabular form itself won't get at its story.

The film's statement of formal inadequacy stems from the kernel within the narrative itself. We catch a glimpse of it when Guido, carrying his sleeping son, is walking in the mist, having "taken a wrong turn" in the concentration camp trying to find his barracks. In the fog, he comes across a distorted pile of corpses. He stops in the fog before the bodies can become distinct and then slowly backs away, deliberately keeping Giosué's back to the scene. This moment of Guido seeing has no witness. The sleeping child's back is to the bodies and there is no evidence that the game fiction is broken for him the next day. Interestingly, this scene punctuates the film retroactively. As the film begins and the first voice-over is heard ("This is a difficult story to tell . . ."), we see a man holding a child walking through fog, the same scene leading up to the corpses. Now we have no context for this at the outset, just the initial voice-over. But to bring forward this scene above all others, the only scene where we see Guido bear witness to what happens to those selected, is significant. This is the only moment of seeing in the entire film, but it is embedded in a narrative that otherwise refuses to show such acts of seeing. In this sense, the opening voice-over and its respective images subjectify the difficulty of telling such a story at the outset, punctuating the then unknown narrator's own comments about how difficult it is to tell this story with a clear tie to the one real moment of seeing in the film. It is this one moment of witness, that one kernel of traumatic encounter, that the fabular form of the film cannot bear.

The narrative itself continues to circle around the kernel that the "like" dimension marks. In the first half of the film, Guido almost magically shapes the world around him through a series of coincidental encounters with his future wife, Dora. He courts her by giving agency to such coincidences, showing himself to possess the ability to make keys fall out of the heavens or strangers to obey his most idiosyncratic wishes. Guido is "like" a magician; he seemingly has special powers. Importantly, the film never shows any recognition by others of Guido's "like"-ness, though, that there is anything else there except for magic, at least not until the scenes in the concentration camp. Of course, we see how Guido is able to fabricate his magic, but Dora does not, nor does Giosué, nor does anyone else except for the silent faces in the concentration camp of those who observe Guido's constructing the game fiction for his son.

Throughout the entire story, the lack of narrator presence in the body of the film allows us to ignore the thorny questions of witnessing since we don't even know who's telling the story until the very end; it defers its knowledge until then. And the film itself follows this tactic throughout its development. We don't know that Guido is a Jew until about a third of a way through the film when he remarks about painting "Jewish Waiter" on his chest in response to his uncle's fear of rising anti-Semitism after his horse has been defaced with Nazi symbols and the words "Jewish Horse." In fact, even when Guido is giving his "lecture" on the new race laws in the guise of a fascist official at Dora's school, pointing out his ears, belly button, and "muscular" features, we don't know he's Jewish. One's identity as a Jew was not *necessarily* the defining part of one's identity, especially in Italy, where Jews often completely assimilated into Italian culture. But there's a dissonance between Guido's obliviousness to his own Jewishness and the constant reminders of Jewish persecution that Benigni invokes: the anti-Semitic graffiti, the store signs forbidding Jews from entering, the harassment by officials. The film takes pains to show the rise of anti-Semitism around Guido. But at the same time, in order for the romance of the story to develop, Guido and his immediate family cannot actually see it. All we see of what Guido or his son or even Dora sees is wrapped in the one scene in the fog. And at the very end of the film, when there is a chance to remark about Guido's murder or even the Holocaust more broadly, Benigni chooses not to show us recognition. The film closes down emphasizing not a moment of witness (which we never see in the eyes of the child) but with a denial of witnessing, an identification with the constructed narrative as a means of survival. This totalizing fiction is possible only with the denial of the moment of seeing, of the witness.

But there is an odd sort of awareness of this in the very form of the film. In fact, the film itself ends with a freezing of the final scene of Giosué and his mother; the only way the film can prevent a movement back to the horror is to stop the film. We don't get to see Giosué find out about his father's murder, to recognize the limits of the fiction that his father had preserved for him. Instead, after the voice-over finishes the camera remains focused on Dora and her son embracing, with Giosué telling her about winning the contest: "A thousand points to laugh like crazy about! We came in first! We're taking the tank home! We won!" The only evidence of Giosué's own recognition is in the telling of the story, which itself breaks down considering the reporting of things that Giosué could not in fact have seen.

❧

The elevation of a particular testimony to cover over all possible renditions of a traumatic encounter is the final end of a certain view of pedagogy. Shoshana Felman, for example, describes the experience of such moments of intrusion, a moment of witness, in her own classroom when teaching a seminar on trauma, a moment of witness that results in a similar "need" to speak in her students and herself. But for Felman, these moments require a working through, a move inevitably arbitrated by the discourse of the teacher, where the teacher's question is about "how to contain [the crisis], how much crisis [the class can] sustain" (Felman 54). Such a claim puts the teacher in the position of knowing what the limits of trauma are for each one of her particular students. Such a universalizing of trauma already misses or forecloses the particular horror. This is not to say that Felman's class did not encounter something, did not experience a moment of witnessing. But it does turn its back on the moment of seeing, and the disruption it causes, in favor of knowledge and of identity. This is precisely what *Life is Beautiful* does in its rendering of the Holocaust, especially in the version with the added voice-over narration. What makes

Life is Beautiful so palatable, so consumable, is the way in which it "rein-tegrates" the crisis of the Holocaust within a "transformed frame of mean-ing," a family narrative that binds the child together with a loss that is seemingly forever deferred. In the end, though Spielberg's film has been accused of doing exactly the same thing, *Schindler's List* is more cannily willing to offer up moments in which the traumatic kernel, glimpsed at once by characters and by the audience but which cannot be reintegrated into knowledge by either, is left merely to be seen. Resnais and Lanzmann, in trying to obey the demands of history, nonetheless recognize that de-spite their best intentions, the didactic nature of their films—their status as testimony—rests on a foundation of that which cannot be told but only seen. For Primo Levi and other survivors, the pedagogical end of their tes-timony rests not in covering over their traumatic encounters with memory or fiction. Rather, their texts suggest that the end of teaching rests in the traumatic kernel itself, in prioritizing the moment of witness over that of the specifics of testimony. Both Benigni and Felman begin by stressing the unrepresentable, that which form cannot hold or the falsity of that which has been given to us as knowable. Both end by foreclosing the witness's encounter in a fiction that might be more livable but that ultimately denies the insistence of trauma.

Notes

1. Selections from Jean Cayrol's text to Night and Fog are taken from the published version rather than from the sketchy subtitles. See Jean Cayrol's "Night and Fog" in *Film: Book 2 Films of Peace and War*. Ed. Robert Hughes (Grove Press: New York, 1962): 234–55.

2. The complete text of *Shoah* can be found in Claude Lanzmann's *Shoah: An Oral History of the Holocaust* (New York: Pantheon Books, 1985). We have in-cluded the page numbers from this edition for ease of reference.

6

Museums and the Imperative of Memory: History, Sublimity, and the Divine

One's first encounter with the photographic inventory of ultimate horrors is a kind of revelation, the prototypically modern revelation: a negative epiphany. . . . Indeed, it seems plausible to me to divide my life into two parts, before I saw the photographs . . . and after. . . . Some limit had been reached, and not only that of horror. . . .

Susan Sontag, cited in Linenthal

Outside the Hall of Remembrance in the United States Holocaust Memorial Museum (USHMM), just before visitors leave the exhibit and proceed down the long stairway to the main hall of the museum, there is an open, loose-leaf binder in which visitors are asked to record their thoughts. These thoughts range from the sublime ("I cannot believe what I have just seen; and yet I know it has happened and understand it because of my disbelief") to the obscene ("If only the Jews had not murdered Jesus Christ and accepted Him they could have been saved"). They record what people believe they have learned at the museum about the Holocaust and about their encounter with the artifacts and testimonies there. In this chapter we will examine how two museums—the United States Holocaust Memorial Museum, on the national mall in Washington, D.C., and the complex of museums and memorials to the Shoah in Jerusalem known as Yad Vashem—negotiate the historical imperative to construct a knowledge (or, if you prefer, a narrative) of the events of the

131

Shoah and the traumatic kernel whose trace is made present in those narratives. The differences in the two museum complexes—as well as the tensions that exist within the museums—reside in the ways they construct the museum visitor, situating them inside narrative or a community that either naturalizes that "residency" or defamiliarizes it so much that the visitor is forced out of historical time and place altogether and into an encounter with moments shot through with what Benjamin calls "messianic time." Such moments are experienced as shock but reveal history's *inaccessibility* as something learned.

We'll argue further that there is a connection between these moments that rupture history and what could be called the divine. It is possible to understand how history works by means of presenting the incommensurable, forcing the reader or viewer to come face to face with objects that seem to present time out of time. This is the divine, in the sense that it is what precedes the naming of time as history, the naming of a self as a subject. It is what originates the utterance but is not coequal with the utterance, with history or the name, itself.

There is the often-cited scene in Elie Wiesel's novel, *Night*, where, after a youngster is hanged for failing to implicate another inmate, a man watching asks, "Where is God now?" Wiesel replies to himself and to the reader, "Here He is—He is hanging here on this gallows" (62). But the Holocaust does not so much mark a departure of the divine and the historical, or God's turning away from his creation in the face of that creation's desecration of life, as it marks the rearticulation of the connection between the divine and the human, the divine and the experiential. But that connection is a connection of incommensurability, of—in Kant's terms—sublimity. It is in that incommensurable connection, in the trauma that forces us to say things we did not mean to say or to remember things we could not have imagined, that something intervenes to provide us with a sense of the structure not of the event—Shoah—but of the human capacity for knowledge and ethical action in the face of trauma.

Questions surrounding how we represent trauma, how we consider memory within acts of representation, are certainly not new. We can simply look at the Second Commandment's imperative of not making an object out of the divine: one cannot represent what defies knowledge, what transcends the very possibility of signification. This simple assertion of course leads to highly complex problems with regard to how we speak about anything that lacks the possibility of signification, how we can know anything about it through representation. Jewish and Christian traditions have wrestled with this issue throughout their histories: the kabbala, as we've suggested, addresses ethical action in light of an unrepresentable divine, while scholastic discussions of the trinity similarly attempt to trace out the known and the unknowable in terms of a coherence that one cannot make whole. These are both attempts to consider action in relation to knowledge when the very foundations of such knowledge must be left open, and where there is an imperative for signification working within an imperative against it. In other words, these are both attempts to situate a knowledge—a history or logic—in the face of some divine or traumatic kernel that resists any such possibility of knowledge.

We can see more recent confrontations with this problem of representation in the work of poststructural theorists ranging from Derrida to Baudrillard as well as in the American pragmatists following Rorty. Each offers ways of cutting through knowledge in the face of the unknowable that always lurks beneath the surface. The effects of such thinking ground Holocaust studies itself, where foundational works by such scholars as Lyotard and Adorno focus explicitly on this epistemological issue. Lyotard's *The Differend*, for example, traces the problems associated with the inability/ imperative of language to remember for us, to situate the past in light of the present. Lyotard begins his examination with a core question: How can there be witnesses when the act of witnessing cancels out the object itself? He then offers a way towards tracing the epistemological breakdown between those who were not there and those who were. Similarly, Adorno's now axiomatic assertion that poetry after Auschwitz can only be barbaric rests on the very same problem of representation: When memory itself attempts to capture an origin, a beginning that is both unrecoverable and yet insistent, representation must fail and must become something that at best is horribly disfiguring and at worst blatantly false.

Following Lyotard and Adorno's lead of linking Holocaust representation to crises of language and knowledge doesn't take us very far however. Neither theorist grapples with the realities of representation, the results of the imperatives that stories must be told. In fact, there is a clear division between those who examine issues of "there-ness" and those like Lyotard and Adorno who are more concerned with epistemology. James Young's work, for example, focuses on what actually is represented in Holocaust memorials and writings. Like Lawrence Langer before him, Young collects and examines the representations that different communities and individuals put into practice, materials that constitute testimony about the event. Both Adorno and Lyotard avoid the ramifications of "there-ness" to witnessing itself, that kernel of trauma that requires some sort of testimony. In this chapter, while addressing the "there-ness" of trauma, a divine horror that forecloses the possibility of representation even while demanding it, we want to locate the creation of "Holocaust history" at the moment where an individual subject (a visitor in one of the museums) directly confronts the remnant objects of the events of the Shoah. It is as a moment where testimony is made to stand in for the event or for the trauma that subjectifies the viewer. Such representations are necessary for history since they take the place of the purely barbaric or void of memory. History, then, both recovers and covers over the event with representations, attempting to carve out a space for a knowledge that allows for its very possibility.

I. *Yad Vashem and the Imperative of History*

One of the founding moments of the state of Israel came quickly upon independence. In 1953, the Knesset passed a special law founding the memorial complex that would commemorate the victims of the Holocaust. The memorial's name comes from a passage in Isaiah: "I will give in my house and within my walls a place and a name (*Yad Vashem*) (LVI, 5). Over the years Yad Vashem has grown to fulfill not only its charge to join place with name, to serve as a memorial to the six million and their families and communities, but also to gather materials to document the Holocaust and to educate Israelis and non-Israelis, Jews and non-Jews. And these tasks are central to the state itself, a conclusion drawn by James Young in his survey of Holocaust memorials. Young concludes "that as the state grows, so too will its memorial undergirding" (*The Texture of Memory* 250), marking the political nature of the memorials at Yad Vashem which, as the state evolves, need to grow in number. To this end, Yad Vashem includes a museum that situates the memorials within an historical context, showing the rise of anti-Semitism in Europe, tracing Nazi acts of genocide to the eventual migration of Jews to Eretz Israel at the end of the war. Yad Vashem functions to place a subject within a history that marks the very beginning of Israel: it is the first stop on any state visit by foreign dignitaries and is a mandatory part of the training for the Israel Defense Force. Over the past fifty years, Yad Vashem's construction has followed the plan of both memorial and museum. Situated on one side of Mount Hertzl, the home of Israel's national cemetery, Yad Vashem is both cemetery and museum, placing each name within a founding national narrative, offering a place where those without physical remains might reside. Thus, Yad Vashem ties together the imperative of speaking with place markers that represent the horrors of bodies never to be found, the never to be completely signified. Unlike the graves on Mount Herzl, Yad Vashem doesn't hold the physical remains of victims. Unlike those killed in the Six Day War who are buried on Mount Hertzl, the Holocaust victims have no physical remains to be put to rest. This alone makes the act of joining place and name difficult, demanding some sort of statement to replace the remains. But although most of the grounds are dedicated to memorial sites—the Hall of Remembrance, the Valley of the Communities, the Avenue of the Righteous Among the Nations, etc.—the most visited site within the complex is the Historical Museum. It is what supplies context to the very act of remembrance at Yad Vashem.

The Historical Museum begins with "M'shoah l'tkumah" ("From Holocaust to Rebirth"), a sixty-square-meter bas-relief sculpture in aluminum on black by Israeli artist Naftali Besem. In the first of four sections, we encounter *Holocaust*, which depicts a woman turning shabbat candles against herself, inverting them onto her breasts as smoke bellows out from a chimney above her. To the right, connecting the first section to the next, a winged fish with its head bent or broken floats on its back. The second frame is *Resistance*, which depicts a chaotic and fragmented image of a man holding a flaming spear and a ladder while flames engulf his surroundings. The third image is *Ascent*, illustrating a survivor's travel to Israel. This less fragmented figure rests in a boat with elongated rudder, paddle, and wheel extending out of the boat's bottom. The final image is titled *Rebirth*, which concludes the four by depicting the shabbat candles now righted and lit, resting on the back of a lion, illustrating the Jewish people in Israel. As a sculpture, Besem's piece is powerful, juxtaposing four images that when taken together outline a movement that includes signs of the complexity of the survivor's journey out of the horrors of genocide, marking different spaces for memory without applying a singular narrative to bind them together. In fact, Besem's work seems to carve out a space within narrative that each bas-relief can only situate. *Holocaust*, for example, ties together elements of mourning and self-destruction with the familiar image of the smokestack. Although the next image repeats the fire of the first now used to represent resistance, how one moves between these images is left unimagined within the work. The bas-relief is tied together by the repetition of symbols, like the fire in all four frames. While the work might represent specific moments within an historical progression, it does so through juxtaposing symbols that dramatize the gaps within any unifying narrative.

The historical museum follows the overarching structure of Besem's sculpture, tracing anti-Semitism, the pogroms, and the extermination camps, followed by the resistance fighters and liberation, and concluding with immigration and the rise of the state. In fact, immediately following Besem's sculpture, the museum offers an organizational exhibit that illustrates historical images that follow the sequence that Besem's work compartmentalizes. Before even entering the full exhibit, the museum presents a more detailed overview of what the specific documentation that follows means in the context of its historical narrative. But unlike Besem's metaphoric rendering of the event, the museum fills in the details, the symbolic pieces that Besem's sculpture invokes. Instead of the inverted candlesticks, here we have scenes of Kristallnacht—images of broken glass and fire. Instead of Besem's symbolic image of the passage to Eretz Israel, the museum depicts images of masses of Jews being detained by British authorities. This is not to say that the museum's history is inaccurate. Rather, the museum narrates the moments of tension within Besem's work with specific historical documentation.

Perhaps the most clearly historical moment in the Historical Museum at Yad Vashem comes just before the section describing liberation from the camps. Before turning a corner around which we encounter the famous picture that includes Elie Wiesel lying in a bunk at Buchenwald, the museum narrates the political problems for Jews immigrating to Palestine during the war. Before we see the liberation, we are confronted with pictures of the Palestinian Mufti stating support for Hitler's Final Solution. Next to this come images of British forces detaining Jewish immigrants in Cyprus. Situated between the resistance fighters and the liberation of the camps, Yad Vashem points toward the trauma of the event through the politics of the founding of Israel, a founding that, as we know, is still very much in negotiation. But pointing toward trauma through historical narratives is ultimately a permanent diversion from the real trauma, a bait and switch that actually occludes the very object of the museum's representation. The narrative of the museum places the state as the solution to the unrecoverable victims, those whose remains were destroyed in the ovens of Auschwitz or the pyres of Chelmno. The state replaces the loss of such remains with its founding narrative, holding a symbolic position that names absence as annihilation. In this regard, speaking against the writing of the museum's history—against the state or the museum's manner of signification—becomes akin to denying the very trauma of the Holocaust.

When leaving the Historical Museum at Yad Vashem, having passed through the images of liberation and immigration and culminating in a memorial to the numbers of dead from each nation, we confront a warning from the Baal Shem Tov: "Forgetfulness leads to exile, while remembrance is the secret of redemption." This final statement punctuates the

Historical Museum at Yad Vashem, marking not only the ends of both remembrance and forgetfulness, but also situating each witness historically. The ends of remembrance; its points of articulations; its origins and its object; its goal and its termination: all of these shadings of meaning are invoked in this passage. For if we define redemption in terms of an act of remembrance, Yad Vashem must offer a way into memory in order for redemption to be realized or fulfilled, in order that individual traumas may be gathered up and imbedded into history. And in this context, remembering the correct history—all of its details and motivations—becomes the only way to avoid exile. This is the final imperative of the Historical Museum at Yad Vashem and directly following the plaque with the Baal Shem Tov's words, the visitor exits into the bright Jerusalem sun.

But, as the Baal Shem Tov equally stresses, the other side of remembrance is forgetfulness, a position that predicates exile itself, making it a place whose ends are more difficult to trace than those of remembrance. We see this in the simple statement "Never forget!": It is significant that when invoking the Holocaust we say "Never forget!" rather than "Remember . . .", in contrast to, say, "Remember the Alamo." Unlike the positive imperative "Remember . . .", "Never Forget!" negates an absence and thus offers up a more complex epistemology. For what are the limits of forgetting? From where does it originate? Where lies its terminus? These are crucial distinctions since, as the Baal Shem Tov asserts, redemption lies on the side of remembrance, not forgetfulness; exile lies on the side of forgetfulness, not remembrance. The very ends of forgetfulness become the boundaries between exile and redemption, chaos and history, absence and signification. This of course presumes to mark an opposition between remembrance and forgetfulness. Such a position suggests that we cannot remember and forget at the same time, that one marks the absence of the other. Or rather, forgetfulness is the extreme of the two: we don't "completely remember" (as in "I completely forgot to . . ."). In this sense, remembrance can be partial, whereas forgetfulness seems to mark an absolute. In addition, opposing remembrance to forgetfulness implies that forgetfulness isn't even a thing in itself, that it's only an absence of remembrance. So "Never forget!" is an imperative to identify with the trauma that is a prerequisite to history, that comes before any specific testimony. "Never forget!" requires that trauma itself be memorized into a unifying imperative whose object—unlike "Remember the Alamo"—is to bind a community in opposition to some loss. Whereas nonnegated imperatives require identity along a specific narrative, a specific object to the verb, "Never forget!" requires no such object, since any namable object is an effect of an absence of such an object. Problematically, this epistemological position places power in any narrative that becomes marked as the one to stave off forgetfulness. Whereas "Remember . . ." presumes an ideological position that defines a community relative to itself, "Never forget!" itself is not ideological, does not refer to a specific narrative in place. Rather, "Never forget!" sets up a structural position relative to loss that goes beyond any one particular narrative that might fill it. More simply, "Never forget!" signifies no universal object, only an infinite number of radical particularities. However, when a singular narrative is elevated to fill such a gulf between knowledge and absence, the narrative becomes foundational to the very identity of the community and any variation becomes an attack on identity itself. Similarly, we often consider remembrance as a choice of will while forgetfulness is either an accident or is forced upon us. If we choose to consider forgetfulness/exile as a choice, we need to consider what kind of choice it might be. Who would deliberately choose exile over redemption, forgetfulness over remembrance? So at the very least, considering forgetfulness as a choice makes it always already a false choice. For Yad Vashem, the choice of forgetfulness is predicated on choosing *not* to remember—which is a particular act of remembrance itself: denial. By seeing remembrance as oppositional to forgetfulness, the Historical Museum at Yad Vashem places the event of the Holocaust itself in the same position as Texans do the Alamo. It offers a universal history of the event that can then stabilize a whole host of other identifications. Placed in these terms, the Historical Museum at Yad Vashem defines a remembrance that attempts to close out all possibility of forgetfulness, attempts to extricate remembrance from any origin in—or even relation to—forgetfulness itself.

Yad Vashem certainly means this way of defining forgetfulness when it cites the Baal Shem Tov. By considering remembrance a presence and forgetfulness an absence of such a presence, the museum situates its telling of the Shoah in direct opposition to what it sees as the only other alternative, denial. But what if forgetfulness does not end in remembrance nor remembrance in forgetfulness? Or what if there is materiality to forgetfulness, a kind of nothing that's something? If we posit forgetfulness as a something that is comparable to the something of remembrance, we lose the simple divisions between exile and redemption, forgetfulness and remembrance. In addition, we problematize both remembrance as a positive (history) and a negative (denial), both of which may have no relation to forgetfulness. We can now see history as a means of testimony whereas witnessing, a prior moment that marks a point of intersection between epistemology and ontology, between knowing and being, occupies a place relative to forgetfulness. In this theoretical rendering, witnessing is the point of trauma in which all possible testimonies or memories originate. It is a moment of the real that is only accessible through testimony, but which is not reducible to any one testimony. In *The Differend*, Lyotard's conception of the witness as one who cannot fill in the forgetfulness with remembrance implies such a model. Similarly, Blanchot's comment on forgetfulness takes it out of the realm of an absence:

> If forgetfulness precedes memory or perhaps founds it, or has no connection at all, then to forget is not simply a weakness, a failing, an absence or void (the starting point of all recollection but a starting point which, like an anticipatory shade, would obscure remembrance in its very possibility, restoring the memorable to its fragility and memory to the loss of memory). (85).

Witnessing, then, is not an historical position. One does not witness history. Rather, one's testimony might constitute history. Witnessing is neither an act of remembrance nor an act of testimony. Returning to the Second Commandment, divinity itself can only be witnessed; it cannot be constituted with an act of testimony (the very problem Augustine addresses when he considers the difficulty of teaching that which cannot be found whole in testimony: how does one learn of God when one hasn't witnessed God?). In this sense, the Shoah demands that one prioritize witnessing over testimony, that testimonies are important only insofar as they point back to the witnessing of the six million.

Unlike the Historical Museum, the memorials throughout Yad Vashem resist narration and thus point us towards witnessing rather than testimony. The most visited memorial at Yad Vashem is the Children's Memorial. On a hill above the Historical Museum, we enter the memorial from the summit, moving down into a corridor that turns from being open to the sun into a dark enclosed structure, the movement out of sunlight being accompanied by quiet music. The first images in the structure are the faces of children, illuminated faces whose eyes meet ours as we leave the brightness for the dark. The rest of the memorial is quite simple: we turn a corner into an even darker chamber where candlelights are reflected infinitely in glass around us. And as we contemplate the reflection of the lights, a voice reading the names of children murdered during the Holocaust echoes through the chamber. We exit the memorial at the base of the hill, moving back into the sun after leaving the chamber.

Of all the memorials at Yad Vashem, this one causes the most personal confrontation with the horror of the event—most people leave visibly shaken—and it does so by very simple representations of names and images. Unlike the museum, the Children's Memorial makes no attempt at constructing a history of children's lives or experiences. It offers no real connection to current politics nor to issues of Jewish immigration to Israel. More specifically, it offers no testimony; it doesn't speak about particular traumas. Instead, the Children's Memorial constructs a space from which a viewer might see something, witness something that itself goes beyond any story. What makes this monument so effective as a way toward recognizing something about the Holocaust resides in what is not itself portrayed. We don't know any actions of these named children; we aren't given any history or narrative. The memorial refuses to remember these children's stories: to do so would reinvoke the horrors that they suffered. In this instance, the memorial functions neither as a political nor historical act; the Children's Memorial simply gives place to names, names to place. Unlike the Historical Museum, the Children's Memorial as an act of remembrance does not insist on remembering all things; it does not present the absolute distinction between memory and forgetfulness, since it does not function to represent the lives of children or even to give their deaths a specific knowledge. This lack of specified (that is, reified) meaning allows a certain element of forgetfulness and hence exile to remain resonant in the lack of narrative: we cannot know or even recognize what these names might have been. The memorial constructs a space that cannot be remembered or filled in by some universal narrative. For this memorial, there isn't the imperative "Remember . . .", since the object of such a remembrance is itself only a seemingly endless list of names, a set of infinite particularities. The Children's Memorial can only mark a space for these names, not redeem them in the way the Historical Museum's invocation of the Baal Shem Tov seems to demand. However, as a means toward bearing witness, the Children's Memorial is fundamentally redemptive.

In terms of an ethics of memory, the Children's Memorial represents a material presence of forgetfulness in remembrance. In this instance, the act of remembrance signifies a witnessing, where one posits a name in relation to an event without eliding the two. Within that very act of placing a name, of signifying a moment that is only present in the act itself, the space for the absence of memory—forgetfulness—is opened up. In reading the names of children in a darkened room with candlelights reflecting infinitely we open up the possibility that that name—that child—could be forgotten, especially considering that the name itself only lasts in the air until the next name is read. The power of the memorial is one that brings us to the very real brink of forgetfulness, the forgetfulness that is an effect of memory, not something that memory can itself replace. In the memorial, the name must be spoken for the absence of the name to be felt, for there to be both a name and a place. The way out of exile requires such a relation to forgetfulness, a redemption whose origin rests in an act of witnessing. In this sense, a remembrance built on witnessing, not history, is the secret of redemption.

The Historical Museum, on the contrary, eradicates the forgetfulness that is so necessary for witnessing. By leading the viewer through a scripted narrative—the rise of anti-Semitism and the Nazi Party, the pogroms, the genocide, the redemption in the state of Israel—the Historical Museum loses meaning in favor of knowledge—a knowledge that forecloses forgetfulness by reifying memory as transmissible absolutely. In Blanchot's terms, we have lost "unknowledge": "Unknowledge is not the lack of knowledge; it is not even knowledge of the lack but rather that which is hidden by knowledge and ignorance alike: the neutral, the unmanifest" (63). No longer do we have the place for a name in such an act, since a name itself is not enough to articulate such a complete narrative. By "telling it all," the place and the name are no longer articulable as distinct positions, but instead their separation is dismissed with a narrative of identity.

At this moment, Yad Vashem shows us the dangerous ease of remembrance without witnessing: epistemology solves problems of ontology; knowledge becomes being. Remembrance—whether affirmation or denial—elevated to replace forgetfulness—knowledge covering over unknowledge—denies the difficult nature of the field of representation, denies the very act of representation in the process of constructing a past. In this sense, the Holocaust itself really does reside in the Historical Museum, really is located and pinned down by the act of similarly eradicating the names that cannot be remembered. Put another way, the Historical Museum only bears witness to itself; it does not place a name in relation to an event, save the merger of the state and the place, the loss of all other names in favor of the one name to name them all. This is the beginning of history and the end of the six million as particulars. The rhetoric of the museum thus places the viewer in the position of having to give up her name in the face of the state, to identify with Israel's history instead of any particular victim.

Redemption lies not with the ideological fiction, the covering over of the impossibility of origins. Rather, redemption rests in keeping the knowledge of trauma/the trauma of knowledge open and thus signifying. For redemption from the past, or from what we feel or believe or remember the past to once have been, places us in the mundane realm of exile. In this sense, the words of the Baal Shem Tov must be taken in light of Adorno and Lyotard's warning against falling into the grotesque or the blatantly false. Remembrance is the secret to redemption, but only as an unfilled term, a space that lacks a knowledge that coheres. Put another way, where the Historical Museum of Yad Vashem fails and where the Children's Memorial succeeds is in how the metonymic representation refers to something that is ultimately metaphoric. Whereas the Historical Museum uses metonymy to represent the whole, the Children's Memorial uses metonymy to show that the whole itself is already removed from the realm of representation, that there is no whole. The faces of Jewish children function to invoke metonymically all children, even as what they signify—the lives of those envisioned—cannot be known or remembered.

II. *The USHMM and the Imperative of Memory*

James Young argues that "what is remembered" and what is archived in places like the Yad Vashem Memorial in Jerusalem and the United States Holocaust Museum, "necessarily depends upon *how* it is remembered" ("The Texture of Memory" 173, emphasis added), and Young goes on to map the interpretive activity that takes place between "event," "memorial," and "viewers" (see, especially, *The Texture of Memory* 283–349 for America's memory of the event). This, however, assumes that there is any access to the "events" represented or the objects housed in museums at all. Theodor Adorno worried this point: by stripping artifacts and even—he might argue—survivor testimonies[1] from their contexts and placing them in museums, one risks separating the viewer's lived life from the manifold characteristics available in the objects' relation with lived life (see Adorno, "Valery Proust Museum"). As objects housed in museums, even survivor testimonies are representations, and as such are subject to manipulation because they reflect not an event or a moment of creation, but "reflect upon their own autonomy and upon the formal law unique to each" object (Adorno, *The Culture Industry* 101; see also "Valery Proust Museum").

But if we take someone like Hayden White seriously, even the contextualization of an event places it into a narrative, and provides it with a plot. Objects placed into museums without context are dead on arrival, and so are historically valueless. Objects placed into a museum in a well-defined context are emplotted and valuable insofar as they can be interpreted according to already understood narratives or plots, but are valueless insofar as they pretend to provide understanding of the event itself. On the view of history in which events are only available in narrative, we learn about interpretation (what Jauss might have called the reception history) of the narratives spawned by the event, but not the events themselves.

To suggest only one brief example to which we'll return in more detail later, seeing a desecrated Torah ark, with or without the accompanying description and photographs of the synagogue from which it was taken both before Kristallnacht and after, teaches us about a museum curator's criteria for the evaluation of evidence, and it teaches us about what we may or may not have known about the violence of the events in Germany in 1938. It does not provide us access to the events that culminated in the desecration of the ark, and certainly not understanding of them. But it may do something more important: force the viewer out of knowledge by rupturing history. The relation between the historical object and the traces left by it is what concerned Walter Benjamin, whose interest in history was grounded in his attempt to understand the relation between "truth content" and "material content" of an object or (as in the case of his essay on Goethe) work of art. For him the material content is the trace of a fleeting historical moment in time and the truth content is the suprahistorical significance of that moment. It is the relation between the historical, momentary, and palpable objectivity of the object and the suprahistorical meaningfulness of that same object that reveals the divine nature of truth. What one learns from the objects, like a desecrated Torah ark, or from historical narratives of survivors is only material content; what one learns from one's encounter with such objects or narratives is only truth content. Beyond these two moments, or in the relation between them, it is possible to recuperate the eventness of the event itself (and, for Benjamin, its divine origin).

The historian's job is to force into relation the moment as it is embedded in historical time and the moment as it has significance as "now-time," as an inseparable part of the observer's own life world, the observer's own language and memory. The redemptive philosophy of history isn't interested in the possibility of recuperating the events that, in Pierre Vidal-Naquet's terms, "precede discourse" if by that we mean getting the historical moment right. The events of history are heterogenous because they *aren't* easily plotted, and they aren't easily plotted because their interpretive significance and their effect upon the participant's and observer's lived lives are by definition incommensurable. But they have an *effect*, an effect that is palpable, and capable of being mapped as effect. That effect takes place in the impasse between spoken language, survivor testimony, desecrated Torah scroll, and the lived life of the observant Jew or the Lithuanian emigré. And this gap, this impasse, is "the strait gate" in kabbalistic terms, "through which the Messiah might enter" (264). In the impasse, in the terms an historian might use, we have a sense, though not evidence, of the event as it disturbs and marks history.

As in the Children's Memorial at Yad Vashem, part of what is pre
sented at the U.S. Holocaust Memorial Museum is both more and less than
evidence. It is a constellation of evidence, memory, and the traces of an
event so horrible that it disturbs the history it narrates. The visitor enters an
elevator on the first floor of the museum, which takes her to the fourth
floor and the beginning of the exhibit. The visitors travel from there down
through the third and second floors of the museum, each devoted to an historical period of the events in Europe: from the time leading up to Hin-
denburg's handing over the German chancellorship to Hitler in 1933 to the
beginning of the War (on the fourth floor); from the beginnings of the
move to exterminate Jews in the pale in Poland and the Ukraine in 1939
to the end of the systematic killing of all the European Jews and the liberation of the camps in 1945 (on the third floor); and the aftermath of the
Holocaust in Europe, the United States, Israel, and elsewhere, from the end
of the War (on the second floor). Though the visitors to the museum are
free to walk around in any sequence in each of the floors, our experience
has been that they instead follow the people, usually strangers, standing in
front of them, along the walls of the exhibit. As described by Weinberg and
Elieli, the purpose of the narrative arrangement of the building is so that
visitors "project themselves into the story and thus experience it like insid-
ers while at the same time remaining at a distance. . . . Drawn into the flow
of the narrative, visitors view the display with their senses tuned to sequence, coherence, and transformation" (49).[2]

But this really is only a point of departure for the museum, and we
would argue that what makes the exhibits function *historically*—what enables the viewer to have access not to the events of the Holocaust but to
the set of material and ideological markers upon which meaning is
founded—are those interruptions that Weinberg and Elieli (and, before
them, the planners and architects of the museum) take pains to recontex-
tualize: the glass walkways between sections of the exhibit floors and the
watchtower rooms, one of which contains the "wall of faces," photographs
collected from an east European shtetl wiped out in the 1940s. It is these
interruptions that most clearly mark the point of intersection in which the
visitor's sense of history-as-narrative is ripped apart.

One of these points of intersection is found in a small area on the
fourth floor of the exhibit devoted to the events leading up to Kristallnacht. In a glass case about eight feet high, in the middle of the floor,
stands the wooden arch that was the front of a Torah ark from the synagogue in Essen, Germany. Immediately next to it is a six-by-six-foot photograph of the interior of the synagogue on the morning of November 10,

1938. Both of these items take as their context the Nuremberg laws, established in 1935, and the stepped-up ostracism of the Jews in Europe from 1935 through 1939. Along the wall behind the photograph and ark are framed identification passes carried by Jews; nearby are photographs, taken by members of the Dusseldorf police in the 1930s, of Jehovah's Witnesses, homosexuals, and others who were rounded up along with prominent Jewish business people during the suppression of those years. In a glass case, in the middle of the floor some paces removed from the ark, are desecrated Torah scrolls. Clearly this section of the museum is intended to lead visitors to understand the series of events that culminated in the violence of Kristallnacht and the sanction the German state provided to individual acts of persecution of Jews and others covered under the Nuremberg laws. The plot of this section of the museum might be as follows: laws were passed ostracizing Jews and others in Germany and the territories; this sanction led to spontaneous and state-led destruction of Jews' personal property and places of business; and this sanction in turn led to deportations from Germany and the territories and, later, full-scale removal and extermination of Jews and others from the newly conquered lands in Poland and the east. The evidence of this narrative is ensconced in the museum: the text of the Nuremberg laws is presented in translation, photographs of Jews lined up for exit visas and identification cards are hung on the wall like living-room paintings, and the recovered remains of synagogue interiors are displayed like wounds.

But what this teaches us is far and away less complete and less compelling than accounts some visitors may know from Hilberg's or Dawidowicz's books on the trajectory of the Holocaust in Europe. The artifacts may make the train of events more accessible to visitors who may not know those works, but they are presented as a narrative under a traditional view of the purpose of museums. But if you understand the ark and the photographs of the Essen synagogue as *interruptions* in the documentary evidence of the deportation of European Jews, or even state-sanctioned anti-Semitism, then this section of the USHMM doesn't exactly teach: it forces us out of knowledge, interrupts it, and allows for the possibility that we might recognize a trace of a moment. And the ark does act as something of an interruption: to non-Jews, it may require something of an explanation to say why the ark is important in a synagogue in the first place; to Jews, coming upon a sacred object in the midst of legalese and the bureaucratic trappings of a government bent on suppression is a bit disconcerting. But the immediate effect of the ark—with the marks of an axe effacing the Hebrew characters that were seen as evidence of the profane by Germans in the early hours of November 10—is to draw attention away from the bureaucratic and to the place of the ark itself. The paint on the ark is unblemished, smooth as the day it was painted in blues and greens, and there is only a moulding missing over the opening from which the Torah scrolls would have been removed. What has been hacked away is the part of the ark that marks the point of connection between the congregants in Essen and the individual, particularly the Jewish individual, museum visitor: the words that mark the moment of the opening of the ark and the removal of the Torah scrolls—"Remember before Whom you Stand"—on a Saturday morning.[3]

There are, in Walter Benjamin's terms, two narratives here, both of which are supported by historical evidence, historical artifacts, and testimonial evidence of those who were there, all placed into relation. There are several items here that might be taken for the "material content" of the display—the desecrated ark, the photograph of the interior of the synagogue, the documentary and tangible evidence of the ostracism and deportation of urban Jews in the late 1930s—and several elements that might be taken as its "truth content"—the significance of the ark and the Torah to Jewish daily life, the significance of carrying government-issued documents that identify individuals by "race." But what access is available to the historical event of Kristallnacht, or deportation, or even something called "the Holocaust," is found between them. Edward Linenthal describes the purpose for collecting artifacts like the scroll and the front of the ark as providing visitors with the everyday significance of the details of life in Europe during the Third Reich and the Holocaust (see *Preserving Memory*, esp. 171–92). Like the faces of the children in the Children's Memorial at Yad Vashem, this constellation of artifacts displaces the possibility of a narrative—of "preserving memory"—by facing the Museum visitor with too many competing narratives. The ark and the Torahs have an everyday significance to observant Jewish visitors to the USHMM, and perhaps a sacred "otherness" to non-Jews: reading from the Torah forms the central aspect of Saturday morning services, and the opening of the ark, even without the removal of the scrolls, obliges congregants to stand in respect. The opening of the ark and the prayers said during the readings are common parts of the daily life cycle of Jews. Likewise the photographs of the synagogue interior may appear to a Jewish visitor as only partly out of the ordinary: the Essen synagogue was lovelier than many synagogues in the United States, but its architecture and layout is very much like that in any other conservative or reform synagogue in the country. It is simply the place to pray and observe holidays and shabbat. (To some it may be a second home.) For a Jewish visitor, to see what marks her identity as part of a historical narrative of systematic destruction—a narrative that visitors may know only too well—disrupts both the narrative of worship and the received narrative of the Holocaust, and burdens these details with far more than the "everyday significance" they would have under ordinary circumstances. It is, in fact, the ordinary circumstances that short-circuit one's ability to contextualize this section of the permanent exhibit, and make history the point of departure in a sense the museum's curators may not have anticipated. Both the material content and the truth content of the display denaturalize the emplotted narratives—religious, everyday, historical—in such a way that the observer learns not so much about the Holocaust as she learns about the limits of figure: the parts in this instance do not indicate a whole, but what lies beyond them.

In effect, the metonymic function of this portion of the exhibit is meant to displace an easy equivalence that visitors may make between their own circumstances and those of the individuals whose identity cards they pick up at the entrance to the museum (see Linenthal 187–9), or whose faces they may believe they recognize in photographs, or whose actions and behaviors they repeat in their own lives. In a book on the relation between events, their images, and history, Edith Wyschogrod examines the epistemic function of the disaster as Blanchot understood it, how what eludes discourse nonetheless has an effect upon it. The disaster—the events of history as they impinge upon and affect individuals prior to becoming an image or an idea—cannot be accessed. It becomes what she calls a "non-event." To illustrate what she means, she refers to an archival photograph of a child—neatly dressed and well fed, apparently unaware of his surroundings—walking on a road in the woods past corpses strewn outside what the caption tells us is Bergen-Belsen. Of the photo she says, "so long as the boy in his uncanny flight is permitted to break into the narrative of what is depicted"—and, presumably what is depicted is the destruction of the Holocaust—"the child's face becomes the escape route for an unsayability that seeps into the . . . image and contests any narrative articulation of what the camera captures, a world where death and life are virtually indistinguishable" (142). This is the position of the viewer in this and other places in the USHMM: she matches narrative to narrative, imagined incident to incident, in a repetitive association of images and words that we have come to associate with the Shoah, and which, placed together, form a tapestry of destruction. Yet the individual pieces themselves when looked at one at a time, or in succession apart from the tapestry, seem to fall apart: there is something uncanny behind them that resists telling or saying. Individual descriptions "break into the narrative of what is depicted" and contest any narrative articulation, any reasonable sequence of events, that we may wish to attribute to it.

Wyschogrod, citing Emmanuel Levinas, also notes the elusiveness of language and the persistence of what lies behind it. She writes,

> [T]he image is not to be grasped as simply indicating an absent object. [Images occupy] the place of objects "as though the represented object died, were degraded, were disincarnated in its own reflection." . . . The image . . . , by holding beings and discourses in abeyance, bracketing them, opens a space of disclosure beyond iconicity that is homologous with the non-discursiveness of the face. (91)

Whether it is the destruction of a synagogue in Germany during Kristallnacht, or the willingness of a museum visitor to imagine her daily life to be disrupted by events like those in Europe during the war, the events called up by the display in the USHMM have died. They are degraded and disincarnated, are forever lost to memory; what is left is the image that stops the event and, though it opens a space beyond representation that is "homologous with the non-discursiveness" of the face or the event itself, it cannot be said to mark the occurrence of the event. There is something else, beyond any equivalence we might assign between the opening of the ark in our synagogue on a Saturday morning and the same action in Germany over sixty years ago; something beyond the equivalence we may be reminded of in the bombing of a synagogue in Sacramento, California. But it is called up by the impossibility of resurrecting a disincarnated event and the painful image simultaneously incarnated as possibility in the mind of the observer.

In one of the towers of the museum, a three-story structure through which a passageway leads visitors from one section of the display to another on the fourth and third floors, there hang more than a thousand photographs taken between 1890 and 1941. These photographs are completely unremarkable portraits: some are posed, others are informal. Some are candid shots of people and families gathered together for picnics, or strolling down streets of a single small town in what is now Lithuania. The photographs are what is left of the life in a shtetl community that was eliminated in two days by an SS mobile killing unit.

The passageway is designed to allow visitors to pass from one portion of the exhibit to another, an exhibit that is arranged chronologically. Yet, the passageway has the effect of interrupting the narrative of the museum, something the planners of the museum did not exactly want, but which they understood they could not avoid. As the founding director of the museum put it, museum planners worried that the passageways "might dissipate the emotional impact of the exhibition on visitors," that it might interrupt the potential hermeneutic effect of the historical narrative. What you notice in that passageway is that visitors seem to find themselves more, not less, "emotionally engaged." This is one of several places in the museum where visitors are seen openly to weep—though there are any number of points here where this happens—and also to smile, oddly, out of a recognition of someone or something. During one visit to the USHMM, a couple and (we presume) their teenage daughter made their way through the passageway, and at once they stopped, all three of them looking, apparently, at the same photograph. The older woman pointed to the photo, which could not be identified by us, and all three of them smiled broadly. This reaction is understandable: one of us remembers another photograph, a posed sitting of a mother and daughter in front of an arras, taken probably during the 1930s. The mother had dark hair and was holding her daughter in front of her. The daughter was around two, and had remarkably fair skin and brilliant blond hair. It would have been easy to mistake the woman for his mother, and the little girl for his older daughter. It was an impossible equation, made all the more so because these two people, amid other people and families and memories of relatives and friends, had been exterminated fifty-five years ago in the context of something even the survivors of such an event can't make sense of.

But it is precisely this impossibility of equation—the repetition of historical circumstances, as signs in metonym, that cannot be made to stand in for the whole they presumably represent—that stands in the way of the historical narrative that would allow this woman to be his mother, or that would allow the family to recognize a woman as their bubbie or an infant as their cousin. It's not just the fact that these people were killed by the *einsatzgruppen*; the fact is that the moment frozen in time by the photograph is, in Levinas's terms, disincarnated, as is the one called to mind by the viewer. What is called up, however, is the image of the other, in the vocabulary of a Levinas or a Blanchot, the trace of the event that cannot be captured by a narrative or an image, but has its place held by the narrative or image as if by proxy. It is this event-as-other, held at the crux of the material content and the truth content of the artifacts found in the Museum—the abyss between sign and sign in metonym—that is called up in the hallway in the USHMM, and that is mistaken for empathy or recognition by viewers and by us. Both these reactions—ours and that of the family—

and the reactions of anyone else who may have stopped short in this passageway, or any other spatial or temporal location in the museum, are interruptions of the historical narrative that the designers of the place laid out so painstakingly to provoke a relationship with the event. But they don't exactly provide a "way in" to the event itself; they don't allow the visitors who could not have been deported or subjected to systematic annihilation in Auschwitz to "experience the atmospheric impact" (Weinberg and Elieli 26) of it by proxy. They evidence a shattering of the narrative, and rearrange the fragments of one's own lived life and of others' lives so that, even for a fleeting moment, they indicate something outside human reason, something understandable in terms of an effect but that can only be partly named, and then only incorrectly. This is an interruption of historical, narrative remembrance by a moment that could be called sublime, or that could be called divine.

III. Sublimity and Redemption

Where, you might ask, is the divine in the recognition of a life not your own, a life that is only a glimpse represented by a photograph or set of photos—or, in other places, by testimony, artifacts, or displays, all arranged to produce an effect, though one different, perhaps, than that intended? In the USHMM, the designers were quite clear to liken its Hall of Remembrance, a large and empty hexagonal space near the exit to the permanent exhibit, to a cathedral: it implies an overwhelming sense of greatness, one that "mak[es] the individual feel small and insignificant" (26). But something quite the opposite is occurring here: the individual's relation to the trauma caused by reference to the events surrounding the Shoah is opened up rather than closed down in the face of the terrible or all-powerful. The trauma here forestalls the individual's ability to name the event—"I've seen something like that before, and it is . . ."—and forces the viewer to confront an element of the unnamable not just in the experience, but to confront the limit of her ability or desire to name at all.

There is another way to understand the moment that interrupts our ability to name the events of the Holocaust. It is tempting, on a traditional theological view, to understand the rhythms of daily life as something like the manifestation of God in human life. In walking to work, in the details and moments of enjoyment you experience in the work itself, in contemplation or prayer, in watching your children grow up, it's very easy to say that the collection of individual moments from the lifeworld is a reflection, in some small way, of the divine in our lives. And if you think about the lives alluded to in the artifacts that remain from them in a museum, either in the posed photographs of yeshiva students or in the faces of people strolling to no place in particular, you can imagine the points of connection between the intention you believe you see in a person's gait and a similar intention when you smile for photographs at weddings or family reunions. You can also see the horrible accidents of life—crime, the death of a child, the destruction of one's property—as the reverse of this reflection, and there are innumerable instances of such reflections in the museum: the unimaginably huge piles of shoes taken from victims at Majdanek, or the photograph of a ten-year-old boy with his hands raised in surrender at the point of a gun during the uprising in the Warsaw ghetto. But this understanding of one's lived life ties together the divine and the human or historical in such a way that we are able to see one in the other. The phenomenal world (the world of life and death, the world of stories, of laws, of our experiences), and the conceptual (that aspect of life that provides for our capacity to even describe our lived lives as such), and the noumenal (that which we cannot see but can only think, the events themselves) become oddly commensurable. We come to make an easy equation between them: God lives here or, in the reverse, God has died here.

The relation established in such moments, and in such places, in the museums is something else: in the terms Benjamin uses in his essay on translation, it is the relationship between the language of the narratives of history, the languages of our narratives of ourselves, and the idea of "something that cannot be communicated": the pure language that Benjamin imagined was the voice of the divine as it spoke the world into existence. Like the fragments of the broken vessel that are pieced together not to form the whole—this, of course, is not possible—but to convey a *sense* of the vessel as a whole, such displays force the visitor to confront the fragments of a vessel scattered to oblivion by the *einsatzgruppen* that swept through the pale and the Baltic region and later by starvation and gas in the death camps. But Benjamin isn't interested in recuperating the single language of the original or of the translation; his method doesn't hope to recuperate a sense of the culture whose members are caught, fleetingly, in photographs and other artifacts that have been recovered from attics and basements and mantels and archives and fields in Europe, Israel, and the United States. Such a recuperation isn't possible. Instead, what may be redeemed or pieced together are the faces and the experiences evoked by them and the annihilation that acts as the historical backdrop of the exhibit and the memories of the viewer. They

don't form an historical whole, but only the disturbing, traumatic sense
that what you have here precedes and troubles history.

Representations of the Holocaust like the ones we've enumerated here
indicate the division among the noumenal, the conceptual, and the phenomenal, between our capacity to render or name the event and the event as
it is understood by us *as* an event. Far from uniting us with those whose lives
appear to be made accessible to us through the photographs taken by family
members or friends, far from linking an imagined horror in our own lives
with the unseen and unimaginable horror that we know only through the
liquidation of a shtetl, the relation established by that moment of interruption rips a seam in the fabric that could be seen to weave together those moments. The opening that it provides, violent and traumatic enough to reduce
visitors in a public museum to tears, also manages to provide warmth to others. It does so by providing an experience that *cannot* be explained in terms
of the name of the divine, that cannot be explained in the name of God.
This is where the traditional lamentations and questions—"Where was
God?" "God has died on the gallows in Auschwitz"—are instructive: the
name of God would not allow such a thing to happen. But to think in these
terms is to wonder aloud why God isn't as good a person as I am.

Thus Kant's odd statement in the *Critique of Judgment* that "the
most sublime passage in the Jewish law is the commandment: thou shalt
not make unto thee any graven image, or any likeness of any thing that is in
heaven or on the earth" (135). In Hebrew, God is referred to as "hashem"
(the name); Peter Haidu and others who write about the Holocaust refer to
the historical series in Europe from 1933 to 1945 as "the event." It is this
same refusal to name, what Gertrud Koch (referring specifically to film) and
others have recognized as the problem inherent in mimesis, that Kant recognizes in the sublime: naming the event or the divine domesticates it.
(Miriam Bratu Hansen's essay, "*Schindler's List* is not *Shoah*," alludes to the
bilderverbot to say that to argue that Spielberg's film is either too mimetic
or not mimetic enough misses the point: Spielberg's film, whether you like
it or you hate it, works by manipulating the conventions of mimesis, not
by discarding them in favor of direct representation—which is, of course,
impossible, and to which Lanzmann's film eloquently attests.) In all three
cases—Kant's analysis of natural objects or events that cannot be brought
reasonably under conception, the theologian's sense that to presume to
name God is a blasphemy, the Holocaust historian's recognition of the
enormity of the tragedy of the Shoah—there is a recognition that any attempt to represent the traumatic or the excessive object or event tends to
dampen its effect upon our neatly packaged lives. And yet, as Plato recog-

nized (and which most readers of Plato don't), there is at least the possibility that certain representations produce a sense of the irrational capacity of the mind and of being, a possibility that you miss if you try too hard to say what it is. The resistance to the name, the univocal, is the very thing that Kant's third critique points to as the essential quality of art, but also of the human capacity for knowledge.

Representations of the Holocaust—in photographs, in writing, in places like the Children's Memorial at Yad Vashem or in the USHMM—do not reinstantiate the divine by providing the event with a name and a system through which it can be described. Representations of the Holocaust do not mark the point at which inhuman or vastly unethical acts can be explained. Rather, representations of the Holocaust mark the point at which human activity and the capacity to understand it part company. But because one requires a capacity to render narrative sense to activity before one actually renders it, that capacity and the narrative itself are intimately related but not at the level of narrative. They are related at the level of excess, at the point where it is impossible to equate my sense of my daughter, and my imagined view of life in a shtetl in Lithuania, and my knowledge of the events comprising the Holocaust, because they produce an effect that works beyond reason.

The photograph of the woman holding her child, and the desecrated ark of the covenant—or in the case of the Children's Memorial at Yad Vashem, the voices of the children and the litany of names of those who have been extinguished—correspond to two languages and two narratives, fragments of a vessel whose words are spoken not by the dead but which are read by the living. The narratives that one can provide when proceeding through the exhibits at the musems are derived in part from one's family, or national, or religious contexts. And there is the language of the synagogue, whose rhythms and significance are unmistakable in the earnestness of congregants, the reverence shown in the covered heads and in the attention paid to whether the Torah is visible behind the ark's curtains, or to the prayers in the new year that ask God to inscribe us into the book of life. There is another language, a language read over and over again in documents and memoirs of those who survived and those who didn't that names the magnitude of the event of the Shoah and fails to capture it as it is displaced by the individual experiences that comprise it. It is the language of Lucy Dawidowicz, of Raul Hilberg, of Abraham Lewin, and Primo Levi.

In the deafening babel of these languages, none of which corresponds to the others, and none of which can be clearly read or heard, the fragments lie side by side like those fragments of the broken vessel to which Benjamin alludes in his essay on translation. And as they do so, the viewer can imperceptibly make out a sense of the vessel as it may have looked before the fall, before the scattering of languages. The vessel, as it momentarily makes itself apparent, is not the event itself. It is not, as Benjamin took pains to make clear, the *ursprache*, the language of God. It is nothing like the experience of the event of the Shoah or of one of the moments that comprised it for individuals whose faces appear in the recovered Lithuanian photographs or who handled the artifacts arrayed in the Historical Museum at Yad Vashem. What can be read, though, between the image of one's own or one's daughter's life and the lives of the dead is an idea of what works beyond reason, what cannot be said, and how it forms the foundation of what can. You cannot read the thing itself, or the divine in these languages of the living and the dead, but you can read the limit of history and of knowledge. One is left with the sense that the event of the Holocaust and the moments that comprise it cannot be invoked by memory, by narrative, by bringing it to presence, except in the silence, the trauma, that interrupts it—a moment that in Dwight Eisenhower's words as he reported what he saw when American troops liberated the camps, "beggars reality."

Notes

1. The best account of the social, cultural, and political implications of building the USHMM is still Edward Linenthal's *Preserving Memory*. One of his strongest arguments is that the Museum is a peculiarly American construction whose narrative produces a memory that is at least as much universal as it is uniquely "Jewish" or that belongs to the survivors. We did not want to take issue with what we think is a strong argument, since our task here has to do with the structure of memory itself rather than with that memory's content.

2. On the second floor of the USHMM, just beyond the Hall of Memories, is the Wexner Learning Center. Over two dozen computer terminals are connected to a database of text, sound, and video files that can be accessed by visitors. One of the larger sub-files in the database comprises survivor testimonies, some of which run several minutes; a few of them are unbelievably compelling. It is unclear what sense some viewers, seeing faces that remind them of parents or grandparents, will have of the testimonies of Jews who, as children, were sent away to live with Christians and who became bitter and angry when they learned, decades later, that they were Jewish. It depends, one might guess, upon whether the visitors had already proceeded through the Museum's permanent exhibit or visited the Learning Center while waiting to enter it.

3. We are reminded here of a scene early on in Spielberg's *Schindler's List*: as they are being rousted from their well-decorated and ornately furnished apartment in Kracow, a husband and wife try to recover and take with them as many valuables as they can put into suitcases. The camera focuses on silver trays and soup tureens, paintings and vases, left unpacked. As the man passes through the threshold of the apartment with an impatient German soldier behind him, he abruptly stops, wheels around, pulls a penknife out of his pocket, and pries the mezuzah off the lintel, kisses it, and puts it into his pocket. As with the ark in the USHMM, this moment interrupts the sequence of Spielberg's narrative with a simple act that might be recognized by Jews (and many non-Jews) as significant insofar as it juxtaposes one object (the mezuzah) and its significance with the already recognized sequence of events (the deportation to the ghetto).

7

Conclusion:
The Ethics of Teaching
(after) Auschwitz

The Holocaust challenges the claims of all the standards that compete for modern [people's] loyalties. Nor does it give simple clear answers or definitive solutions. To claim that it does is not to take burning children seriously.
Irving Greenberg, "Cloud of Smoke, Pillar of Fire"

We want to start this chapter by asking a simple question: what do we hope to accomplish when we teach, or write about, the Shoah? In the years since 1945 we've heard a lot of answers: so that we never forget; so that something like this could never happen again; so we remember those who perished; so that we can heal or redeem the damage done to the world through anti-Semitism or racial hatred or any number of other symptoms of genocide. We'd like to suggest that although these answers, and others like them—answers that focus our attention on the events of the Holocaust and the broad ethical consequences of it—are compelling and useful, they are nevertheless impossible. They're impossible for two important and connected reasons. The first is that what we have come to understand as knowledge and learning don't so much provide access to an event as they occlude access to it; by allowing us to believe that the event—or any object of knowledge for that matter—can be retrieved, such imperatives elide the symbolization of an event with its occurrence. The second is that the objects through which we do have access to the event—testimony, documentary evidence, museums and memorials, poetry and fiction—are representations of a traumatic, sublime object that is resistant to such attempts to create knowledge. Taken together, both points circle around the same kernel of impossibility, the same occlusion of supposed knowledge and event. And this impossible and traumatic kernel forces us to reconsider what we mean by "learning" about the Holocaust.

Take the fifty-year-old response to the question, why teach or write about the Shoah: to remember, to memorialize the dead so that what they suffered will never happen again. We see this imperative enacted concretely at Yad Vashem in Israel. The historical museum itself contextualizes the Holocaust and the events immediately before and after in terms of a redemption through community. The museum not only covers the rise of Hitler and the beginnings of the Final Solution, but also addresses the ghetto and camp communities as well as the resistance movement. The last quarter of the museum ties these communities to those that attempted to immigrate to Eretz Israel. And as we exit the historical museum, we are confronted with the translated words of Baal Shem Tov: "Forgetfulness leads to exile, while remembrance is the secret of redemption." The museum fulfills these words by defining redemption as the end of exile and the formation of a state. Throughout the museum we move through a narrative history of the Holocaust that both rests in and points towards the state itself. Yad Vashem presents redemption as the building of community.

This circularity of being situated in while pointing towards is the same impossible kernel occluded in all attempts to universalize remembrance. For knowledge in the face of trauma is the very beginnings of community. Universal constructions, however, may not redeem the dead since they do not address the particularities of trauma itself, the individual lives and experiences of those who suffered. Nor are they universal outside of any particular history or system of knowledge. If we think of the history of the Holocaust as a singular set of events that involves not just our capacity to write those events but to have some sense of the lives that were caught up, one by one, in those events, then history itself both demands explanations of particular traumas and complicates the possibility of such explanations. History constructs community or community constructs history by occluding the particular trauma of an event. And those within the community, those who have knowledge, know what they know. This implies a certain barrier to seeing based on an identification with knowledge. Within a community, one must overcome knowledge of oneself, of the community in order to bear witness. Otherwise, one identifies with a given testimony. On the other hand, those who are not within such a community carry the burden of a complete lack of context, of not knowing what's at stake in a given representation, of not being put in the place of ever having to see. Both positions show the complicated epistemological ends to bearing witness: on one end we have those with not enough knowledge, who know nothing of deportations and genocide; at the other end, we have those who know too much, or rather who are too much within knowledge to see what they have already seemingly recognized. In both cases, redemption as we have defined it becomes impossible.

If knowledge is never complete, never wrought so well as to replicate or even directly represent that object or event, then this is especially true of the events comprising the Holocaust. While there is clear documentary evidence available to suggest to us the operations of the mobile killing squads that followed behind the invasion of the Russian and Polish pale, for instance, and there is enough testimonial evidence to suggest to us the experiences of individuals involved in the killing (both survivors and collaborators), that evidence is not enough to provide us with a knowledge of the events. When we teach—and when we learn—we engage in a naming operation that involves discovering new words, regardless of whether we think of learning as transmission or as creation of knowledge. Augustine puts it this way when discussing his own teaching:

> So it is that we bear these images in the deep recesses of the memory as witnesses, so to speak, of things previously experienced by the senses. . . . But these images are only witnesses to ourselves. If the one who hears what I am recounting has seen these things for himself and was there on the spot, he does not learn them from my words, but recognizes them himself by the images he took away with him from these things. But if he has not experienced them with his senses, then it is clearly a matter of his believing my words rather than of learning. ("De Magistro" 53)

Augustine goes even further still, saying that when we understand an object or experience in terms of objects or experiences we have already understood and experienced on our own terms, we have only remembered what we already knew.

Augustine here marks the very impossibility of transmitting the object of knowledge, of offering a singular or even pluralistic way of achieving recognition of an event. One may arrive at an understanding—a universalized position—but something is missing in such an understanding: the encounter with the object is itself not recognizable within knowledge. It is to this problem that purely historical accountings of the Holocaust fall prey, where the trauma of the event is covered over by principles of accounting.

Some representations of the Holocaust avoid such an accounting since they need not attempt to construct adequate universals in and of themselves. Rather, they present a limit to such universal constructions, pointing toward the necessarily impossible nature of a universal knowledge within a universal language (a language that communicates without loss). In other words, these representations defy the epistemological foundation on which academic discourse—teaching discourse—resides. In this sense, representations of the Holocaust transcend any attempt at constructing academic knowledge, subjectifying the very limit that academic discourse must by definition foreclose.

Knowledge and community cannot recover the lives of the six million, let alone allow us to understand the fact of their murder so that nothing like it ever occurs again, because even the recovery of the fragments of the vessel cannot recover the vessel itself, nor can it retrieve the moment of its shattering. The implications of learning as naming are more severe for most of us, who were not there on the spot and who have no point of experience to ground that which we learn: the destruction of a shtetl or the desperation of realizing that there will be no one alive to say kaddish for you can only be understood by encountering these events or moments in terms of events or moments we have already named, or experienced. Presumably we cannot teach or learn that which is beyond memory.

I. Wilkomirski, Ethics, and Teaching

Now, what happens when we learn that a discourse or a testimony of an event to which we have no access, a discourse whose integrity we had taken for granted, turns out to be a lie? This is what happened in the Wilkomirski case when, in Zurich in early 1994, a literary agent received a copy of the manuscript that would eventually become *Fragments*. It is a harrowing account of bewilderment and confusion, murder and atrocity witnessed by a child who was so young at the time that murder and atrocity seemed to be all life—survival—had to offer. The narrative itself moves starkly between the disorientation and horror of the camps to the equally disorienting, normal world of orphanages, foster parents, and "the ordering logic of grownups." More so than in many memoirs, this one seemed to replicate the associations common to involuntary memory, in which a flash of recollection calls up times and places that have only tangentially to do with the spatio-temporal location that could only be called the memory's source. The agent was so affected by the manuscript that she sent it almost immediately to Suhrkamp Verlag in Frankfurt, where it was picked up for publication less than a year later.

Until 1998, *Fragments* stood as an example of the now familiar genre of Holocaust memoir, though a profoundly moving and well-written one. For Daniel Ganzfried, it didn't ring true. He found, and then published, evidence that changed the status of the memoir: it was written by Bruno Doesseker, a clarinet-maker who was born in early 1941 to Yvonne Grosjean, daughter of an unmarried Swiss woman who along with her brother was separated from poor parents as a child. Yvonne gave her son up to foster parents, Kurt and Martha Doesseker, in 1945, and they adopted him twelve years later. The boy's father had paid toward the cost of his son's care up until that time, and in 1981, Doesseker—who now called himself Benjamin Wilkomirski—inherited a small estate on the death of Yvonne Grosjean. From the 1960s until publication of the book in 1995, Doesseker had been obsessed with the Holocaust, and has in his home a substantial library full of memoirs, photographs, and historical accounts of the atrocities committed against Jews and others during the war. Max Grosjean, his natural uncle, was found during Ganzfried's research, and if DNA from a blood sample matches the author's, Ganzfried's case of a forgery would be proved. Doesseker has so far refused to take such a test.

For much of the reading public, and for many scholars of the Shoah, *Fragments* is no longer an instance of memory; it is a lie. As one writer has put it, it now contaminates the Holocaust archive and stands as a testament to the fraudulent use of the events of the Shoah. But even Wilkomirski's staunchest critics seem to think that something horrifying resides at the center of the book, though it may not be the events of the Shoah. Elena Lappin provides one plausible explanation: that as a child Doesseker tried on alternate stories of origin—one friend recalls that "'he used to say that his adoptive parents wanted him as a medical experiment,'" and a couple says he told them in the 1960s that "'he had been in the Warsaw ghetto and was saved from the Holocaust by a Swiss nanny'"—as a way of dealing with the separation from his mother. Worse, if his mother's status as *Verdingkinder* involved her "sale" as indentured servant and involved "beatings and sexual abuse," did the child's separation involve similar horrors? Israel Gutman, himself a Holocaust survivor and a historian of the Shoah, says that Wilkomirski "has written a story which he has experienced deeply, that's for sure" (Lappin 61). Though the story may not be true, and though the onus is on Wilkomirski to clear up the controversy, Deborah Dwork said in an interview with the *New York Times* that Wilkomirski is clearly "a deeply scarred man" who "believes in his identity" (Carvajal). Though the authority of the writer, Bruno Doesseker, has been undermined, the book's status as a testament to witness is so far unimpeached.

One way to sort through the controversy is by asking what we think *Fragments* teaches. If we take Ganzfried's charges at face value, and see the memoir as a fraud—the record of events imagined but not experienced by the author—then clearly we have in Doesseker a deeply flawed man and, in passing off this fiction as memoir, a severely unethical act. But what Lappin and Gourevitch note, and what Deborah Dwork, Israel Gutman, and many others say in spite of themselves, is that the memoir itself indicates the site of a trauma (though perhaps not the trauma of the Holocaust) and that the figural intensity of the book is what provides it authority. This latter view is consonant with Cathy Caruth's work, the focus of which is the victim of "a shocking accident" who "gets away, apparently unharmed" (16), a person whose knowledge of events, and whose ability to transfer that knowledge to others, is ambiguous at best. "[T]he victim of the [accident] was never fully conscious during the accident itself. . . . The experience of trauma, the fact of latency, would thus seem to consist, not in the forgetting of a reality that can hence never be fully known, but in an inherent latency within the experience itself" (17). The testimony of the victim or the survivor is marked by absences or gaps—seen, often, in gestures or pauses or fits of anger or weeping in videotaped testimonies of Holocaust survivors that leave, through their repetition, a sense of the event that has been lost.

Shoshana Felman's understanding of trauma parallels Caruth's, though her work focuses more on the language that follows the occurrence of the event. The individual "speaks in advance of the control of consciousness, his testimony is delivered in 'breathless gasps': in essence it is a *precocious testimony* . . . that speak[s] beyond its means," that testifies to the event "whose origin cannot be precisely located but whose repercussions, in their very uncontrollable and unanticipated nature, still continue to evolve even in the very process of testimony" (Felman 29, 30). Though the witness is, in Felman's words, pursued by the obligation to speak, she is not necessarily pursued by the obligation to provide an historically accurate accounting of the event, because the event as such has disappeared. Felman recognizes that such testimony has a "freeing" effect (see 47–8), one like that cited by Wilkomirski as well as by those familiar with his "story": he says "I wanted my own certainty back, and I wanted my voice back, so I began to write . . . [in] an attempt to set myself free" (154, 155).

What complicates matters is that, for Felman, the trauma that pursues the witness also pursues witnesses to the witnessing. In her seminar at Yale, her students experienced what she calls a "crisis" of witnessing, in which—after reading poetry and narratives of witness, and after viewing several videotaped testimonies from the Fortunoff Archive—her students became profoundly ill at ease with what they were seeing, and broke into an "endless and relentless talking" about the class, talking that Felman heard about through phone calls at odd hours, letters, questions from students' roommates. The accident, the "disaster," whose representations had been read and viewed by the class—which, by implication, were not records of the events but were instead their detritus, their trace—had, according to Felman, "*happened* in the class, happened *to* the class. The accident had *passed through* the class" (52, Felman's emphasis). The trace or abyss of the event that made itself evident in the "stuttering" of the texts—their silences, their incommensurabilities, their figural displacements—produced an anxiety in Felman's students. Texts that bear witness to the forgotten event, the disaster of history, keep the reader from making sense of the narrative and what results is a break or a crisis. The resulting talk—the testimony of the secondhand witness—can only "be made sense of" (Felman's terms) by connecting this uncanniness to the individual's own experience, to "work through" the resulting chaos by producing a narrative that puts it in its proper place (see Felman 54–7; see also LaCapra, *Representing* 211–20). Two of the end-of-semester papers cited by Felman make the point. One student achieves closure by bridging the abyss of the event witnessed by the writers she had read by referring to her father's experiences during the Chinese civil war. "What sorts of burdens has this passed on to me?" the student asks. She continues, "I feel a strange sort of collectivity has been formed in this class." A second student, "caught between two contradictory wishes at once, to speak or not to speak, I can only stammer." He will turn, as a result, to literature, and "read as if for life" (58). Both students have found a need to fill the abyss of the event, what has been forgotten and irretrievably lost to history, with language, though a language not their own—in the first case, the language of a parent whose narrative of his experiences succumbs to the same discursive problems as any other testimony, and in the second case, the language of literature.

It is not the traumatic act—the murder of infants or the moment when a child realizes that he no longer has a mother—that is visible in the memoir of a Holocaust survivor. What is visible is the structure of trauma made apparent in these painful narratives that try but fail to muster a language capable of making the viewer, the reader, see. Wilkomirski's "memoir" does not so much teach events that, taken together with others, comprise the Shoah; instead it points to "another reality," the event as it washes over the memory of the author and stands in the way of the narrative recollection of history. The content of the memoir as a marker of the writer's authority is tenuous at best: Gourevitch and Lappin both found troubling evidence that it was impossible for Wilkomirski to be where he claims to have been. But the effect of the memoir, as it indicates a destruction both of narrative and of consciousness that seems to evidence a trauma consistent with that of someone who "got away apparently unharmed," seems to grant an authority to its author in spite of our questions about his status as a survivor of the historical circumstances of the Shoah. The words of the victim "do not simply refer, but, through their repetition . . . convey the impact of a history precisely as what cannot be grasped" about the event itself (Caruth 21). The words of the victim do not teach the event; instead they act as a reminder of the event as it precedes the survivor's ability to bring it to language at all.

Of course, such a view of testimony gives us no way to adjudicate the competing claims of Bruno Doesseker and Daniel Ganzfried, because to compare the authenticity of the narrative with the facts of history would be to confuse the narrative with the events themselves. If the adoption records provided by the Swiss government are genuine and show that Wilkomirski was born in Switzerland, this extrinsic fact does not only undermine the speaker's authority if, as Wilkomirski writes, children who survived the Shoah were often "furnished with false names and often with false papers" so that they would not be shipped to the East as stateless persons. It also serves to complicate the matter of history further. As for the narrative itself, and its depiction of events that bore it, its gaps cannot be said simply to represent inaccuracies; rather—as Caruth suggests, speaking of Freud—they also represent and "preserve [another] history precisely within this gap in his text" (21).

II. Teaching, Ethics, and Denial

But how do we teach the events if even testimonies themselves provided by people who were there are subject to the dynamic of trauma and forgetting that the Wilkomirski text—as an extreme and controversial example—suggests? As much as we endeavor to bring students and peers to recognize the difficulty inherent in creating knowledge of what could only be called a limit event, that endeavor is met with incredulity, frustration, and—if Felman is right—a correspondent trauma in our audience. One way to respond, in the face of the complexity of the issues at hand, to what Blanchot calls the "utter burn of history" is to turn your back on it: "Gets on your nerves, seeing that every day" (*Shoah* 93). The logic of denial, political and racial agendas notwithstanding, is founded on this premise: something so horrible and counterrational simply cannot be contained by means of the conceptual or logical categories we have constructed for the sense data of everyday occurrences. The events of the Shoah, then, must therefore have conformed to some logic that we have overlooked: the Nazis were responding to the threat of Jewish Bolshevism; Jews were not systematically killed but died of the starvation that comes in wartime.

We want to describe here an instance of just such an occurrence of denial, and to suggest its implications for ethics and pedagogy. This was in a course on the Holocaust that was focused specifically on the problems inherent in writing the event—and here we had in mind not only the difficulties suggested by contributors to Berel Lang's book of a few years ago, but more fundamentally the ones suggested by Lyotard and Blanchot. The course began with clear documentary evidence that laid out the operations of the Final Solution and with testimonial evidence that suggests the *experiences* of individuals involved in it. What we realized, and what students in the course began to realize, is that this evidence is not enough to provide a comprehensive knowledge of the events and the experiences of the survivors or perpetrators. Knowing the events of the Shoah cannot possibly be equated with the horror of the events, with the irrationality of its logic, or with the pain it brings to those confronted with its representation.

Rather than focus attention on what can be learned from representations—from writing—of the events of the Shoah, class members examined, instead, the degree to which any attempt to make sense of the event would be marred or disrupted by what might be called the event's trace. We read, in the first third of the course, a number of memoirs written by survivors, and sections from several historical accounts—by Hilberg, Dawidowicz, Gilbert, Browning—of the events remembered; assignments were designed to examine not simply how writing "conveyed" knowledge but how writing stood in the way of the event. As in the case of the Wilkomirski "memoir," we encouraged students to investigate, through writing, the relation between the traumatic or sublime event and the (sometimes precocious) testimony that gave historians and laypeople access to, and in some cases occluded, it. By the tenth week of a sixteen-week semester, many students were extremely frustrated. Coming into the class, many of them had assumed that we would find a way to name the events of the Shoah, to pin it down once and for all so that it could be put at a safe distance, or so that they could at least work to place it there. It was, after all, more than fifty years in the past, and so the imperative to remember seemed urgent to many—how could such a thing have happened, and how can we prevent it from happening again? But by putting pressure on the language with which the events of the Shoah were described, we were also putting pressure on the easy relation of language and event, and of experience and knowledge. Far from being able to understand the Holocaust, many students found that as they tried to write what they had learned, they were confounded by the trace of the event, that aspect of the Shoah—its irrationality, the vertigo of unreason—that prevents it from being written, named, or known.

It was in the face of this frustration that one student proposed, over an electronic listserve devoted to class members, a paper that attempted to prove that the Holocaust had not occurred. The course instructor responded, again publicly, that such a paper would not be allowed: in part because of the problems inherent in proving a negative, and in part because of the disruption such a topic (and the attendant discussion) would cause in the class. The student was advised to choose another topic. The proposal, and the discussions that took place in the wake of its disallowance, uncovered a curious ethical dimension of pedagogy. It focused our attention on the ways in which universal knowledge—even a knowledge that insists upon the nonoccurrence of an event—stands in the way of the moment of seeing, the seeing that occurs when representations break down in the face of what can't be adequately represented.

Given that the course we offered was focused particularly on the kinds of pressures exerted on writing by the Shoah, it may seem like something of a contradiction to disallow a paper that so clearly responds to that pressure by invoking trauma's inverse: denial. And, in fact, the issue was raised by students in the course, on the grounds that by writing the argument that it did not occur one would learn the futility of the argument and, in turn, of the event's occurrence. But such a position ignored the ethical implications of the issue, by which we mean the particular instances of seeing as opposed to the ways in which we build a systematic approach to dealing with what we have seen. We anticipated that this was not going to be a paper on what one could not know or how a given knowledge was inadequate to a real trauma. Rather, by offering to write a paper that disproved the Holocaust, a paper that cancelled out the trauma before it could begin, the student was attempting to avoid the very messy and uncomfortable encounter with representation itself, with the trace of horror that resides in knowledge. (This problem, of course, was the objective of the class.) Even more, the student's proposal aimed to reify the notion of ethics as a *knowledge*-based system, a system that avoids questions of temporal disturbances like seeing. In other words, we were concerned that in arguing that the Holocaust did not occur, or that it was exaggerated, the student would simply be building another knowledge, using discourse as a way to keep trauma at bay. This kind of learning comes at the expense of (ethical) effect, an effect that has little to do with logic, but which has everything to do with the extralogical, irrational, traumatic underside of events like the Shoah. Whatever one may learn through the deniers' argument, one does so at the expense of seeing. And it is precisely the effects of seeing—seeing the traces of the event itself, or the way in which the event mars the lives and the histories we build for ourselves to fend off the disaster—that the denier will attempt to foreclose for everyone, both by his "knowledge" and by the reaction it provokes in others to construct a "better" knowledge that cannot be undermined, that would be barren of un-knowledge.

It is unwarranted to suggest that it is unethical to teach a course on the Holocaust that does not lead to a certain trajectory—that the Holocaust, and other holocausts, should be prevented; that "Jew" and "gentile" are categories that should best be abandoned in favor of a kinship of people; etc.—because ethics maps individual instances of seeing, of witness. As we have tried to show, representations of the Shoah present us with a challenge to traditional notions of ethics as a rational system of choices moving us—as a "we" or a community—toward the good. What we see in films like *Shoah* and *Schindler's List*, in both the USHMM and Yad Vashem, in Lyotard and Blanchot, is inevitably a *failure* of an ethics based upon a "good." What we have in those cases is an ethics based on a point of impasse, a moment before the establishment of a foundation, a foundation that we'd call "moral". In this sense, an ethics of representation—and thus an ethics of pedagogy—rests in providing a moment where the "good" fails, where morality fails, where knowledge fails, where one's very community, identity—the "we" of community—fails. As soon as one chooses what "the good" is, what one knows or is, one risks counting out one's fellows and one's neighbors, and what choices one makes may well be harmful to them in accordance with the logic of that good.

To found a pedagogy of the Holocaust upon morality is to ignore that the Shoah was a fundamentally extralogical event and that events of history resist interpretation or methodological neatness. The decision to rule out a paper denying the Holocaust was an attempt to forestall a series of choices: writing such a paper—even in the best of circumstances— would inevitably have forced its writer into the position of affirming the existence of the Holocaust in terms of certainty, knowledge, categories of distinction that rest on the foundation of logic at the exclusion of the very real and excruciating traces the event leaves not just on the survivors but on anyone who comes into contact with the event. Ruling it out of court was designed to maintain the ethical possibilities of the classroom, not to close them down. In effect, the choice was designed—at the expense of frustration and at the expense of the imperative to create a memory of the event that rests on things we already know—to leave open the gap between our ability to name and the name itself.

Ethics is a system of choices but it is also a moment in which one takes a single path. The ethical moment is brief, and it is unique—your choices are going to be different from mine, though perhaps only slightly so, because the moment in which you do the choosing is different, though perhaps only by seconds, from the one in which I choose—and it can't be determined. For all the planning a teacher does, for all the thinking that a legislator does in making the laws, there will be choices s/he cannot have imagined before the fact. Laws have loopholes; ethics do too. As much as we'd have liked for everyone in our class to come away with the sense that the Holocaust was horrible, should never have happened, but can happen again unless we are vigilant, we could never guarantee it. We can set up, responsibly, a set of choices. But we can't force students down any single path. To do so might be the *moral* thing to do. But to force a moral upon a person leads to certainty, and it was certainty—that Jews were subhuman, that the thousand-year Reich was the culmination of history—and its logic that led to the Final Solution.

There is a moment in which the events of history, or the moments of a lived life—the look on a parent's face that implies unconditional love for a child and that cannot foresee that child's moment of annihilation—and the name we provide for it meet at an impasse. This impasse is the limit of knowledge: it is the moment of recognition during prayer where the kabbalist's recitation of the attributes of the divine is transformed into the recognition that the divine exceeds the capability to name them. It is the moment in which we at once seem to recognize in the faces in a photograph something like moments in our own lives—in which we provide for ourselves a certain, stunning knowledge that the lives of those living in Ejzsysky are like the lives of our grandparents or our own two generations later—while realizing with the force of history that their destruction was utterly unlike anything that we might try to name. This is not the redemption of, or learning about, the events we imagine occurred in 1941 in Lithuania, or in the sixty years before their abrupt end. This is a redemption that forestalls the individual's ability to name the event—"I've seen something like that before, and it is . . ."—and forces the viewer to confront an element of the unnamable not just in the experience, but to confront the limit of her ability or desire to name at all. It was just this sense of redemption that we were trying to hold open in our pedagogy.

III. Teaching (after) Auschwitz

We want to conclude by briefly drawing out some of the implications of the foregoing. The first has to do with claims that Wilkomirski's text is tantamount to Holocaust denial, and the second has to do with contemporary claims about the relation of writing and reality. What if, as Ganzfried, Hilberg, and others claim, Doesseker's "memories," and the trauma that he so clearly seems to have experienced, are patently false? This is all the more disturbing if it leads, as Philip Blom has suggested, to an "ero[sion of] the very ground on which remembrance can be built" (Blom) and leads eventually to "a new revisionism that no longer attacks the truth of the Holocaust but only individual claims of survival" (Peskin). Does the ambivalent relation of testimony to knowledge and learning allow for such a radical reading of the Wilkomirski memoir? It is, in fact, entirely consistent with what we have said so far that the nature of events rendered in discourse can only be established individually: that it is impossible to understand whether or not "the Holocaust" occurred in all of its horrible detail because any rendering of the event—either through eyewitness testimony or with the broad brushes of history or panoramic films like *Schindler's List* or *Shoah*—risks giving us the mistaken impression that what we hear or see in the testimony is what the eyewitness herself saw, or that the individual narrative can stand as a substitute for the larger historical narrative. This was the point made during the debates that followed the release of *Schindler's List* in 1994. Reviewers in the roundtable discussion printed in the *Village Voice* in March of that year worried that the American viewing public would equate the movie with the event, and conclude that, in the end, it wasn't all so terrible. What was remarkable about that roundtable discussion, and about nearly every discussion that took place after the film's premiere, is that every participant in the debate "saw" something quite different in the film. This is partly due to the nature of the pedagogical enterprise.

Since Richard Rorty told us once and for all that we do not establish truth through discourse as much as we produce arguments for a certain view of it, we have simply taken for granted the idea that no argument, no matter how strong and no matter the integrity of the speaker, will settle a matter once and for all. Arguments produce contingent truths that can be later tested for consistency, but those contingent truths are established through the argument itself. It is significant that in this view of knowledge there are few guarantees that what is learned in one "conversation" or testimony will be learned the same way in another. This view of the pedagogical enterprise is not new: in the *Phaedrus,* Plato's Socrates is at pains to show that, ideally, writing is indicative of what lies behind knowledge rather than productive of knowledge. The successful teacher is the one who is able to convince his students not that what he says is true, but that what he says, while not true, has an effect that points to what language fails to represent. And this effect—writing as a reminder of what was once inherent in the soul but is now inaccessible to it (*Phaedrus* 277e–278a)—is a radically individual one, an effect that is different from soul to soul, from listener to listener, from witness to witness. To return now to Philip Blom's worry that the Wilkomirski narrative introduces a new sort of Holocaust denial that questions not the occurrence of the event but individual testimonies that, taken together, might testify to it, he is right to be concerned. He is right to say that if we can undermine the authority of the writer of a Holocaust testimony, and say with certainty that he was never there and that he did not see what he claims to have seen, we have eliminated one piece of evidence that we can use to argue that the atrocities of the Shoah occurred. Such testimonies—in the form of eyewitness accounts, documentary evidence, trial transcripts, and diaries—taken together form the tapestry of suffering that we have inherited as the narrative of the Holocaust. But such testimonies, as accounts of traumatic events that are inaccessible even to the memories of those who survived, let alone those who claim to have done so or those who read their accounts, function in similar ways and have similar effects: they establish the credibility of the speaker, and indicate an event as it occurs prior to her ability to speak it, not so much in their accordance with the facts of history (facts that are accessible only through narrative) but in the way they disrupt the narrative of history and force the reader, or the interviewer, to see something horrible, perhaps a trace of the traumatic event itself. These effects are *only* available one witness, one reader, one student at a time. In the case of the Wilkomirski memoir, we may well be able to undermine the authority of the speaker if we take him to be trying to establish a narrative of the circumstances of the Holocaust that will settle the matter once and for all. The converse is also true: his lack of credibility does seem to throw open to question the veracity of testimonies of other survivors. But this is not to say that it lessens the traumatic effect of the testimony, or the testimony's ability to indicate something about the nature of the disaster, though that disaster may not be the historical events we call the Shoah. Elena Lappin suggests that Bruno Doesseker has indeed suffered some shocking accident in the events surrounding his separation from his mother, or the years in which he lived in orphanages or foster care or in the care of adoptive parents. Such an event renders the uncanny effect of the memoir's metonymic language as an indication of an event that is not only inaccessible to his readers but inaccessible to himself as well. As we have said, Philip Blom has reason to worry about the effect of Wilkomirski's lack of credibility. But he should worry about the very same problem in each and every survivor testimony.

The pedagogical implications of this are complicated. We have paid a good deal of attention in the last several years to the Holocaust in high school and university classes, particularly to the ways in which the events, as rendered in fiction and in testimonial accounts, can be seen as points of departure for discussions of diversity, or race hatred, or the role of resistance, or any number of other controversial topics. The assumption we generally make in courses like these is that their goal should be the production of knowledge of the events of the Shoah and, whenever possible, to connect that knowledge with other knowledges—of the dynamics of poverty, or of racism, or of other disasters or genocides. But while there is clear documentary evidence available to substantiate the occurrence of events like the gassings at Chelmno, and though there is enough testimonial evidence to suggest to us the *experiences* of individuals involved in the killing (both survivors and collaborators), that evidence cannot bring knowledge into accord with the events themselves. We've seen this time and time again in writing classes associated with the Holocaust: faced with the enormity of the events as described in halting, incomplete, and yet horrifying testimonies and documents, students have a very difficult time evaluating that writing, let alone trying to find language with which to write themselves. How can you possibly assess the authority of the sources you read, and the character of the witnesses who have written them, when you are absolutely shattered by their effect?

This effect is hardly knowledge, or at least it doesn't qualify as knowledge of the events the testimonies provide. To return to Augustine's *The Teacher*, we could say that he is attempting to show that what we know we know in terms of either disciplinary or communitarian senses of the world. We may avoid the myopia of a single discipline's paradigm through what Sandra Harding and others have called "standpoint epistemology," an examination of an object or event from the perspective of more than a single conceptual scheme, but in the end the tendency is to provide the event (or its components, or its facets) with a name.

The effect of a discourse, of a testimony, cannot function as evidence of the authority or veracity of the witness, if by that we mean "getting it right." But if we take seriously the idea that learning occurs when a witness indicates the event as it exceeds her ability to write or name it, then perhaps the goal of writing courses that account for the events of the Holocaust should not be to produce knowledge—either through analysis of documents, testimonies, and literature, or through the production of essays linking anti-Semitism to contemporary racism—but to indicate the elusiveness of the traumatic experience that is in some cases indicated by written language. If Cathy Caruth is right about the nature of trauma, then it should be no surprise that evaluating the effectiveness of a witness's account of the horrors of the camps and evaluating the veracity of the account point in two opposing directions. And though it's plausible that Bruno Doesseker is a charlatan, it's also plausible that the testimony he provides of the experience of a child by the name of Binjamin Wilkomirski is a narrative account of a trauma to which he has no access but whose effect is visible in the metonymic, repetitive effect of its language.

IV. Testimony and the End of Teaching

Returning to Adorno's comment about the music of the SS drowning out the screams of their victims, we see the problems of defining a narrative—of making sense—of the impossibility of trauma, of screams. By reading representations of the Shoah solely in terms of testimony (or knowledge) we miss the moments of seeing, the moments of witnessing. Such a perverse vision of the Holocaust—as a knowledge that we can see and know and speak and understand—rejects the real epistemological significance of representations like some of those we have discussed in this book, representations that consistently point towards the inconsistency of knowledge itself. In this way, such representations are founded on an epistemology of the impasse, on that which cannot be expressed by the historical or the factual since it is the impasse that must be narrated over as cause of knowledge, as cuts into the symbolic or historical, as responses to an irresolvable question of identity. A movie like *Schindler's List*, for example, places the viewer in the position of having to recognize the ends of knowledge itself, of seeing the misperception necessary for understanding and thus questions the very foundations from which testimony is spoken, not in terms of historical fact, but in terms of the inability to represent trauma *as* trauma.

For representations of the Holocaust, the end offers a means by which we can see the relationship between history and memory, between understanding and recognition. Witnessing involves the recognition of the silence necessary in the act of speaking or understanding, situating one structurally in terms of a movement from the impossible to the actual and back to the impossible. Here is the ethical position inherent in Adorno's negative dialectics and Lyotard's differend and Blanchot's utter burn. In this sense, Berel Lang is correct to rewrite "the limit of representation" as the "the representation of limits." But even in this move we need to go further in thinking about how the end of representation, its eradication, is ultimately the goal of representation, that the limits of representation are both its constraint and its object. And fiction, testimony, and other representations of the Shoah show the gulf inherent in narrative representation, the limits of the classical mode by which it constructs the diegesis.

What does it mean to consider representation in terms of its ends? In reactions to *Schindler's List* and *Life is Beautiful*, people attacked the films for their focus on certain kinds of survivors and their exclusion of others. Such attacks define the narrative of the film in universal terms, as the music of the SS, as constructing a "we" that excludes (as all "we"s do). But what if the end of representation is not the construction of a we, but its foreclosure, its impossibility in the face of some trauma? It is this end that Adorno prioritizes and Lyotard recognizes: that in the construction of a we or an I in the face of the Holocaust there remains a kernel that resists such a construction, that both causes and eludes the identification necessary for all representation. This is the distinction between being in the place of bearing witness and in the place of testifying. The first is a position of nonknowledge, of not knowing or understanding, only seeing. The second position takes the place of witnessing, of bearing the burden of not knowing by attempting to know.

So what does Holocaust representation and its ethics tell us about teaching? If the end of representation is a nonknowledge, a position from which one cannot speak, how do we teach such a moment without falling into knowledge as a universal answer that erases an encounter with trauma, an encounter that must be particular? Academic discourse—teaching discourse—necessarily works from the position that the teacher has something to teach, that an encounter with knowledge is universal rather than particular (otherwise we wouldn't have tests or other means of evaluation). So, it

seems inevitable to say that the Holocaust marks the end of teaching (a termination of teaching) or that teaching is an impossible profession (both of
which we believe). We need to teach *that what we are supposed to know we do
not know*, that the most crucial—hence most radically particular—learning
is not to be found in the fabric of our lectures, tests, essays, understandings,
or knowledge of the event. Rather, for students to learn particularly they
must be able to recognize that teaching involves the making of Schindler's
and Stern's lists, that the lesson or the point or the difficulty rests not in
terms of what is actually on such a list, what we know, but the gulf that surrounds it, that which the list necessarily silences, the cost of what we know.
Otherwise we run the risk of teaching our students that knowledge solves
difference, that they can identify with a "we" or an "I" that will be enough
to silence the screams. And it is this entry into a "we" that Levi sees as the
first step in the syllogism whose only logical conclusion is the Lager. Perhaps
this pedagogy is best represented by Michael Berenbaum, who begins and
ends his *The World Must Know* with the words of another teacher:

> A veteran prisoner in Sachsenhausen would inform new arrivals of
> the rules of camp life, of the difficulties they would have to endure,
> of the darkness that awaited them. He told them what was to be—
> honestly, directly, and without adornment. He concluded his re-
> marks with the words: "I have told you this story not to weaken you.
> But to strengthen you. Now it is up to you!" (Berenbaum 3)

Bibliography

Adorno, Theodor W. "Commitment." *Notes for Literature*. Trans. Shierry Nicholsen. New York: Columbia University Press, 1992. 76–94.

———. *The Culture Industry*. Ed. J.M. Bernstein. New York: Routledge, 1991.

———. *Negative Dialectics*. Trans. E.B. Ashton. New York: Seabury Press, 1973.

———. *Prisms*. Trans. Samuel and Shierry Weber. Cambridge, MA: MIT Press, 1981.

Alkana, Joseph. "'Do We Not Know the Meaning of Aesthetic Gratification?': Cynthia Ozick's *The Shawl*, Akedah, and the Ethics of Holocaust Literary Aesthetics." *Modern Fiction Studies* 43.4 (1997): 963–90.

Appelfeld, Aharon. *Age of Wonders*. Boston: David Godine, 1981.

———. *Badenheim 1939*. Boston: David Godine, 1980.

———. *The Immortal Bartfuss*. New York: Grove Press, 1988.

———. *To the Land of the Cattails*. New York: Weidenfeld and Nicolson, 1986.

Ankersmit, F. R. "Historiography and Postmodernism." *History and Theory* 28.2 (1989) and 29.3 (1990).

Augustine. "De Magistro." *Fathers of the Church*. Trans. Robert P. Russell. Vol. 59. Washington: Catholic University of America Press, 1968.

Bartov, Omer. "Spielberg's Oskar: Hollywood Tries Evil." *Spielberg's Holocaust*. Ed. Yosefa Lishitsky. Bloomington: Indiana University Press, 1997. 41–60.

Benigni, Roberto, dir. *Life is Beautiful*. Universal Studios, 1998.

Benjamin, Walter. *Illuminations*. Trans. Harry Zohn. New York: Schocken, 1968.

———. *Reflections*. Trans. E. Jephcott. New York: Harcourt, Brace, Jovanovich, 1978.

———. "Theses on the Philosophy of History." *Illuminations*. 253–64.

Bennington, Geoffrey and Robert Young. "Introduction: Posing the Question." Ed. D. Attridge, G. Bennington, and R. Young, *Post-Structuralism and the Question of History*. Cambridge: Cambridge University Press, 1987.

Bernard-Donals, Michael. "Beyond the Question of Authenticity: Witness and Testimony in the *Fragments* Controversy." *PMLA* [forthcoming].

Berenbaum, Michael. *The World Must Know*. Boston: Little, Brown and Company, 1993.

Bernstein, Michael Andre. *Foregone Conclusions: Against Apocalyptic History*. Berkeley, CA: University of California Press, 1994.

Biale, David. *Gershom Scholem: Kabbala and Counterhistory*. Cambridge, MA: Harvard University Press, 1979.

Blanchot, Maurice. *The Writing of the Disaster*. Trans. Ann Smock. Lincoln, NE: Bison/University of Nebraska Press, 1980.

Blom, Philip. "In a Country . . ." *The Independent* (London) 30 September 1998, Features 1+.

Borowski, Tadeusz. *This Way for the Gas, Ladies and Gentlemen,* 2nd Ed. Trans. Barbara Vedder. New York: Penguin, 1967.

———. "A Day at Harmenz." *This Way for the Gas, Ladies and Gentlemen.*

———. "This Way for the Gas, Ladies and Gentlemen." *This Way for the Gas, Ladies and Gentlemen.*

Browning, Christopher. "The Decision Concerning the Final Solution." *Unanswered Questions: Nazi Germany and the Genocide of the Jews*. Ed. Francois Furet. New York: Schocken, 1989. 96–118.

———. "One Day in Jozefow: Initiation to Mass Murder." *Lessons and Legacies: The Meaning of the Holocaust in a Changing World*. Ed. Peter Hayes. Evanston, IL: Northwestern University Press, 1991. 196–209.

Cantor, Jay. "Death and the Image." *Tri/Quarterly* 79 (Fall 1990): 173–95.

Caruth, Cathy. "Unclaimed Experience: Trauma and the Possibility of History." *Yale French Studies* (1991) 79: 181–92.

———. *Unclaimed Experience: Trauma, Narrative, and History*. Baltimore: Johns Hopkins University Press, 1995.

Carvajal, Doreen. "A Holocaust Memoir in Doubt." *New York Times* 3 Nov. 1998, E1+.

Cayrol, Jean. "Night and Fog." *Film: Book 2, Films of Peace and War*. Ed. Robert Hughes. Grove Press: New York, 1962. 234–55.

Certeau, Michel de. *The Practice of Everyday Life*. Trans. Stephen Randall. Berkeley: University of California Press, 1984.

Crowther, Paul. *The Kantian Sublime: From Morality to Art.* Oxford: Clarendon/Oxford University Press, 1989.

Dawidowicz, Lucy. *The War Against the Jews, 1933–1945.* New York: Holt, Rinehart and Winston, 1975.

Denby, David. "In the Eye of the Beholder: Another Look at Roberto Benigni's Holocaust Fantasy." *The New Yorker* 15 March 1999, 96–99.

Eckhardt, Alice and A. R. Eckhardt. "Studying the Holocaust's Impact Today: Some Dilemmas of Language and Method." *Echoes from the Holocaust: Philosophical Reflections on a Dark Time.* Ed. Alan Rosenberg and Gerald E. Myers. Philadelphia: Temple University Press 1989.

Felman, Shoshana and Dori Laub. *Testimony: Crises of Witnessing in Literature, Psychoanalysis, and History.* New York: Routledge, 1992.

Finkelstein, Norman. *The Ritual of New Creation: Jewish Tradition and Contemporary Literature.* Albany: State University Press of New York, 1992.

Fortunoff Video Archives for Holocaust Testimonies, Yale University.

Freud, Sigmund. *Moses and Monotheism.* Trans. Katherine Jones. New York: Vintage, 1955.

Friedlander, Saul. "The 'Final Solution': On the Unease in Historical Interpretation." *Lessons and Legacies: The Meaning of the Holocaust in a Changing World.* Ed. Peter Hayes. Evanston, IL: Northwestern University Press, 1991.

———. "Historical Writing and the Memory of the Holocaust." *Writing and the Holocaust.* Ed. Berel Lang. New York: Holmes and Maier, 1988. 66–77.

———. *Memory, History, and the Extermination of the Jews of Europe.* Bloomington: Indiana University Press, 1993.

———, ed. *Probing the Limits of Representation.* Cambridge, MA: Harvard University Press, 1992.

———. *Reflections of Nazism.* New York: Harper and Row, 1984.

Funkenstein, Amos. "Collective Memory and Historical Consciousness." *History and Memory* 1 (1989): 5–26.

———. "History, Counterhistory, and Narrative." in Friedlander, *Probing the Limits of Representation,* 66–81.

———. "Theological Interpretations of the Holocaust." *Unanswered Questions: Nazi Germany and the Genocide of the Jews.* Ed. Francois Furet. New York: Schocken, 1989.

Gilbert, Martin. *Holocaust: A History of the Jews During the Second World War.* New York: Holt, Rinehart and Winston, 1985.

Ginzburg, Carlo. "Just One Witness." *Probing the Limits of Representation: Nazism and the "Final Solution".* Ed. Saul Friedlander. Cambridge, MA: Harvard University Press, 1992. 82–96.

Gourevitch, Philip. "The Memory Thief." *The New Yorker* 14 June 1999, 48–68.

———. "What They Saw at the Holocaust Museum." *New York Times Magazine*. 12 February 1995, 44–5.

Greenberg, Irving. "Cloud of Smoke, Pillar of Fire," in *Holocaust: Religious and Philosophical Implications*. Ed. John K. Roth and Michael Berenbaum. New York: Paragon House, 1989. 305–45.

Haidu, Peter. "The Dialectics of Unspeakability: Language, Silence, and the Narratives of Desubjectification," in Friedlander, *Probing the Limits of Representation*, 277–99.

Handelman, Susan. *Fragments of Redemption*. Bloomington: Indiana University Press, 1991.

Hansen, Miriam Bratu. "*Schindler's List* is not *Shoah*: Second Commandment, Popular Modernism, and Public Memory." *Critical Inquiry* 22.2 (Winter 1995): 292–312.

Hatley, James. "Impossible Mourning: Two Attempts to Remember Annihilation." *Centennial Review* 35.3 (Fall 1991): 445–60.

Hartman, Geoffrey. "The Book of the Destruction," in Friedlander, *Probing the Limits of Representation*, 318–34.

———. "The Cinema Animal." *Salmagundi* 106/7 (Spring/Fall 1995): 227–46.

Hecht, Anthony. "More Light! More Light!" *The Hard Hours*. New York: Atheneum, 1967.

Hilberg, Raul. *The Destruction of the European Jews*. Chicago: Quadrangle, 1961.

———. "I Was Not There." *Writing and the Holocaust*. Ed. Berel Lang. New York: Holmes and Meier, 1988.

Hoberman, J. "*Schindler's List*: Myth, Movie, and Memory." *Village Voice* 29 (March 1994): 24–31.

Horowitz, Sara. "But is it Good for the Jews? Spielberg's Schindler and the Aesthetics of Atrocity." *Spielberg's Holocaust*. Ed. Yosefa Lishitsky. Bloomington: Indiana University Press, 1997. 119–39.

Howe, Irving. "Writing and the Holocaust." *Writing and the Holocaust*. Ed. Berel Lang. New York: Holmes and Maier, 1988. 175–99.

Idel, Moshe. *Kabbala: New Perspectives*. New Haven: Yale University Press, 1988.

Jabes, Edmond. *From the Desert to the Book*. Trans. Pierre Joris. Barrytown, NY: Station Hill, 1990.

Jay, Martin. "Of Plots, Witnesses, and Judgments." *Probing the Limits of Representation: Nazism and the "Final Solution."* Ed. Saul Friedlander. Cambridge, MA: Harvard University Press, 1992. 97–107.

Kant, Immanuel. *The Critique of Judgment*. Trans. Werner Pluhar. Indianapolis: Hackett, 1987.

———. *Prolegomena to Any Future Metaphysics*. Trans. James Ellington. Indianapolis: Hackett, 1985.

Kaufmann, Yehezkel. *The Religion of Israel: From its Beginnings to the Babylonian Exile*. Trans. Moshe Greenberg. Chicago: University of Chicago Press, 1960.

Kauvar, Elaine M. *Cynthia Ozick's Fiction: Tradition and Invention*. Bloomington: Indiana University Press, 1993. See "The Magic Shawl," 179–202.

Kikhiwczak, Piotr. "Beyond Self: A Lesson from the Concentration Camps." *Canadian Review of Comparative Literature* 19.3 (September 1992): 395–405.

Koch, Gertrud. "Mimesis and *Bilderverbot*." *Screen* 34 (Autumn 1993): 211–22.

Kracauer, Sigfried. *History: Last Things Before the Last*. Oxford: Oxford University Press, 1969.

LaCapra, Dominick. *History and Memory After Auschwitz*. Ithaca, NY: Cornell University Press, 1998.

———. *Representing the Holocaust: History, Theory, Trauma*. Ithaca, NY: Cornell University Press, 1994.

Lang, Berel. *Act and Idea in the Nazi Genocide*. Chicago: University of Chicago Press, 1990.

———. "The Representation of Limits." *Probing the Limits of Representation: Nazism and the "Final Solution."* Ed. Saul Friedlander. Cambridge, MA: Harvard University Press, 1992. 300–317.

———, ed. *Writing and the Holocaust*. New York: Holmes and Maier, 1988.

Langer, Lawrence. *The Holocaust and the Literary Imagination*. New Haven: Yale University Press, 1975.

———. *Holocaust Testimonies: The Ruins of Memory*. New Haven: Yale University Press, 1991.

Lanzmann, Claude, dir. *Shoah*. NYF, 1985.

———. *Shoah: An Oral History of the Holocaust*. New York: Pantheon, 1985.

Lappin, Elena. "The Man with Two Heads." *Granta* 66 (Summer 1999): 7–65.

Levi, Primo. *Survival in Auschwitz*. New York: Vintage, 1995.

Lewin, Abraham. "Diary of the Great Deportation." *A Cup of Tears*. Ed. Antony Polonsky. London: Blackwell, 1988.

Linenthal, Edward. *Preserving Memory: The Struggle to Create America's Holocaust Museum*. New York: Penguin, 1995.

Lishitsky, Yosefa, ed. *Spielberg's Holocaust: Critical Perspectives on* Schindler's List. Bloomington: Indiana University Press, 1997.

————. "Introduction." *Spielberg's Holocaust*. Ed. Yosefa Lishitsky.

Lyotard, Jean-Francois. *The Differend: Phrases in Dispute*. Minneapolis: University of Minnesota Press, 1988.

————. "Discussion, or Phrasing 'after Auschwitz.'" Ed. Andrew Benjamin. *The Lyotard Reader*. Oxford: Basil Blackwell, 1989.

————. "Presenting the Unpresentable: The Sublime." *Artforum* (April 1982).

Magurshak, Dan. "The 'Incomprehensibility' of the Holocaust: Tightening Some Loose Usage." *Echoes from the Holocaust: Philosophical Reflections on a Dark Time*. Ed. Alan Rosenberg and Gerald E. Myers. Philadelphia: Temple University Press, 1988. 421–31.

Maier, Charles. *The Unmasterable Past: History, Holocaust, and German Nationalism*. Cambridge, MA: Harvard University Press, 1988.

McLaughlin, Thomas. "Figurative Language." *Critical Terms for Literary Study*, 2d Ed. Ed. Frank Lentricchia and Thomas McLaughlin. Chicago: University of Chicago Press, 1995. 80–90.

Mink, Louis O. *Historical Understanding*. Ithaca, NY: Cornell University Press, 1987.

Mintz, Alan. *Hurban: Responses to Catastrophe in Hebrew Literature*. New York: Columbia University Press, 1984. See "The Appelfeld World," 203–238.

Novick, Peter. *That Noble Dream: The "Objectivity Question" and the American Historical Profession*. Cambridge: Cambridge University Press, 1988.

Ozick, Cynthia. *Metaphor and Memory*. New York: Knopf, 1989.

————. "Rosa." *The Shawl*. 11–70.

————. *The Shawl*. New York: Knopf, 1989.

————. "The Shawl." *The Shawl*. 1–10.

————. "Toward a New Yiddish." *Art and Ardor*. New York: Knopf, 1983. 151–77.

Patterson, David. *Sun Turned to Darkness: Memory and Recovery in the Holocaust Memoir*. Syracuse: Syracuse University Press, 1998.

Peskin, Harvey. "Holocaust Denial: A Sequel." *The Nation* 14.269 (19 April 1999): 34.

Plato. *Phaedrus*. Ithaca: Cornell University Press, 1998.

Resnais, Alain, dir. *Night and Fog*. Images, 1955.

Roskies, David. *Against the Apocalypse: Responses to Catastrophe in Modern Jewish Culture*. Cambridge, MA: Harvard University Press, 1984.

Scholem, Gershom. *On the Kabbalah and its Symbolism*. Trans. Ralph Manheim. New York: Schocken, 1965.

Spiegelman, Art. *Maus, A Survivor's Tale I: My Father Bleeds History*. New York: Pantheon, 1986.

———. *Maus, A Survivor's Tale II: And Here my Troubles Began.* New York: Pantheon, 1991.

Spielberg, Steven, dir. *Schindler's List.* Universal Studios, 1993.

Stanovick, Lucy. Interview with Mary R. St. Louis, MO. March–April 1997.

Steiner, George. "The Great Tautology." *No Passion Spent.* New York: Faber, 1996. 348–60.

Strandberg, Victor. *Greek Mind/Jewish Soul: The Conflicted Art of Cynthia Ozick.* Madison: University of Wisconsin Press, 1994. See "*The Shawl*: A Tale of Two Cities," 139–51.

Vidal-Naquet, Pierre. *Assassins of Memory: Essays on the Denial of the Holocaust.* Trans. Jeffrey Mehlman. New York: Columbia University Press, 1992.

———. "Theses on Revisionism." *Unanswered Questions: Nazi Germany and the Genocide of the Jews.* Ed. Francois Furet. New York: Schocken, 1989. 304–19.

Weinberg, Jeshajahu and Rina Elieli. *The Holocaust Museum in Washington.* New York: Rizzoli, 1995.

White, Hayden. *The Content of the Form: Narrative Discourse and Historical Representation.* Baltimore: Johns Hopkins University Press, 1987.

———. "Historical Emplotment and the Problem of Truth." *Probing the Limits of Representation: Nazism and the "Final Solution."* Ed. Saul Friedlander. Cambridge, MA: Harvard University Press, 1992. 37–53.

———. *Metahistory: The Historical Imagination in Nineteenth Century Europe.* Baltimore: Johns Hopkins University Press, 1978.

Wiesel, Elie. *Night.* New York: Bantam, 1982.

Wilkomirski, Binjamin. *Fragments: Memories of a Wartime Childhood.* New York: Schocken, 1996.

Wirth, Andrzej. "A Discovery of Tragedy: The Incomplete Account of Tadeusz Borowski." *The Polish Review* 12.3 (Summer 1967): 43–51.

Wirth-Neser, Hana. "The Languages of Memory: Cynthia Ozick's *The Shawl.*" *Multilingual America: Transnationalism, Ethnicity, and the Languages of American Literature.* Ed. Werner Sollors. New York: New York University Press, 1998. 313–26.

Wolin, Richard. *Walter Benjamin: An Aesthetic of Redemption.* Berkeley: University of California Press, 1994.

Wyschogrod, Edith. *An Ethics of Remembering.* Chicago: University of Chicago Press, 1998.

Young, James E. *The Texture of Memory: Holocaust Memorials and Meaning.* New Haven: Yale University Press, 1993.

———. *Writing and Rewriting the Holocaust.* Bloomington: Indiana University Press, 1988.

Index